WHY MEN DON'T GET ENOUGH SEX AND WOMEN DON'T GET ENOUGH LOVE

WHY MEN DON'T GET ENOUGH SEX

and

WOMEN DON'T GET ENOUGH LOVE

Dr Jonathan Kramer
and Diane Dunaway

Virgin

This edition first published in 1994 by
Virgin Books
an imprint of Virgin Publishing Ltd
332 Ladbroke Grove
London W10 5AH

First published in Great Britain by Virgin Books in 1991

First published in 1990 by Pocket Books, an imprint of
Simon & Schuster, Inc., New York

A catalogue record for this title is available from the British Library

ISBN 0-86369-739-9

Printed and bound in Great Britain by
Cox & Wyman Ltd, Reading, Berks.

To lovers everywhere,

*with the hope this book will help you
to live more happily ever after.*

Acknowledgments

We want to thank the many people who directly and indirectly contributed to the creation of this book. Those who deserve special mention include:

Margaret McBride, agent supreme, for her brilliant intuition and expert literary midwifery;

Linda Marrow, senior editor at Pocket Books, for her immediate and continuing enthusiasm and her invaluable editorial polishing;

Hank Stine, for the spark of an idea that got us going;

Loretta Barrett, for her powerful encouragement and an important course correction;

Nancy Sayles, for her promotional expertise;

Paula Detmer Riggs, for her invaluable suggestions and advice throughout the manuscript;

Pat Adams-Manson, Lee Faver, Nick Kramer, Dr. Chuck Moss, Dr. Richie Sobel, Winifred Golden, and Barbara Faith for their friendship, support, and encouragement throughout the writing process.

And to the hundreds of individuals and couples who helped us better understand our subject, either through being in therapy or by participating in interviews, we offer a heartfelt thank-you.

Names and identifying characteristics have been changed to protect the privacy of interviewees and therapy clients.

Contents

PART THREE

MORE HAPPILY EVER AFTER

Introduction

We want this book to change your life for the better, and we're certain it can. *Why Men Don't Get Enough Sex and Women Don't Get Enough Love* tells men the secrets women have always wanted men to know. It tells women what they've always wanted to hear. And it offers couples hope for a new, more loving relationship.

Why Men Don't Get Enough Sex and Women Don't Get Enough Love penetrates deep to the root of the male/female conflict, and offers a solution that faces the facts.

Why Men Don't Get Enough Sex and Women Don't Get Enough Love is the result of exhaustive research, twenty years of clinical experience, interviews with several hundred couples and individuals, and our own personal explorations during our fifteen years together as a couple.

Part One lays out the problem between men and women, and gives a prehistorical and historical background to help understand the natural reasons for the battle of the sexes. And it discusses the truths about men and women, as well as the illusions men and women have about each other.

Part Two is our program to help men and women get beyond the battling and the frustration to a relationship that creates great love and great sex; it is designed to be done either together or individually.

Part Three shows how to continue the changes into daily life in the future, and points toward a deeper meaning of love and sex.

In the past, men and women didn't know how to end their personal battle of the sexes, but now we do. It's not necessarily easy, but it's possible. We've done it, others have done it, and so can you.

It is our sincere hope that you will benefit from the understanding we've gained and the program we've developed to solve the dilemma faced by every man and every woman who wants a truly fulfilling relationship, and that by doing so you, too, will live more happily ever after.

PART ONE

TOO LITTLE SEX, TOO LITTLE LOVE

1

The Eternal Struggle

IMAGINE BEING DEEPLY
IN LOVE

Imagine being deeply in love.

If you're a woman, imagine what it would be like to meet your partner at the end of a long day. Maybe it's in a magical, secluded vacation spot or perhaps it's in the privacy of your own home.

He smiles as he walks up to you. He looks at you, really seeing you, his eyes caressing your face in an adoring way. You feel his caring and attention. His hand brushes your cheek.

"Hello," he says, "I missed you." Then, bending down, he kisses you tenderly, lovingly, in the way he knows you like best.

Your arms go around him; you pull him to you, feel his closeness, return his kiss.

Perhaps he says something to make you laugh or brings you a small surprise. A rich feeling of oneness is between you, and whether you've planned to enjoy a special dinner, take a bubble bath, see a movie, or go straight to the bedroom, you're filled with the golden glow of the love you share.

If you're a man, imagine meeting your partner this way. Imagine the warmth you feel, the sense of acceptance and caring. Imagine seeing her joy that you are with her and feeling your own. Imagine her welcoming your touch, your caresses, and imagine knowing that sometime during the evening, perhaps now, perhaps later, she will open her arms to you and will welcome your lovemaking.

Many of us have experienced this kind of love and oneness with someone. Perhaps for you it was only briefly or long ago, or perhaps this oneness is still part of your relationship from time to time. But however much we've experienced this, most of us wish we could live all our lives within the glow of deep love and satisfaction. Unfortunately, however, even in "good" relationships the following conversation is far more familiar.

SEX VERSUS LOVE

BOB: You never want to do it!

JULIE: We just did it on Wednesday.

BOB: Right! And you didn't want to do it then, either. You never want to make love.

JULIE: Don't accuse me of that. I *do* want to "make love." All you want is to have sex.

BOB: What's that supposed to mean? I'm so sick of this argument. At thirty-five it's healthy to want sex. You make it sound like I'm a sex fiend.

JULIE: I don't think you're a fiend. I just think there's a big difference between making love and having sex. I want to know you love me, not that you just want to have sex with me.

BOB: But I do love you. Why do you think I married you and bring home my paycheck every week?

JULIE: That's what I mean. You think that's all there is to it. I want you to really *show* me that you love me.

BOB: Show it? I'm here. I'm not with someone else.

JULIE: Maybe not, but you still don't pay attention to me—not the way I really want you to.

BOB: Exactly what do you want me to do? I sent you flowers for your birthday, and I took your car into the shop for you just last week. And anyway, what does this have to do with the fact that you don't ever want to have sex? You know, before we were married you were a lot more interested. Sometimes I think it was all just an act to get me to the altar.

JULIE: If I've changed, Bob, it's because you have, too. Maybe I'd be more interested in sex if you were more interested in love.

Bob and Julie's conversation rings a familiar note for nearly everyone who's ever been in a long-term relationship: he wants more sex; she wants more love.

Julie feels resentful because Bob seems so focused on sex. Like most women she wants more love, but she has no idea how to explain this to him so that he will understand it or how to help him fill her need. She wishes she were more interested in having sex and knows she would be if only she had the love she needed. But because he doesn't understand this, she feels their relationship is doomed never to be all she hoped it would be. She's disappointed and she's hurt.

Like most men, Bob doesn't understand why his wife isn't more interested in having sex and why she seems to want something more from him, something he doesn't understand and can't seem to give. He's also becoming less and less willing to discuss a subject that so often leaves him feeling confused, discouraged, annoyed, and frustrated. He, too, wants to be sexually satisfied and feel deeply in love, but he isn't sure what to change or how to change it. He's disappointed and angry.

Bob blames Julie; Julie blames Bob.

Bob is thirty-five and owns an auto parts store. Julie, who is thirty-one, is a teacher working at night to earn her real estate license. They've been married for four years and their problems had been growing steadily worse for over a year before they came for therapy, hoping to avoid a separation.

In their first counseling session it became clear that their problems—Julie not feeling loved and Bob feeling sexually frustrated—were like a whirlpool sucking them down, adding power and emotion to all their other problems.

"When Julie first stopped being interested in sex, I thought it was only temporary," said Bob, "but now it's become the norm. You know, we used to have small arguments every time my mother came to visit or when we were short of money, but now the same fights that used to end in our making up with a kiss never seem to end at all. Now every skirmish becomes a war."

It became clear after this conversation that Julie and Bob, like many couples, were having problems in their sex life that were fueling all their other relationship problems, which, in turn, made their love-sex conflict worse.

Bob felt that Julie never wanted to have sex. "You say you love me, but when we get in bed it's always 'Not tonight,'" he told her during the first session. "I don't think you really love me or care about what I want. Then you complain about how hard I'm working and how I should make more time to talk to you."

Julie was equally frustrated that Bob seemed so interested in sex but so uninterested in making love and being romantic.

"When you come home at night you hardly say a word to me and you don't listen to anything I say," Julie told Bob. "Then at bedtime, you just crawl in and expect me to be as excited and as ready for sex as you are. Why should I be interested in having sex with you when you aren't even interested in talking to me? Sometimes I think you don't even care who's lying there as long as you have someone to put it in."

Bob wasn't getting enough sex. Julie wasn't getting enough love. Both were frustrated. The result was a relationship in crisis. Neither of them felt sure their marriage could last.

"The problem has already gone on too long," said Bob, "and maybe it's impossible to solve. I know no matter what I do there's still no pleasing Julie."

"It's true the hurt has gone on too long," added Julie. "The thing that makes me feel it's hopeless is that everyone else I know seems to have the same problem."

Unfortunately, Julie was right. This "not enough sex, not enough love" frustration seems to plague virtually every couple to one degree or another.

ROCKS IN THE MATTRESS

As the old saying goes, "When the marriage goes on the rocks, the rocks are in the mattress." Men want more sex than they usually get. Studies show, for example, that men think about sex an average of 6 times an hour; that's 750 times a week, not counting dreams.[1] In contrast, the average married couple has sex 1.5 times a week.[2]

Given such a degree of male sexual frustration, it's not surprising to discover that *Playboy* and *Penthouse* are the most popular men's magazines, with combined sales of nearly 6 million copies a month, or that a survey by *Psychology Today* found that 55 percent of the men surveyed were dissatisfied with their sex lives.

It's no wonder, then, that couples argue most often about sexual frequency—or, perhaps worse, they don't discuss their frustrations at all, letting them fester and grow into a permanent wound.

Estimates say that from 26 percent to 66 percent of all married men have affairs[3] and about 51 percent of all new marriages ultimately end in divorce.[4]

Some 64 percent of women say they are dissatisfied with the amount of love they receive and 98 percent want to make basic changes in their marriages and in their emotional relationships with men.[5]

In short, men want more sex; women want more love. The vast majority are dissatisfied, and yet even as this dissatisfaction pushes couples apart, the desire to have a relationship makes couples do their best to overcome the difficulties. The problem is that a good sex life and a good love life go hand in hand to make a happy relationship. You don't usually get one without the other.

SEX AND HAPPINESS

The reality is that when people have a happy relationship they express their contentment sexually, and their sexual satisfaction in turn makes them happier in their relationship.

A *Playboy* survey found that a large majority of married men and women who felt their marriage was very close also said their sex lives were very pleasurable. In addition, a *Redbook* survey found that frequency of sex was connected to sexual satisfaction for women.[6] We also know that women living in "very happy" marriages report being more highly orgasmic than women in less happy relationships.[7]

Sex and happiness go together.

SEX AND LOVE

Sex with love is better than sex without love. People find greater satisfaction when sex is in an intimate, caring relationship.

After studying 12,000 couples, Philip Blumstein and Pepper Schwartz summarized the situation: "Our findings lead to the overwhelming conclusion that a good sex life is central to a good overall relationship. Couples who have sex frequently say they have a good sex life. Moreover, infrequent sex is associated with conflict for everyone . . . those who say they have [sex] with their partner infrequently tend to be dissatisfied with their entire relationship."[8]

Good relationships equal good love and good sex, but as Julie noted, everyone does seem to have the same problem: women want more love; men want more sex. Everyday problems, be they over money, in-laws, or children, only exacerbate this apparently unavoidable human dilemma, and the underlying dissatisfaction over sex versus love makes the everyday problems seem worse.

No matter what other problems a couple may have, the love-sex frustration is often just beneath the surface, never really settled, brewing perhaps for years, and erupting whenever the relationship is strained.

It is like an unavoidable corrosive force eating away at the underlying good feelings that brought the couple together in the first place until the relationship is no longer a refuge of peace, but a battleground filled with tension and open conflict, or perhaps a cold war that can last forever. (As we'll see later, the way men and women have been taught to relate to each other virtually guarantees that this battle of the sexes will occur).

This runs directly counter to our ideal. People want to get married and stay married. In fact, a full 96 percent of all Americans hold the ideal of two people sharing a life and a home together.[9] Only a few couples (19 percent)[10] actually achieve this ideal, however. Happiness in relationships, then, is the exception, not the rule. Sex-love frustration is a factor for nearly everyone. And when this inevitable clash occurs, not wanting to get divorced, people try to solve the problems in their own ways.

MALE SOLUTIONS

Later, in a private session, Bob admitted that he loved Julie, but said he was confused. "I want us to stay together, and so I've just tried to ignore this problem with Julie and sex. But I can't keep ignoring it forever," he said. "I'm young, and there are women everywhere. For example, there's a dress shop right next to my store. Sometimes I'm so frustrated that just seeing one of the women coming out of the shop gives me an erection. You know, you can't go through many days like that. I decided to try to exercise my frustration out. I went to the gym, but seeing all the women there in tights made it worse.

"I decided to just get my mind off it and try working harder and building the business. Julie's father is a doctor, and she expects nice things. Her parents didn't think she should marry me, so I've always been determined to prove I can make it big for us. I figured work would keep my mind off our problem. But when I stayed longer at work, Julie accused me of caring more about the store than about her.

"Then I joined a softball team after work. I played really hard and discovered I could play off some of my frustration. I thought not asking for sex so much would make a difference to Julie and would make us happier. But the evenings away from her only seemed to infuriate her. She accused me of not coming home because I wanted to be with her only if we were having sex. It was ridiculous. Can you imagine anyone misunderstanding someone she supposedly loves so much? Well, after that I really began to give up. In fact, to tell you the truth I've been considering having an affair with the dress shop owner. Maybe I should just get the sex I need somewhere else."

Having an affair is a common solution among men. An estimated 26 to 66 percent of men have affairs in which they are primarily seeking sex.[11] The problem with this is that people value monogamy, and affairs erect walls of dishonesty, disloyalty, guilt, hurt, and anger.

Some 85 percent of couples say they highly value monogamy and would not condone sex outside of marriage under any circumstances.[12] This means that when men have affairs, they're violating their own principles and thus harming themselves as well as their relationships. Nevertheless, millions of men, like Bob, aren't sure what else to do to get their sexual needs met.

Other men attempt to solve the marital dilemma by ignoring the problem, hoping it will somehow resolve itself. Or they bury themselves in an activity, like watching TV, playing sports, doing hobbies, or working harder—in the hope of keeping their "minds" off their lust.

Of course these are all Band-Aids that don't even begin to cure the underlying wound. So there it sits and festers, manifesting itself in irritability, in silence, and in a deep sense of hurt because, while men want sex, they also want love, and as we'll see, for a man, this loss of sex also means loss of love.

FEMALE SOLUTIONS

In private, Julie said she was extremely frustrated—not sexually, but emotionally. "I love Bob," she said, "and I wish I were as interested in having sex as I used to be. At first I blamed myself. I thought maybe there was something wrong with me. Maybe I'm frigid or something. But then I talked to my best friend and found out she feels the same way and her friends do, too. The truth is I want more from Bob. I want him to be interested in me, the person, but he's hardly ever interested in talking about anything, and when I finally get him to talk it's about his store and how his business is going. Success is so important to him, but not people, really, not even me. It's as if he expects shop talk to turn me on or something.

"Then I decided—look, you want him to care about you more. Why not look better for him? I started going to an exercise dance class, but it didn't make him more loving. Instead he said I looked 'hot' in my leotard. He was even more demanding about sex and called me a tease if I didn't want to. I stopped going to the dance class.

"Then a girlfriend said that I was going about attracting him in the wrong way. She quoted the old adage, 'The quickest way to a man's heart is through his stomach.' So I tried cooking more, being more domestic, even ironing his shirts (and I hate ironing), just so he'd realize I loved him. He assumed I was trying to save money and said he'd rather pay the difference because the cleaners did a better job. I said, 'Bob, I did it to show you I love you.' 'Okay, that's nice,' he said, 'but take them to the cleaners next time.' Can you imagine anyone so misunderstanding the woman he supposedly loves? 'You can take them yourself,' I said. I was really mad, but he couldn't understand. He just wanted us to make up, and of course you know how—by having sex.

"I've thought about having an affair. A man at school is interested in me. He talks to me about himself in a personal way Bob never does, and he seems to really listen when I talk and says I'm beautiful, and you know he really looks at me like he cares. Then he told me he is married, and he said his wife has a sexual problem, but he has three kids and can't afford a divorce. That's when I realized it was the same thing; he just wants sex.

"I realized then that if I wanted love there were people who loved me. I started getting closer to my friends and my sister and mother, and it helped to feel they truly care about me. But in talking to them and hearing their problems, I realized we're all the same. We all want man-woman love. We all even want sex. But we all want men to show they love us, too. We want them to listen to us and to be romantic and exciting. But it's so hard to make them understand. The problem is really a deep one.

"Women aren't automatically excited the way men are. But men seem to expect us to be turned on, and they're annoyed when it doesn't happen. Of course, it's the same for everyone. I've told myself that. Sometimes I think I should just give up and let him have sex when he wants it, fake an orgasm, and be done with it. Anything to keep the peace.

"The problem is if I force myself to have sex and pretend to enjoy it, I feel like a prostitute. I don't want to feel that way, but I don't want to lose him, either. Some of my friends tell me to find someone more compatible, but who? Even they admit their husbands are all the same. My mother had the same problem with my father and finally divorced him. But my stepfather wasn't any better and she learned to, as she says, 'live with it.' The problem is can I live with it? Things have changed. It used to be that women were forced to put up with whatever problems they had with their husbands because they couldn't support themselves. For a lot of women, that's just not true anymore. Women can get out of a marriage now, and if things don't change, I know that's where Bob and I are headed. Still," she said with a sad shake of her head, "I remember our beautiful wedding day and how happy and hopeful we were, and I don't want our marriage to end. I want us to have a *real* marriage that's full of life and sharing and fun and, yes, sex, too, but this conflict with him wanting more sex and me wanting more love is ruining everything."

Julie and Bob are a typical example of the love-versus-sex problem. It seems almost inescapable, doesn't it? Didn't you and nearly everyone you know start off with high hopes for a loving, intimate relationship? Sooner or later, though, most couples end up with overwhelming problems, even if, like Julie and Bob, they still love each other underneath it all. The spark that brought them together in the first place has diminished for Julie and Bob in much the same way it has for so many others.

It's as if there is some marital "disease" that, in time, turns nearly every bright new relationship into something difficult and strained, full of misunderstanding and pain.

There is, in fact, an inevitable force beneath all these problems. Like an unseen hand, it works to make difficulties virtually unavoidable. Fortunately, however, they are not incurable.

A few couples do find their own way out of the difficulty and back into a happy marriage. But for many couples the problems only grow worse, making the situation intolerable. About half of all couples divorce. But an all too common alternative is what we call *marital coma*.

MARITAL COMA

Marital coma is marital brain-death. It is the result of the erosion of love and closeness. It is a stagnation brought on by a lack of intimacy, by being wounded and disappointed, by smothered anger and resentment, by a sense of hopelessness, a belief that it's impossible to resolve the situation. And yet most couples are unwilling (sometimes for financial or family reasons) to dissolve the relationship. In short, marital coma exists when a marriage is technically dead but no one pulls the plug.

Couples in a state of marital coma are easy to spot. Eating in a restaurant, they often stare uninterestedly past each other, and if they do speak, it is in monosyllables. At home they often lead separate lives, have separate friends, pursue separate hobbies, and take separate vacations. At social events they may not interact at all, or they may display a studied appearance of congeniality, which they drop the moment they are off stage. Alone with friends, they may indulge in subtle or not so subtle put-downs of each other.

Some marital comas resemble a cold war that occasionally breaks out into open battle before returning to its normal state of truce, each outbreak causing the couple to draw further and further apart. Other marital comas are simply devoid of any vibrant or positive connection or sparkle as the partners go through the motions of a life together and immerse themselves in routine.

While some divorces are years in the making, marital comas are almost always the result of an accumulation of many small events rather than a few large ones.

One common sign of approaching marital coma occurs when he becomes increasingly uncommunicative and unable or unwilling to express himself emotionally. He may then turn off sexually as well.

SHE: Honey, let's dance.
HE: I don't like to dance.
SHE: Tell me how you feel about your job (the neighbors, the new apartment).
HE: It's fine.
SHE: What's wrong?
HE: Nothing.

Meanwhile she becomes less willing to express herself sexually and emotionally.

HE: Honey. Let's go to bed early.

SHE: The kids are having friends over tonight. Maybe when they go to college we'll get our privacy back.

HE: The kids are out for the evening.

SHE: I know. But I've got a million things to do.

HE: You've been on the phone all evening.

SHE: I've got lots of people I have to talk to. Anyway, you're busy watching television.

In marital coma, the man and woman avoid each other and no longer bother to discuss their problems. They may have simply given up, or they may have found that trying to deal with the difficulties only makes matters worse.

She increasingly avoids contact with him, particularly sexual contact, except perhaps when her own libido demands it. She may not do or say anything overtly aggressive or negative for which she could be blamed or attacked. Instead she will withhold expressions of caring, particularly physical expressions, and she'll begin to depend on friends, children, co-workers, relatives, or outside activities to meet her need for closeness and communication.

The situation gradually deteriorates. Both may forget anniversaries and birthdays, or make little of them, and both, in their own way, may feel sorry and resentful that things aren't different.

He will probably feel helpless to change the situation and have no idea how or why things got to such a state. Hopelessness often results. Or he may not even admit to himself that they have a problem. She is more likely to have some idea what's wrong, but she doesn't know the solution and may also feel it is impossible to change. Depending on what her own expectations are, she may feel increasingly willing to accept the situation, or increasingly infuriated that this is what her hopes for a good relationship have come to. Ultimately hopelessness results, and finding no way to breathe life into their relationship, they remain stuck in a lifeless marital coma.

George and Rita are such a couple. They came to therapy wanting to revive their relationship. They are in their early fifties and their last daughter has just left for college. For years now Rita has been a housewife and mother, filling up any spare time with volunteer activities. She considers herself a good mother, housekeeper, cook, and wife. She has done her part, and together she and George have raised four children.

She always imagined that after their job as parents was done they would have time to travel and be together without the worries and pressures of children and money. But now she is only beginning to realize that the relationship she so looked forward to having is not available.

"I'm not even sure how it happened," says Rita. "The pressures of just living, I suppose. It seemed George was so busy supporting us he didn't have time for anything else. And I was busy with the kids. Then later, when we had more time, he was just interested in going fishing or golfing with his friends. He certainly didn't seem interested in me and the children. If I complained, he reminded me he was doing his job by providing for all of us. Sometimes I felt so unloved; I was just going through the motions of life, instead of living it. Sometimes I'd think of leaving him, but that was impossible. I had a nursing degree, but I hadn't worked at it in years and couldn't have supported my kids on a nurse's salary. Anyway, what right did I have to deprive the children of a father just because I was unhappy?

"My mother told me the same thing. 'George is a good man,' she said. 'Whoever promised you a perfect life? Stay with him. A good father is hard to find.' And so I stayed. But now the kids are gone, George and I are further apart than ever, and I'm realistic about my slim chances of finding someone else: men my age want women twenty years younger. It's so ironic that now, when we have the time and money to live happily ever after, we've grown so far apart that we're going to live unhappily ever after."

Though George was usually a man of few words, he was concerned enough about his marital problem to try to solve it even though he wasn't optimistic. "I gave up years ago," he said. "She didn't have the time for me. I was just a means to an end: she wanted a houseful of kids and I gave that to her. She wasn't much interested in what I wanted, so I just shut up and watched a lot of TV. She was never much in bed, if you know what I mean, but I put up with it and shut up as much as I could to keep peace. Don't get me wrong; Rita's a wonderful person. She's been a great mother, and we've accomplished a lot over the years. But she sure didn't have time for me. I know she blames me for our problems, and maybe I should have talked to her more, but she didn't exactly do right by me, either. She wanted us to come to therapy because she thinks now that the kids are gone things can change between us. But I think it's hard to change a tiger's stripes. I know plenty of men who it seems to me are in the same boat. From here on out, we'll just put in our time."

We see this same problem between men and women over and over again. We recognize it as universal. But while many have examined the problem and it is fully recognized, the real underlying cause of the problem has been ignored.

Why do couples have the love-versus-sex conflict to begin with? How does it come about? Is it simply an innate difference between men and women? Are men and women destined to have different and ultimately conflicting needs? Or does something in our society or our circumstances make us this way?

Instead of looking for this underlying cause, most books and discussions on the subject focus on what occurs as a result of the difficulties that arise when men don't get enough sex and women don't get enough love. Instead of looking beneath the problem to see what's causing it, they focus on the pain, on the frustration, on the fact that women love too much or that men are angry.

THE SEX-LOVE
EROSION DISEASE

This problem is so common it seems like a universal disease.

Some couples seem to catch SLED—sex-love erosion disease—on their honeymoon, and they go metaphorically downhill from there. Just what is this universal marital "disease" that is devastating so many relationships? Why have so many couples succumbed to divorce or to the living death of marital coma? What is at the bottom of this battle of the sexes? Is this disease really unavoidable, or can we cure it if we understand the cause? Before men can get more sex and women can get more love, we need to understand the underlying reason for men's apparent resistance to love and women's apparent resistance to sex. Are men just selfish and uncaring, as so many women claim? Or is there some deep force that drives men, without their knowledge or consent, to crave sex and withhold love?

Do women use sex to attract men and trap them into marriage before turning off sexually, as many men suspect? Or are they simply behaving in a certain way without their understanding or awareness?

To find the underlying answers to these basic questions, it isn't enough to look at men and women in the present day. Instead, it is essential to look more closely at our origins as well. How did the battle of the sexes begin and develop? And what led to the genesis of this sex-love erosion disease that is still infecting our society and our relationships?

In order to better understand marital coma and ultimately cure it, it's necessary to understand some basic facts about men and women and why they are who they are, not just as they exist today, but into the deepest past to discover the root of the battle of the sexes and how the sex-love erosion disease came into being as well as how these facts set men and women at odds today.

NOTES, CHAPTER 1

1. Karen Shanor, *The Shanor Study: The Sexual Sensitivity of the American Male* (New York: Dial Press, 1978), p. 253.
2. William Masters, Virginia Johnson, and Robert Kolodny, *Human Sexuality*, 2nd ed. (Boston: Little, Brown, 1985), p. 247. In the first year of marriage frequency of intercourse is 3.7 times per week, dropping to 2.2 times in the fourth year, 1.5 in the sixth and continuing to fall with time together and age.
3. William Masters, Virginia Johnson, and Robert Kolodny, *Masters and Johnson on Sex and Human Loving* (Boston: Little, Brown 1988), p. 334.
4. *American Demographics*, Dow Jones, Ithaca, NY, 1989.
5. Shere Hite, *Women and Love* (New York: St. Martin's Press, 1989), pp. 100, 26.
6. Masters, Johnson, and Kolodny, 1988, p. 330.
7. P.H. Gebhard, "Factors in Marital Orgasm," *Journal of Social Issues* 22 (4): 88–95, 1966.
8. Philip Blumstein and Pepper Schwartz, *American Couples: Money, Work, Sex* (New York: Pocket Books, 1983), p. 201.
9. Robert N. Bellah, Richard Madsen, William M. Sullivan, Steven M. Tipton, Ann Swidler, *Habits of the Heart* (Berkeley: University of California Press, 1985), p. 90.
10. Hite, *Women and Love*, p. 61.
11. Masters, Johnson, and Kolodny, 1988, p. 334.
12. Francesca Cancian, *Love in America* (Cambridge, England: Cambridge University Press, 1987), p. 150.

2

The Facts About Men

W hy do men behave the way they do? That question is asked over and over, most often by women.

There is hardly a woman alive who hasn't spent hours discussing the male psyche—who he really is sexually, emotionally, physically, and how to better understand and deal with him. And though some women feel they understand their men better than their men understand themselves, they still feel baffled by certain male traits.

The truth is that men are not as baffling when viewed in the context of forces in the past that created and shaped men as they are today. Indeed, looking at these forces not only explains who men are; it also explains the male contribution to the battle of the sexes.

Ten facts about men follow. They will help to explain who men are today, how and why they got this way, and how they are changing.

Fact #1: Men have warrior spirit

"Last week my two nephews, eight and nine years old, came to visit," a woman told us. "I have two girls and I'd forgotten what boys are like.

"First they climbed our apple tree and stood at the top pretending they were space men ready to blast off. I was sure they were going to break their necks. The next thing I knew they were redirecting a stream right through our backyard. They spent the entire week fighting, each one trying to prove he was better than the other, and they refused to play with my eleven-year-old girl, calling her stupid because she didn't want to do some of the crazy things they were doing. I thought I would lose my mind. My husband only shrugged and said, 'Boys will be boys.' But that didn't seem like enough of an explanation to me. Why are boys like that?"

The truth is that both boys and girls are born with basic energy to go forward, to understand their environment, to explore, and to shape things and situations to their own will. However, most men use this energy differently than most women do. There is evidence to suggest that part of this difference is something children are simply born with. Certainly whatever these distinctions are at birth, they are greatly molded and shaped after birth to make boys and girls use this basic energy in distinctly different ways. A woman's basic energy is usually channeled into "nurturing spirit," while a man's is usually channeled into "warrior spirit."

This warrior spirit, can be molded and directed. Warrior spirit is essentially raw energy that is capable of being channeled into an infinite variety of forms. These forms can be violent and destructive or peaceful and in the service of life. Specifically how and to what end warrior spirit is molded depends very much on the social influences the child is subjected to. In our society the molding of a boy's basic energy begins very early.

This is easy to see on any playground. Even small boys are already encouraged and therefore inclined to climb higher than girls, to race each other, and to explore farther afield. As boys grow older they often emulate real warriors, building forts, striving to climb to the top of the jungle gym, fighting to be king of the mountain, or competing to see who has the biggest battle scars.

Boys act this way because, in our society, most men are trained to channel their warrior spirit into being successful, being competitive, being a leader, getting a job done, being unemotional, being the best, being dominant, and if necessary, literally being a warrior capable of combat.

Unfortunately while many of these traits make men attractive to women, they also produce negative side effects that have put men at odds with women and have created the male half of the battle of the sexes, a male-female conflict with such a long tradition that we tend to think of it as inevitable.

An important and central point that we want to make in this book is that the conflicts that arise between the sexes, particularly over issues of love and sex, are *not* inevitable.

The battle of the sexes was and is an outcome of circumstances and of the basic need to survive. This need to survive has forced society to mold the energy of both men and women in ways that foster survival but also foster conflict and frustration between them. Unfortunately, what has helped us survive has not helped us relate best to each other as men and women. Indeed, the social molding we've all undergone for the sake of survival has created and supported the battle of the sexes for thousands of years and hundreds of generations.

The good news is that because the battle of the sexes is primarily a result of circumstances and socialization, it can also change, and is already changing, as a result of new circumstances and a different kind of socialization. Therefore the battle of the sexes is not an unavoidable trap. Just the opposite is true. There is reason to conclude that now, for the first time in thousands of years, the circumstances are right for men and women to learn to live together in harmony. But before we consider this good news further, let's continue to look at how boys' warrior spirit is molded.

Why is it that boys are encouraged to compete, to dominate, and often to fight with each other either literally or symbolically?

A first fact to understand about men is that their basic warrior spirit is molded so as to help them be successful. In peacetime this aggressive, competitive spirit, this drive to dominate, is focused on the workplace and on being successful. In violent times these same traits of domination, aggression, and competitiveness are further molded to prepare a man to kill and to survive. This is the way it has been for as long as anyone can remember. Aggressiveness, competitiveness, and the drive to succeed and dominate are encouraged in boys and are considered natural and appropriate.

"Boys will be boys," people say. But are boys really born this way, or could they be quite different under different circumstances?

The answer, as we see it, is that they could be different.

Indeed, man's basic nature is potentially far more peaceable, more intimate, even more romantic and more inclined to live harmoniously with women than is generally true today.

To support this belief we need only look back to man's early history and note that the male's basic nature is neither particularly violent nor dominant. In fact, noted anthropologist Richard Leakey, among others, suggests that Neolithic man was not the club-swinging, apelike creature so often depicted in cartoons, knocking his mate over the head and dragging her off to enslavement in his camp.

According to Leakey, these early men were not violent, nor did they enslave women. In fact, if we are to judge by these early humans, it is apparently far more natural for men to be gentle creatures who treat women more like equal partners than slaves and whose warrior spirit was focused on fostering harmony and life.

A profile of these early men is given by ethologist Robin Fox in *Sexual Selection and the Descent of Man*. Fox describes early men as "controlled, cunning, cooperative, attractive to the ladies, good with the children, relaxed, tough, eloquent, skillful, knowledgeable, and proficient in defense and hunting."[1] Those qualities we often assume to be inherent in men, such as violence and aggression, are not mentioned in the profile.

Among these early people violence between men was rare and did not usually result in murder. Generally violence was used only to protect the family group from predators or to hunt, and even hunting was frequently done with great spiritual awareness. For example, animals were killed only after thanking the spirits and thanking the animal for giving up its life so the hunter could eat and therefore live.

For at least a million years these men and women lived together in well organized, closely knit tribes of family-oriented hunter-gatherer bands. In many early societies, women, far from being enslaved by men, were honored, respected, and revered for having the great, essential, and uniquely female power to bring forth and nurture life.

In her important book *The Chalice and the Blade*,[2] Riane Eisler explores this long period when people lived in relative peace, prosperity, and cooperation, and women and men shared life more equitably. Eisler offers evidence that a goddess-based culture existed over six thousand years ago in the Neolithic period, during which there was a flowering of art and crafts and a sense of oneness with nature.

There was such respect for motherhood and the essential contributions of women in this early period that a person's power was actually measured by one's ability to create and nurture life. In this early civilization, men could more freely express their love and women could more freely express their sexuality. The female-male frustration resulting from women not getting love from men and men not getting sex from women did not exist as it does today. Therefore, the battle of the sexes did not exist as it does today.

The male-female mutual respect and compatibility so widely expressed in this period points to this being the most natural human state. This harmonious way of life might have continued to this day except for a very important and dramatic social change. This change, lasting for the next six thousand years, not only altered human society and demolished men's equitable relationship with women, but also had a catastrophic effect on man's relationship to himself and remolded his warrior spirit into the form in which we see it expressed today. This change was the introduction of violence.

Fact #2: The need for violence has shaped men to avoid most emotions, particularly tender ones

"Men just don't feel, at least not as much as women do. I'm convinced of it," said Janet, one of the women interviewed for this book. "For instance, the other night my husband Mick and I were watching a movie about a mother losing her child to a kidnapper and never finding the little boy again or knowing what happened to him. It was so sad I was just sobbing, but Mick didn't seem at all sad. He just laughed at me, and when I couldn't stop crying, he said I was crazy to cry over a movie and left the room.

"We have children, and I know Mick would just die if something happened to one of them. I even think that deep down the movie made him sad and upset, too, but he never lets anything show.

"Another time we had a fire next door and had to evacuate our house real quick. I was nearly hysterical, but Mick was calm through the whole thing and hardly said a word.

"When we were first married I used to think it was real sexy for him to be the strong, silent type. For one thing, I always knew he could take care of me, and not knowing his feelings made him seem mysterious. But I didn't expect him to remain so distant. I just assumed that having me and the kids to love would give him something to feel love for, so he wouldn't be so distant all the time. But the only time Mick ever reacts to anything is when he gets mad, and boy, can he blow his top when he's angry. It's a heck of a thing, though, that being angry is the only time he really shows what he feels. I can't remember the last time he told me or the kids he loved us. When I asked him once if he did he just said, 'You should know I do,' and that was it. I guess we do know, but it doesn't seem right for him not to say so. From what I hear from other women, lots of men are pretty much the same. Are all men so distant and so closed with their feelings?"

The second fact about men is that, while they do have feelings, they've learned to keep them covered up. In our society, men have strict rules governing what is considered acceptable male behavior. Men are taught to suppress all emotions except, under certain circumstances, anger. They are to be cool and calm, and to emphasize rational rather than emotional reaction, particularly in difficult or dangerous situations.

Tender emotions are generally rejected as a sign of weakness and vulnerability. If expressed, they are an invitation to other men to ridicule or to attempt to dominate him. Instead, the male tradition dictates that men are to go forward in life, even into dangerous or difficult situations, without flinching, to dominate and defeat their competitors and opponents, and to be strong, independent, competent, in control, and able to stand alone.

In order to do this, men tend to turn away from feelings and concentrate on actions and thinking. This is one of the strongest traditions passed on to generation after generation of males, and it is one of the characteristics a man must demonstrate to gain and retain acceptance in male society.

Any boy who doesn't demonstrate these qualities—who doesn't, at a young age, give up showing his emotions, especially his vulnerable feelings such as sadness, pity, love, and pain—will be labeled a wimp or a pussy by the other boys. He will be given little or no understanding and certainly no respect. Instead, the others will often pick on and ridicule him until he becomes as "tough" as they are.

This emotional "toughness" and all the resulting male characteristics are among the most difficult of the masculine traits for women to understand or relate to. What makes understanding most difficult is that men's reasons for having these traits often remain a mystery even to men themselves. For example, ask a man why he doesn't show emotion and he will probably say something like "Men just don't." He isn't certain why "men don't," he just knows it's so. He learned it from his father and grandfather, from his brothers, male friends, and male heroes in movies, in books, and on TV, and from seeing "weaker" men ridiculed. He can't remember men being any different. If anything, past generations of men seemed even less emotional.

The problem is that because he is restricted from showing tender emotion, he is also restricted from showing love. This is a part of the reason why men don't get enough sex and women don't get enough love, and why there is such a universal male-female conflict and frustration.

But then why, if it causes so much conflict between men and women, does this trait of male emotional restriction live on? And why do women, who after all raise young boys, continue to mold male warrior spirit to this end? Are women just masochists? Are they forced to raise their sons this way by men? Or are they just following a pattern so old that neither women nor men even consider socializing their boys any differently? Fortunately there is an answer that makes perfect sense.

This answer lies buried in the deep past, in a time more than six thousand years ago when men and women lived at peace with each other in relatively equal relationships, probably before this male tradition of denying emotions, particularly tender emotions, had been established.

As we said earlier, it was the introduction of violence that radically altered the human condition. This violence came about when mankind shifted away from hunting and gathering and developed agriculture.

As these early people learned to grow and harvest crops they settled the most fertile lands along the lakes and rivers in the areas that are now Greece, Italy, and other parts of Europe. For at least a thousand years they lived in relative peace and prosperity, until they discovered that, unlike their earlier nomadic way of life, the cultivation of crops and the resulting surpluses had created a temptation that brought forth a whole new type of human behavior—organized large-scale violence.

The violence came in waves beginning at least six thousand years ago as hordes of Kurgans and other tribes swept down from the north, riding horses they had domesticated for war, and carrying battle-axes and double-edged swords they had fashioned from metal.

This Kurgan violence was the beginning of a total reshaping of human civilization as well as of the relationship between men and women. Why? Because now, in order to survive, these peaceable men were forced to learn to kill or be killed. This is a fact that changed man's relationship with himself and his emotions, particularly his tender emotions. Women, on the other hand, faced their own tragedy as they found their previously equal relationship with men falling away before the new necessity to have a male protector at any cost. Suddenly having a male protector was a matter of life and death.

This shift away from peace and toward violence and female enslavement took man even further away from his connection to his inner world. Now, instead of power being measured by one's ability to *give* life, as it had been earlier in the peaceful goddess culture, power was measured by one's ability to *take* life. The power to give and protect life had been supplanted by the power to kill.

Now the "strongest" men—those most capable of violence, and

therefore less compassionate and emotionally vulnerable—assumed leadership. Women—being generally smaller, physically weaker, and responsible for the children—had to be protected. Now a man might do without a woman, but a woman could no longer survive by herself, as she could in the past. In a violent era a woman had to depend on a man.

Now this essential role of protector put men clearly in charge, letting them decide whom they would protect and whom they would not. These men, of course, might have been tender or nurturing to their wives and children, but the value of tenderness and nurturing fell away before the need to survive.

Women were then obliged to seek the favor of those men who were most capable of protecting them—those most capable of violence and therefore least capable of compassion and tenderness. As we will see in Chapter 3, some women to this day prefer the most aggressive and therefore successful men as mates, even though these men may have the least chance of being tender, compassionate, or intimate. In recent years, this tendency has altered slightly, but the fact remains that men are still trained to dominate, to be prepared for war, and to suppress their emotions. And from the beginning of this violent era to the present, power was, and often still is, granted to those most capable of war and violence, and women until very recently remained subservient to men.

The fact, then, that men became dominant over women was not a result of any natural order basic to human nature, nor was it due to men's basic superiority to women, as many have claimed. Rather, it was a result of the introduction of violence, the need to survive, and the resulting social reordering that put men in charge and made women dependent on their goodwill. Women were simply forced to trade their equality for survival.

As infuriating as this may be, however, before we continue looking at the results of this turn of events, it is important to see another truth: it is easy to blame all men for what occurred back at this crossroads of human history. The truth is, however, that, given a choice, most men probably would not have chosen the path of violence.

Many men were forced into physical aggression because, as we have seen, the moment *some* men became violent, *all* men were forced to be equally violent or die. Yes, men made war, but not all men, nor can all men be blamed.

Another essential point, if one is to understand men, is that while men have enjoyed the fruits of their dominance, over women and over society, when men took up the sword, they were also shaped by the sword. And this sword was double-edged. Yes, it has given men power, but men have also suffered, both on and off the battlefield, for this power.

By taking up the blade and killing, men gained dominance, but they found that the blade cut them as well as the enemy, dividing them from themselves, the earth, and their fellow men, women, and children. By being forced to be ready to kill, men have been necessarily separated from their own hearts and souls.

Most women on some level sense this separation of men from themselves. Women often perceive it as a certain sadness or emptiness in men, a lack of love, a woundedness, an emotional incompleteness that often puzzles women and makes them consider their men and wonder, Does he feel, just as I do? Is he just covering it up? Is he truly capable of loving? Does he really love me?

Part of the reason that women are attracted to men, we believe, is that they yearn to heal this "wounded" man and put him back in touch with his emotions, to give him love and help him feel it in himself. It's as if, instinctively, women yearn to give men the pleasurable and essential emotional life that they feel.

The difficulty is that men are trained to feel differently than women are and to experience their feelings, particularly their tender feelings, less intensely. This is because hundreds of generations of men had no choice but to take up arms and suffer through the hell and horror of war. They also had to suffer emotionally by being raised to be capable of doing so.

THE MALE TRADITION OF COMBAT-READINESS

An essential part of historical and modern male training is what we call combat-readiness training. Combat-readiness is both a subtle and an overt training program to prepare men for war.

In a violent world, a man must be prepared emotionally to think clearly and logically even in the heat of a fight. He must, for instance, be able to see a fellow combatant—a brother, a neighbor, or a friend—die. He must experience this without losing control. This is essential, since any uncontrolled response, such as panic or untempered fury, might pose a risk not only to his own but to his fellow warriors' lives.

The ability to control emotion requires a man to develop emotional detachment, even though simultaneously he must learn to work with others as part of an efficient team. Therefore, he must learn to relate without emotion or with very carefully controlled emotion. In essence, then, he must achieve a state of emotional anesthesia.

A combat-ready man uses this anesthesia to permit him to kill a person he has never met before and against whom he has no personal grudge. He must kill simply because that person has been identified as the enemy, and he must do it without reservation or question, without shrinking from the horror of his act, and quickly, before the other anesthetized warrior kills him. So in addition to emotional anesthesia, he must also put on the armor of separateness. He is a more effective and successful combatant if he can suppress all traces of compassion, pity, and empathy.

He also must be able to tolerate hardship without complaining, learn to draw on his reserves of strength, go the extra mile, tolerate pain, and continue to function, and kill if necessary, in spite of wounds.

He must be able to accept orders from a "superior" while being independent enough to work on his own and not ask for help.

He must learn that to accept help or to lack the above characteristics is always suspect and leaves a man vulnerable to being considered a wimp, a sissy, a pussy, or lacking balls. These extremely insulting labels are avoided at almost any cost by nearly all men. Signs of weakness invite domination and ridicule.

If a man does not develop these characteristics, he will fall short of the standards by which society and especially other men are able to identify him as male. Therefore, without these traits, his own ability to see himself as a man is threatened.

But why, so long after the violence of six thousand years ago, are men still combat-ready? The reason is that, six thousand years later, we still have combat.

In our modern Western culture, war has been a common occurrence. In the United States every generation has had a war to fight. Many of our fathers and grandfathers fought in World War II, and because of their combat-readiness their generation and ours survived.

Later wars, in Korea and Vietnam, again required men to be combat-ready. Hence, every generation of American men has been asked to fight, and each war has reinforced the notion that males need to be capable of becoming combat-ready.

The problem that we confront today is that, while this combat-ready style is important to society's survival, it also has an important and very central side effect: combat-readiness ensures problems between men and women because it discourages men from loving, while being loved is exactly what women want.

By blocking emotion and pain and avoiding closeness, a man turns away from a whole realm of emotional experiences—intimacy and love among them. Instead he becomes a master of the Outer World, the world of action and thought, while avoiding the softer, more vulnerable Inner World—the woman's more personal and social world—of emotion, intimacy, intuition, relationships, and nurturing.

This training to suppress the Inner World, however, is arduous and often painful, and rites of initiation begin at an early age.

ARMOR AND ANESTHESIA

We witnessed one such male initiation rite last year when a few families camped together in the local mountains.

An eleven-year-old neighbor boy, Jamie, well known for his love of animals and his often stated desire to one day be a veterinarian, was taken on a hunting foray by his visiting uncle Walt.

Walt, an overtly combat-ready man, brought his .22 rifle along and, after sharpening the boy's marksmanship skills, shamed and ridiculed Jamie into shooting a rabbit.

Neither of us will ever forget the devastated look on Jamie's face when, upon his return, he was again ridiculed into holding up the limp body of the hapless creature for our inspection, or how, afterward, Jamie unsuccessfully tried to wipe the blood off his hands as Uncle Walt was praising his hunting prowess.

This is a common early lesson for young men and one designed to teach them to put aside their softer feelings and learn to kill as a demonstration of skill and male competence.

To kill humans, of course, requires even more powerful anesthesia. Some soldiers, after returning from Vietnam, have told us that they felt their war experience had killed their ability to love. As one hand-to-hand combat vet told us, "It's just impossible for me to love. If I start to feel anything, even the slightest sense of caring about some girl, not to mention loving her—I'm not even sure what loving feels like anymore— it's as if somebody inside me puts a gun to my head and all my danger instincts go off. It's like I get my ass kicked for even trying to care."

The worst part, perhaps, is that the male culture Jamie is being prepared to enter does not permit him to complain, feel sad or scared, or express his revulsion over his forced initiation; this stoicism is another aspect of male combat-readiness training. All Jamie and other boys like him can do, without risking the trauma of being labeled a wimp, is to pretend they don't feel any of these emotions and learn to cover them up. And with every such lesson, every hurt and injury, a boy will learn to protect himself from the pain in two ways: by entering a state of emotional anesthesia in which he does not experience feelings, and by developing armor that allows him to stay distant from others both physically, by pulling away from others and into himself, and emotionally, by not letting others penetrate his emotional barriers.

Not only, then, are men trained to keep their tender emotions controlled through anesthesia, but they are also taught to keep people at an emotional distance so they won't even be tempted to feel tender emotions.

WHY MEN CAN'T SAY THE L-WORD

The problem is that men also have a powerful sex drive that pulls them toward women. Many men try to gain sexual fulfillment from women without allowing themselves any emotional involvement. Fortunately, however, this male training can't suppress the enormous drive to bond with and love another. And so most men do, at some point in their lives, fall in love. The problem is that this goes strongly against their male training.

Historically there have been many warnings, in actual socialization, as well as in myths and stories, about how dangerous it is for a man to lose his heart to a woman and how this takes away from a man's strength. We hear of Adam being seduced by Eve into eating the apple, and of Sampson who, against the advice of others, falls in love with Delilah and ultimately loses his strength.

Love was believed to weaken a man, and this notion has kept men from expressing love in the way most easily recognized by women—that is, by saying "I love you."

But of course love isn't the only emotion that a man's anesthesia deadens. Sadness and fear, except in mild and controlled forms, are also avoided by many men.

MALE LOVE

Here, then, is an obvious question: If men don't open their hearts directly to feelings of love, can they really love at all? And if they can, what form does their love take?

The male style of love is often very different from the female version, and men may not show their love in the way many women expect love to be expressed. Men do, nonetheless, have a way of loving, and while it unfortunately is not often recognized by women—or by society, either, since society generally accepts the female version of love—it *is* love.

As we've seen, many barriers exist even today to keep men from expressing their feelings, particularly their feelings of love. But men can express love in a masculine way that, not too surprisingly, fits their role as the powerful provider and protector.

As Francesca Cancian wrote in her excellent book, *Love in America*, "the qualities judged most important in being a man, according to a large national survey of men and women, are being a good provider, having strong views about what is right and wrong, and being concerned with a woman's sexual satisfaction—qualities that are emphasized in the masculine style of love."[3] This fits perfectly with all we've learned so far.

Male love "focuses on practical help, shared physical activities, spending time together and sex."[4] Men also feel a sense of responsibility for their partner's well-being, and this concern gets expressed through protection, sexual intimacy, helping actions, time spent together, trying to be worthy of admiration, feeling responsible, and being a good provider who brings home the kill (instead of an antelope steak, now it's a paycheck).

This leads us full circle. In order to be considered a man, men are forced to ignore or suppress their softer emotions, their love, and their desire for openness and intimacy. This automatically makes it more difficult for men to relate well to women and to be romantic or show the emotional signals, or love signals, that women need to relate physically to them.

This, then, is the problem men and women face: men don't get enough sex because women don't get enough love; men can't give more love in the way women want because they've been trained not to.

Combat-readiness, then, has become such a part of the fabric of men's personalities and daily lives that it has taken its toll on every man's relationship, not only with himself but with everyone he knows, particularly the woman with whom he is supposed to be the closest, the woman he loves.

Nearly every woman senses this loss, though she probably doesn't understand the reason for it. Part of the attractiveness of men to women, we believe, is a yearning to heal this wounded man and make him whole again, to put him back in touch with his emotions, to give him love, to help him feel love and be renewed by it.

Men are separated from themselves and others. Women realize this but at the same time are frustrated by it, particularly when all of their attempts seem not to reach or heal their men, when the wounds seem too deep for women to mend so that, in effect, a man's wound hurts the woman as well.

Another problem is that when men have emotions, when something breaks through their armor, they have no way to deal with the pain. They often feel ashamed to cry, complain, or express their pain, and the wound therefore remains even more painful.

An example of the male need to avoid emotion came from Gaylord, a World War I veteran we interviewed who, at the age of eighty-eight, told us what he considered the biggest mistake of his life. He said that when he was a young man of twenty-four a dog he'd loved for sixteen years, Bandit, died. He told us that it hurt so much to love the dog and lose it that he vowed he'd never have another dog as long as he lived. Now, as Gaylord neared his own death and was reviewing his long life, he realized that he'd lost over sixty years of the love and friendship of animals for the sake of avoiding emotional pain.

ANGER: THE ONE PERMISSIBLE EMOTION

Men are allowed to feel one emotion—anger. But while the expression of anger is part of their training to kill, men are usually not required to do so. Therefore, many men cannot release this emotion and instead must learn to control it.

This is especially important, since women are very sensitive to the different forms of anger because of their own training to avoid aggression. As a result, men know they have to be careful with their anger and try to contain and control it as much as possible. Keep in mind that controlling an emotion often makes that emotion more intense. Thus, in effect what is also operating emotionally is ferocity control.

Fact #3: Men are driven to succeed

"All Duncan cares about is getting ahead," said one woman in dismay. "Of course I don't mind getting ahead. I like to live in a nice house and have a decent car, but I'm not like Duncan. For him, success is much more important, almost as if it's second to sex and food. He really wants to be successful and he works hard to make it happen. First he worked overtime and played politics at the office. Now he's been put in charge, but still he seems driven to do even better. I do like him being successful, but now that we have so much, why doesn't he spend more time with us? What use is success if you don't spend time with your family? Why is success so important to him? What's going on?"

Few things are so thoroughly trained into men as aggressiveness and the drive to succeed and master the world.

Men are driven to succeed in order to establish their status among other men. In earlier times, status and power meant that a man was less vulnerable to attack, and this fact alone increased his ability to survive.

Today, successful men have a greater selection of women than do men who are not successful. And in primitive cultures, such as the Yanomamo in South America, men who have proven their aggressiveness by killing other men have twice as many wives and, as a result, twice as many children as those men of comparable age who haven't killed. For example, as Edward Wilson points out in *On Human Nature*, a founder of a particular bloc of villages had forty-five children by eight wives. Ultimately, after his very aggressive sons had married, 75 percent of the population were this man's descendants. [5]

Male aggressiveness is one of the few traits that human males from various cultures seem to share. As early as three years old, boys exhibit higher levels of aggression than girls, and boys strive to dominate others at a very early age as well. [6] This lays the groundwork for the drive to succeed in the Outer World.

Today boys and men are acutely aware they are primarily measured by what they achieve. Boys fight to be first in line; men try to get ahead at the office. A man in our society isn't considered worthwhile because of the number of children he produces or because he is loving toward his wife and family, but rather by external symbols of wealth and accomplishment.

How much status does his job have? How much does he earn? What kind of home can he afford for his family? When introduced to a new erson the first question is usually "What do you do?" The question men must answer, the way in which they are primarily judged by others, and the thing that makes them feel good about themselves concerns what they have achieved in the Outer World.

THE BOYS' COMMANDMENTS

The drive to succeed in the Outer World is passed along from man to man, beginning in boyhood.

As Raphaela Best describes in her eye-opening book *We've All Got Scars*, the basic rules of boyhood are: be strong, be first, don't be a sissy, don't associate with a sissy, don't play with a crybaby, don't do housework or participate in any other activity associated with girls, and don't show affection.

Virtually all boys are well schooled in the commandments of the boy culture. These rules are passed along from boy to boy, and are learned from sports, ads, TV, and adults. The phrases used to teach the male drive to succeed include "no pain, no gain," "play even if you're injured," "don't wimp out," "act like a man," "don't be a crybaby," "take it like a man," "don't be a girl," and "don't be a loser."

Boys have, in Daniel Levinson's wonderfully apt phrase, seen in *Love in America* by Francesca Cancian, "dreams of glorious achievement," and they grow into men striving to live out their dreams. Whether they want to be big league baseball players, business entrepreneurs, winners of the Nobel Peace Prize, or President, men strive for success in the Outer World.

Of course, few men live out their wildest dreams, and nearly all are forced to compromise and accept a level of achievement below their dream. When men feel a need for more success than they have, they may seek it by owning an expensive or fast car, winning trophies, building up their muscles, increasing their bank account, or having a great stereo or wardrobe. Not to have recognizable Outer World success is to lose status and to be viewed by much of society as less of a man. Again, too, combat-readiness training is designed to help men act out their aggressiveness in the service of attaining success.

RAMBO AND ROCKY

As a boy grows up, the male combat-preparedness training passes on the combat-ready personality in two ways: directly and indirectly.

Boys receive direct lessons in how to be men when they play with guns and toy soldiers; map out strategy; pretend to be wounded and to shoot and kill others; play on a winning team; and stand on their own.

They learn combat-readiness indirectly through competitive sports and games. (In cultures where warfare is absent, so too are competitive sports.) Competitive sports teach several skills needed for combat-readiness, such as competition for survival, teamwork, the notion of "us" versus "them," the importance of defeating an opponent, and the triumph of identifying with a winner.

Training in the boys' school of life says win, avoid being a loser, avoid incompetence, be self-reliant, ignore pain, suppress emotion, don't ask for help, and to some extent, try to dominate. In other words, be successful in the Outer World, my son, and you will be rewarded.

WARRIORS IN SUITS AND TIES

Men take these same attributes into adulthood, but in our society, they are redirected into other skills during times of peace.

War strategy becomes office strategy, or it becomes the energy to control, to go forward, to "work wounded," to reach goals, to compete, to defeat others by developing better skills, to lead, to organize, and to defeat one's "enemies"—those people or situations that are blocking one's path to success.

In the workplace, then, many men are still combatants, but they are now disguised in suits and ties or hard hats, using skill, strength, education, or power acquired through competence or politics, or both, to establish dominance and to "win."

Now men hunt money instead of meat. The trouble is that, in his drive to seek high status and success, a man often gives his woman a low priority, spending little time and attention on her. The woman often views this as a sign that he loves his job or his success more than her and that it is more important to him to have a new car, for example, than to be with his wife. Therefore men, who often feel that they are being successful as much for their wives as they are for themselves, are shocked to discover that their wives are angry and feel unloved. Nevertheless, many women don't want to have sex with their men because they feel that the man's success is more important to him than she is, that he doesn't love her and is just using her sexually. This is yet another part of the reason why men don't get enough sex and women don't get enough love.

Still men continue to pursue success because they don't understand this about women. What they do know is that success is very attractive to women. Indeed one of the most important rewards for being successful in early times, or in the present, is the reward of being attractive to women. Men who are successful are much more likely to have their choice of women. Having an attractive woman is a point of status for men today just as it was in the past. This brings us to fact #4.

Fact #4: Men want to be attractive to women

Every man wants to be considered desirable, but for men, being attractive doesn't have nearly so much to do with physical appearance as it does for women.

The social message given to men is that while women are attracted to good-looking men, being successful counts far more for a man. This is backed up by studies showing that women select mates for their ability to be a good provider rather than for their good looks.

The truth is that, just as women have spent centuries being selected by men for their desirability as sex objects, women have been evaluating men as success objects. By this we mean women evaluate men both as successful protectors, particularly in violent times, and as successful providers. This, no doubt, began when women first discovered that some men always returned from the hunt with something to add to the family food supplies while others did not. Good looks did little to make up for an empty stomach. Although starvation, at least in the Western world, isn't so large a threat, we have all been trained to want and to consume well beyond simple sustenance. Therefore, the men who can provide goods for consumption are prized more highly than those who cannot.

It seems reasonable, therefore, that men, whether they are consciously aware of the choice they are making or not, tend to focus less on their physical attractiveness than on symbols of strength, power, and success.

We can see this clearly demonstrated today especially when a man and woman are getting ready for an evening out. The man may shave, run a comb through his hair, and dress in a suit similar to all those worn by other men. For women it is usually a very different story. He won't understand why it takes her so long to get ready, and he may assume she is selfish and become annoyed at what seems to him to be unreasonable self-absorption.

"What's wrong with women?" men lament. "Why do they have to make such a fuss? It takes me twenty minutes to get ready to go to a simple dinner party and it takes her half a day of shopping and an hour and twenty minutes to get ready. Why should it matter so much?" He can't understand why looks are so important to her when he has already rejected appearance as unimportant.

Men do want to be attractive to women, however, and they know that the way to do this is to be successful at being a man. Success in the workplace is the most important and the most highly rewarded status a man can achieve.

Unfortunately, this constant drive to be successful is almost never fully satisfied. This is because, no matter how high a level of success a man may reach, he often lacks the ability to feel any real deep satisfaction from this source. Deep satisfaction is not a product of achieving success in the Outer World so much as it is a part of achieving a relationship with one's Inner World.

Fact #5: Most men are continually trying to prove their worth

Among men, and particularly those with a high dose of warrior spirit, there is a constant urge and drive to do more, do it better, do it faster, and have more of it. The basic aggressive drive to survive and succeed pushes men ever forward.

This is true in part because men tend to have few areas in which to demonstrate their self-worth and thereby establish their identity. A woman, by contrast, may have many identities within which to demonstrate her competence and self-worth. She may have a career and also be a mother, a wife, and a social group leader. All these areas give her a sense of self-worth. Men, on the other hand, tend to put most, if not all, of their self-worth eggs in the work-achievement-success basket.

A second reason why men are continually trying to prove their worth is that no matter how much they accumulate, chances are they will never feel fully satisfied. A man may have success, but it is a fact of human life that outer world success tends to offer short and shallow satisfactions rather than those that are long-term and deeply rewarding. Sure he had a success, but that was last week or last month. He can only feel good if he is having success now. The worst part is that men expect success to satisfy them and are surprised and often bewildered when they never feel fully satisfied and fulfilled.

What men don't realize is that a deeper satisfaction doesn't come with Outer World success nearly so well as it comes from Inner World success, the traditional woman's domain of children, home, emotion, contentment, nurturing, and loving. And since he is still operating almost exclusively in the Outer World, he is thus, by definition, lacking in the more deeply fulfilling Inner World satisfactions.

This is another point of puzzlement for women. They often feel satisfied, but sense that their men are not. They often blame themselves —their appearance, their limited domestic skills, or their stressful schedules. Men also will sometimes blame their partners or circumstances as well because they, too, fail to understand the source of their dissatisfaction. They may even have a sense of guilt for having so much and not feeling better. They may decide the problem is with their partner and separate from her and find someone new. A man may change jobs or move to an entirely new place. He may buy a new car, a new wardrobe, or any number of other things to make himself feel better. But all of his attempts are usually for naught because he doesn't truly understand the problem and therefore can't solve it. Men don't even have access to their own Inner World of emotion and feeling to help them figure it out. Therefore men will simply try to fill the void they feel with more Outer World substitutes like success and dominance. This drive for many men is unending and their satisfaction fleeting.

The owner of a yachting company recently told us that it's common for his wealthy male customers to begin by buying a small boat. But soon they feel dissatisfied and, thinking that a bigger boat will satisfy them, a year or so later they buy another, larger yacht. Finally, after buying a third or fourth still larger one, they give up on yachting altogether, having decided it just doesn't give them what they hoped it would. These men then often move on to owning their own plane, hoping this new hobby will provide them with what they seek.

Since most men's signs of success are tightly clustered around Outer World accomplishments, their main energy is directed toward the external world; they strive to accumulate more money, more status, more degrees, more investments, a better résumé, a bigger yacht, or a private plane.

George, whom we mentioned earlier, was a "successful" divorce attorney, but said that he, too, was dissatisfied. Yes, of course he knew he was successful, others said so, but he set his sights higher and higher—on a partnership in his firm, then on a senior partnership. It was never enough. His drive to succeed was endless.

And woe to the man who *does* reach his ultimate success goal, for he then discovers he still has a gaping hole of dissatisfaction inside him, no way to understand or deal with the pain, and no idea what it is or how to cure it.

Another way to feel successful is for a man to identify with a sports team and to feel like a winner when his team wins. Especially for men who have been blocked in other avenues of meeting their success hunger, sports can provide the "food" they crave.

Many women gape in wonder at men's passionate enthusiasm for and devotion to a football team, without realizing the fulfillment he can achieve from the team's success. Rooting for a winner can make a man feel like a winner. That's why so many grown men are able to stand up in public and scream with maniacal fervor at the top of their lungs, "We're number one!"

Unfortunately, however, the combination of stress from being driven to succeed in the Outer World and the feeling of never having enough often leads to more frustration and irritability. And since most men don't feel they're accomplishing enough, a deep frustration often permanently exists inside them, which is supposed to be kept hidden.

Imagine what it's like for the man who feels he hasn't made his "dream of glorious achievement" come true—not to mention solving the more mundane problem of getting by from paycheck to paycheck while being constantly bombarded by a barrage of commercials on TV and radio, in newspaper and magazines saying: Buy, buy, buy. More, newer, bigger. And he wants success not only for himself but for her, too.

As Warren Farrell points out in his insightful book *Why Men Are the Way They Are,* the pressure for men to be successful and to demonstrate that success is greater than ever. For example, over time the diamond ads in newspapers and magazines show men buying bigger and bigger diamond engagement rings for their fiancées.

The result is that men are frustrated not only in terms of what success they can achieve but in how much they can display to others.

This feeling of never gaining enough leaves a man frustrated and under stress and often results in irritation that affects the relationship negatively. This in turn results in him getting less sex and her getting less love.

Fact #6: Men have a powerful sex drive

"Ed and I have our ups and downs, but whenever we are really down, it always has something to do with sex," said Martha, a twenty-nine-year-old woman who'd been married three years. "Why is having sex so important to men? It's like sometimes it's all that Ed thinks about. And he can be so persistent. I like sex, but I don't think about it all the time, and it sure isn't the most important thing to me. I guess that's why Ed's mad so much, because I just don't care about it as much as he does. The funny thing is that it's such a short moment of pleasure for a man and yet for that little time they take up so much energy to get it. Why doesn't he figure out something else to do. It's always sex. He wants to have sex when he feels good, and he wants to have sex when he feels bad. He even wants to have sex when we're fighting. And if I'm upset he's sure that's what I need to make me feel better. The thing is, I can think of half a dozen other things I'd rather do with Ed than have sex. I mean what's wrong with just having a good time together and not having sex? I'd like to sit down and have a conversation with him, go out for a walk, or even play a game of cards more than just have sex. He's so horny all the time that I can't even hug him or cuddle with him or let him touch me without him deciding that it's time to have sex, and if I don't want to, he'll get mad as hell and say that I was acting like I wanted to have sex and now I don't. The thing is that I *wasn't* acting like I wanted to have sex; I was acting like I wanted some love. But everything for Ed is sex. Are all men the same?"

It isn't by accident that there are over five billion human beings on this planet in spite of all the wars, famines, diseases, and disasters. Men like sex and virtually always want more than they are getting.

According to one study, mentioned earlier, men think about sex 6 times an hour and yet they only have sex 1.5 times a week. That's a lot of frustration. Why is sex so important to them?

Sex serves many purposes for men. First of all, it feels good. It's also an outlet for the powerful innate sex drive. It's rooted in the survival of our species and is an inherent drive based in our physical and biological needs, which we share with other animals.

Second, men feel a sense of ego gratification as a result of having sex with a woman, particularly a desirable one. It means, for example, that, while she might have chosen many other men to have sex with, she *has* chosen *him*.

Many men view sex as another form of success. It is another way of having won or of having conquered. It's not surprising that these men, in particular, are frustrated by a lack of sex the same way they are frustrated by a lack of success. No matter how much they have, it isn't satisfying for long.

Third, sex gains importance through the possibility of procreation, as a man passes along his family name and a part of himself. For many generations large numbers of offspring fostered survival, and male sexuality was accordingly encouraged.

Fourth, men use sex as an expression of love. A man often feels a sincere, deep, and meaningful love while having sex with a woman he loves. He can feel good within himself in a central way that makes him feel valuable, desirable, and complete, bringing him closeness and intimacy with the person he most highly values.

Fifth, no one can understand men without understanding that sex, beyond all of the reasons mentioned above, is one of the few, if not the only, means a man has of expressing intimacy and emotion.

A man may want to tell a woman he loves her; he may want to share his feelings, perhaps to seek forgiveness for a past slight; he may want to express how he admires her; he may want comfort in a moment of doubt, or because he is sad or lonely; or he may want to let her know he thinks she is the most marvelous woman in the world. He may have a limitless number of emotional reactions to her and to the world around him, but sex is often the only avenue of expression that he feels comfortable with or feels he has permission to utilize.

He can't talk about how he's feeling. His male training has for so long discouraged him from doing so that he might not know what to say or, worse, he may be so separated from his feelings that he doesn't even know what he feels. This means he is not likely to seek any resolution of his feelings through discussing or expressing them verbally, or through caressing and cuddling, as a woman so often wants him to do. Frequently all or most of his feelings, particularly his tender feelings, are automatically translated into the socially sanctioned male channel of sexual need.

Here, then, is where a big portion of the battle of the sexes is waged. She is waiting for him to show how much he loves her so she will want to have sex. She wants to feel good *before* having sex. He feels good *after* having sex.

This point must be clear because it is basic to one of the most common ways men and women misunderstand each other. Because his combat training discourages him from expressing tender emotions, he doesn't express the caring a woman needs to make her want to have sex. As a result he doesn't get the sex he wants, or he gets less than he would get if he knew how to express love in a way that made a woman want to have sex with him. As a result, both are frustrated.

Unfortunately, since irritation and anger are among the few emotions men can express, that is how the frustration usually manifests itself. Yet most men try to contain and control their irritation and frustration, at least as much as possible. An important reason men bother to control themselves as much as they do is related to the following fact.

Fact #7: Men desire and depend on their relationships with women more than they usually realize or admit

Men need women. If you don't think so, just look at the statistics: 94 percent of all men marry,[7] and they remarry much more quickly than women do after being divorced or widowed. Men also live longer when they're married, and divorced men commit suicide five times more often than do married men.[8]

Men need women emotionally and for practical reasons.

The practical reasons are obvious and centuries old. Very early in our history, men and women divided up the chores. Men were in charge of hunting, while women were responsible for gathering or growing plants and vegetables and preparing food. Men were in charge of defense. Women produced and raised the children. This natural co-dependency based on division of labor still persists into our age, and while many women now pursue careers, they are still in charge of home and children, a task men look to them to perform.

But there is a much deeper and more essential reason men need women. Women represent the other half of the world that many men generally still don't enter—the Inner World.

We have spoken of the Inner World and the Outer World before—the Inner World being that of feelings, home, nurturing, intuition, love, and relationships. The Outer World is the world of conquest, in war or on the job. It is the world of action and thought, of doing and controlling, of mastery and success. In our day it is generally the world of career, and it is a world women have entered only recently.

Still, while women have moved into the Outer World, men, generally, have remained outside the Inner World, blocked from it by their male training. Therefore they need someone to bring this essential part of their humanness to them, and that someone is virtually always a woman.

Few men have close friendships. This is true because part of their combat-readiness training discourages men from being too close to each other emotionally and also because it is often difficult and complex for men and women to be just friends. This means that men have no one to talk to, no one to really share any genuine closeness and intimacy with except their female partner. A woman therefore often serves as a trusted companion to a man, someone with whom he can share whatever intimacy he is capable of sharing. She also may act as his social "glue." Because women have long been good at forming and maintaining relationships, they establish the social network, bringing their men in with them. Men therefore have a social life through their women. They can be friends with the husbands or boyfriends of their wives' friends. Women also provide men with children. It is through women, then, that men can link more intimately with the rest of humanity.

Living in a world of danger and isolation leaves a man yearning for a haven, and he tries to find it in the arms, and the vagina, of his woman. As Andrew Schmookler has said in his brilliant book *Out of Weakness*, "The female thus represents not only the paradise that has been lost, but also a part of the warrior that has been lost in the creation of armored strength. . . . The woman embodies, for the warrior, the core of life."[9]

Another factor in this co-dependency is that women tend to take care of men not only emotionally but physically as well, making sure they eat well, see a doctor when necessary, and generally take care of their health. This, combined with the ability to fill men's emotional needs—however often they deny that they have any—makes the male need for women a powerful and pervading one.

One study found that among men whose wives had died within the previous six months the death rate was 40 percent higher than expected.[10] Therefore, while a man has been conditioned for a lifetime to avoid closeness and feelings, particularly deep emotional and tender feelings, the scientific evidence strongly suggests that, in spite of and because of the emotional anesthesia, the social armor, and the suppression of the

Inner World, men find it difficult to live without women and often die of a broken heart without them.

This suggests that in spite of a man's combat-ready training, which tells him not to want or need the Inner World and not to react to loss, but to stand alone, all these emotions play a primary and very important role in his basic well-being. Still, in spite of this need, however strong, men still find closeness uncomfortable.

Fact #8: Men avoid closeness in relationships

Most men are eager to have a primary relationship with a woman, yet they avoid emotional closeness and dependency. It sounds contradictory, but it actually makes perfect sense when viewed in the context of male training.

As we've seen, men have been trained away from emotional closeness even though they require and crave a certain amount of closeness in order to verify their identity as human beings. Therefore, while they need intimacy, their training keeps them from knowing how to get it.

As Bernie Zilbergeld, clinical psychologist and head of the Men's Program at the University of California, San Francisco, said, "The point is simple and frightening: the socialization of males provides very little that is of value in the formation of intimate relationships."[11]

BOYS WEAR BLUE

The socialization of males begins in childhood when boys are trained to be different from girls.

Most people are familiar with the well-publicized study of the same baby being dressed first as a boy and then as a girl and the differences in how the child was handled by people who were unaware of the child's sex. Little girls received more cuddling, while little boys were expected to require less affection and were given less. Little girls were spoken to in softer, gentler tones, while boys were approached with deeper, stronger voices. But while early training of this sort no doubt is already preparing a boy for a more independent and isolated role, there is an even earlier stage of training than this.

When boys and girls are babies they are virtually always, in all cultures, primarily cared for by their mothers. As they grow, girls realize, little by little, that in many of the most essential ways they are like their mothers.

The situation is quite different for little boys. Very early in childhood, boys get the feeling and eventually the clear message that they are not like their mothers. They cannot identify with her because they are not going to grow up to be like her. Boys are forced very early to separate themselves emotionally from their mothers and to be far more emotionally independent.

MAMA'S BOY

In fact, a boy is ridiculed and made to feel ashamed if he is regarded as a mama's boy. This point was illustrated perfectly at a recent birthday party for three-year-olds to which our own three-year-old, Amanda, was invited.

At some point during the party the mothers, preoccupied with kitchen preparations, allowed two of the children, a boy and a girl, to slip away unnoticed to an older sister's room where they proceeded to put on her clothes and makeup. When they next appeared, the two were wearing dresses, lipstick, and eye shadow, all liberally applied, and both were obviously proud of their work.

The little girl, Tasha, was greeted with approving laughter and told she looked pretty even as she was mildly scolded and told she shouldn't have left the party or used someone else's things. The three-year-old boy, Bobbie, was scolded far more sternly and the makeup was immediately wiped off by his frowning mother, who asked him again and again, "What will your father say when he hears you were dressing like a girl?" The other little boys danced about chanting, "Bobbie is a girl, Bobbie is a girl," until finally Bobbie burst into tears. Two five-year-old boys immediately labeled him a mama's baby and wouldn't play with him for the rest of the party.

Bobbie had done the unforgivable: he had taken on female symbols and trappings.

The sad truth is that Bobbie and all little boys quickly and often traumatically learn that boys are supposed to feel separated from their mothers and from all females. They don't look like them and they must not, under any circumstances, act like them. This means that boys are forced to be distant from their number one person in life—their mother. And the harsh breaking of this central relationship creates a foundation for further avoidance of closeness, through the creation of stronger separation and independence.

ORPHANS IN AN OCEAN OF BOYHOOD

The fact that boys must be markedly different from girls and independent of their mothers forces a boy, often painfully, to stop identifying with her and to identify instead with the parent he will most closely resemble—his father.

This psychological break from the primary parent may be difficult and traumatic enough in itself, yet there is usually a further complication. The vast majority of fathers are emotionally and often physically unavailable to their sons.

Yes, he may see his father occasionally, but the average child, boy or girl, spends less than five minutes a day with his or her father.

In most cases, the boy's father has himself been trained to be separate and to believe that emotional relating—holding, touching, kissing, talking softly, nurturing gently, even to his own son—is not acceptable masculine behavior and is to be avoided.

The result is that boys are frightened, confused, and wounded by their separateness and aloneness, a psychic injury that sets them adrift in the vast, wave-filled ocean of boyhood.

It is true that this casting-adrift does, in effect, build character—as a result of it the boy develops a strong sense of individual identity—but it is also damaging. Small Bobbie at the party for three-year-olds, for instance, was forced to put on a layer of armor and strive to dominate. Even at age three he was suffering through one of the first stages of combat-readiness training as he is wounded and told not to cry.

As a boy gets older the requirements for admission to manhood get tougher and his combat-readiness armor and anesthesia affect him even more powerfully. At a very early age a boy must adopt the ethos of independence and individual strength. He still feels a need to be close to another, but he also has to avoid the seeming threat that intimacy presents to his individuality and separateness. The result is the message many men give out to their women: "Be with me, but don't get too close."

One way that boys and men keep their distance is by turning against others, a common male psychological defense in which a man focuses on how to blame others rather than himself. This separative defense was no doubt used by our great-great-great-grandfathers and has been around for thousands of years. It's another way to hold people off at arm's length. (Women tend to turn against themselves, as we will see later).

Men even keep distance from their supposed friends. Male friendships are based around work or sports, and avoid personal subjects ("Be a man—handle life on your own"). Men have few, if any, close friends in whom they honestly confide. They may have long-standing friendships, but most men do not talk to each other about personal feelings, problems, or relationships the way women do. Men learn to "play their cards close to the chest" and "keep their backs to the wall." It's a rough-and-tumble life in the Outer World for many men today, but as we've seen, it used to be even worse.

We can also see male distancing in a man's choice of entertainment. The danger and the hell of warfare kept men in need of social distance as armor against the pain of losing a fellow combatant and of being able to kill. This same situation is re-created daily in sports. Most men watch football—which centers on competition, mock warfare, emotional control, frustration and energy outlet, team cohesion, and individual skill—rather than the programs most women prefer—those that are concerned with human relationships and emotions.

The social distance a man maintains has obvious drawbacks, since it so often keeps him from getting to have sex with a woman who values closeness. This is also one of the primary contributors to the male-female love-sex conflict. She wants to feel close before having sex. He distrusts closeness and often wants to get close only physically. This makes a woman feel used. She believes that he does not love her but only uses her physically for sex. And so the struggle continues.

The facts we have seen so far—the drive to succeed, the sense of never getting or doing enough, the sexual frustration, the need to be close while still needing to avoid closeness, the emotional control even in the face of pain, danger, and hardship—are a powerful and wounding combination. One result of all of this for many men is a state of unalleviated stress that leads to another fact.

Fact #9: Being a man is dangerous to one's health

The average man lives about seventy-one years, whereas the average woman lives to be over seventy-eight—an additional seven years of life for women.

While part of the reason for this is biological, estimates say that from one-third to one-half of this difference in life span is due to the male life-style and personality. Looking at what we know about male combat-readiness training, we can accurately predict that men will tend to ignore illness (even serious illness), avoid seeking medical help, and fail to take measures that would help them have better health. And though they may accomplish a great deal at work, the stress and the excessive drive cause them to have more heart problems and stomach difficulties than women.

If men are going to take care of their health they usually need help, usually from a woman. Nevertheless, there are signs that many men are becoming better at caring for themselves, relating better with their children and other family members, paying more attention to their nutrition, their need for exercise, and symptoms of health problems. All of which leads us to the final fact about men.

Fact #10: Men are changing

There are signs that men are changing. More fathers are spending more time with their children than previous generations of fathers did. More men are looking for help to find deeper meaning in life and to achieve more emotional connection. Men are able to show more emotions in public, and best of all they're starting to open up to their Inner World.

We can see the beginning of a change that points to the possibility of alleviating the combat training which most men endure and which sits at so much of the root of the difficulties between men and women.

We can already see significant differences between men in their twenties and thirties and older men.

One woman we interviewed has the interesting profession of training and caring for elephants. Teresa told us about the time that Lucky, one of her elephants, was dying. Teresa sat next to Lucky's face and wept at the loss of her old, dear friend. Two young male trainers, age twenty-three and thirty-two, who also felt Lucky was family, wept along with her. Standing apart from them were two older male trainers, age fifty-four and sixty-one, snickering at the emotional state of the three who mourned. While the older trainers were separated from their own emotions, the younger men were far less so.

This is the new reality that we as a society, and men in particular, are moving toward. It is a new way of directing warrior spirit and a new kind of combat training that prepares men for the Outer World, but also takes into account the Inner World. We are seeing this new attitude among many younger men because now, for the first time in thousands of years, the circumstances that supported the combat training men previously received is breaking down and permitting men to be different.

The *Los Angeles Times Magazine* reported on October 1, 1989, that men are now just beginning to change and many "have wandered onto a 'Daddy Track.' Professional men, single fathers, manual laborers—not a lot of men, but more all the time—have discovered a flip side to the women's movement. Where women found new identities and self-respect in jobs outside the home, these men are finding that what really matters to them is life outside the job. . . . They work and provide, but they want, too, to be home to enjoy with their families the fruits of their efforts. Urged on by their wives, haunted by their fathers' example, they are stumbling toward a new balance between work and family."

This phenomenon is growing and is most common among younger men. According to the *L.A. Times* article, "When one thousand men and women were surveyed by Robert Half International, a San Francisco personnel recruiting firm, 74 percent of the men said they would choose a Daddy Track—flexible jobs that offer slower career advancement but more time to give attention to family—over more rigid jobs on a faster track. . . . A national study in May by Opinion Research Corporation of Princeton, New Jersey, found that male managers under forty are the group in the work force least satisfied with the amount of time their jobs leave for their family life. . . . Fathers are saying: 'I'm not going to do to my kids what my dad did to me. I don't want to just be a paycheck to them.'"

Little by little, the traditional male role and specifically the need for combat-readiness training, with its armor and anesthesia, are changing. As John Mueller has written in *Retreat from Doomsday: The Obsolescence of Major War*, by "May 15, 1984, the major countries of the developed world

48 *Too Little Sex, Too Little Love*

had managed to remain at peace with each other for the longest continuous stretch of time since the days of the Roman Empire."[12] Mueller sees this achievement not as the result of a restraint imposed by a balance of nuclear power, but rather as a step in a historical process which has forced us to conclude that war is a futile enterprise, a conviction that has spread among increasing numbers of people in the developed countries. War, which was once considered one of life's necessities, has become "rationally unthinkable" and is now regarded as no less absurd than dueling, slavery, bear-baiting, and human sacrifice. Mueller believes that World War II may come to be seen as the war that ended wars. Certainly in a time of technological warfare—which women could conduct as readily as men, and women are among the soldiers with their fingers on the nuclear buttons—the need for combat-ready men has declined. As our society moves away from hand-to-hand war and into a new era of economic and technological conflict, human awareness, and sensitivity, new opportunities are being created for men.

Men no longer need to be emotionally anesthetized and armored for warfare; they now have the opportunity to explore the Inner World of emotion, relationships, intimacy, and love. They can remain strong and competent, and they can retain the other positive and life-fostering male traits, but they can now drop the negative aspects of combat training. A man can be aware of his own feelings of love, caring, and intimacy, the very feelings that turn women on, both emotionally and sexually. Therefore men now have the opportunity to give women the love they want and in turn to receive more of the sex, and thereby the love, that is so important to men.

NOTES, CHAPTER 2

1. Quoted in Edward O. Wilson, *On Human Nature* (New York: Bantam, 1979), p. 89.
2. Riane Eisler, *The Chalice and the Blade* (New York: Harper & Row, 1987). Eisler's book is based on the pioneering work of UCLA archeologist Marija Gimbutas.
3. Francesca Cancian, *Love in America* (Cambridge, England: Cambridge University Press, 1987), p. 77.
4. Cancian, p. 75.
5. Wilson, p. 119.
6. Carol R. Ember and Melvin Ember, *Cultural Anthropology* (Englewood Cliffs, N.J.: Prentice-Hall, 1988), p. 155.

7. William Masters, Virginia Johnson, and Robert Kolodny, *Masters and Johnson on Sex and Human Loving* (Boston: Little, Brown, 1988) p. 326.
8. Cancian, p. 85.
9. Andrew Schmookler, *Out of Weakness: Healing the Wounds That Drive Us to War* (New York: Bantam, 1988), p. 169.
10. Cancian, p. 82.
11. Bernie Zilbergeld, *Male Sexuality* (New York: Bantam, 1978), p. 38.
12. New York: Basic Books, 1989.

3

The Facts About Women

Poets, philosophers, and psychologists have long expounded upon the mysteriousness of women and the difficulty in understanding the feminine psyche. Women are, however, no more mysterious than men. Like men, women are the way they are because of the biological, anthropological, and social forces that have shaped them.

For hundreds of generations, while men have been masters of the Outer World, controlling and dominating that which is outside of themselves, women have been masters of the Inner World, experts in dealing with home, family, friends, communication, feelings, intuition, intimacy, and nurturing.

These Inner World skills have come naturally out of who she is biologically, as well as who she has been asked to be socially. And, just as men have used their skills in the Outer World to foster their own quality of life and ensure their survival, so too have women learned to use their understanding of the Inner World to foster their quality of life and ensure their survival.

Let's look at the facts about who women are, why and how they became the way they are, and how this all contributes to the women's half of the battle of the sexes and the love-sex conflict that plagues the relationships of men and women.

Fact #1: Women have nurturing spirit

Just as the basic human energy of men has been molded into warrior spirit, the basic energy of women is molded into nurturing spirit. This follows an eons-old tradition.

The most basic role of the female throughout history has been that of nurturer within her Inner World, a world centered around relationships and care-giving, home and hearth.

Early woman may or may not have had a close emotional relationship with the man who impregnated her, but if her infant was to survive, she had to have a close nurturing relationship with her child. The women who were best able to care for and protect their children were the ones whose offspring survived. Therefore the most nurturing women were the ones who passed on their genes as well as the nurturing tradition and training to their daughters who, in turn, stood a better chance of passing on their own genes and training to the next generation of women. In fact, nurturing has become so inherent in women that many women experience physical nurturing "triggers." For example, often when nursing mothers hear a baby cry, even one other than their own, their milk automatically springs forth, a difficult situation for the woman who is standing in the grocery checkout line. Women often feel unmistakable nurturing triggers at the mere sight of a baby, be it human or animal, and automatically want to pick it up, to hold it close, give it warmth, and caress it. This is even more true and powerful if a women sees a baby or any other living creature that is hurt. Something in her makes her want to help.

That is not to say that men don't have some of the same reactions. For women they are simply closer to the surface and usually more readily acted upon, since men are trained not to show tenderness or nurturing qualities, which are identified as female characteristics. A man may therefore spring to the aid of a baby trapped in a burning building. But once the child is saved, he is likely to be uncomfortable holding and comforting it and will probably look for a woman to do so.

Nurturing fosters life, and traditionally women have nurtured not only their children but also their men, other family members, friends, pets, gardens, and often humanity in general. In fact, women often nurture virtually anything and everything, giving help, advice, nursing and medical attention, and whatever else will foster survival and growth.

This basic trait of women, then, has been an essential part of being female, but apart from promoting the survival of others through her ability to nurture, very early in human history woman learned to use this ability to help herself survive.

While men focus on being independent and capable of standing on their own as a way of surviving in the world, women focus on being cooperative and looking to their relationships to help them survive. And of all the relationships women have learned to form, none has been of greater consequence to their survival and the survival of their children than their relationship with men. Throughout history, while a woman might survive on her own (some eras have been more conducive to this than others) she has virtually always found it helpful to have a good man around the house.

Female sexuality contributed to female survival by helping women establish relationships with men. But beyond attracting men sexually, a woman, if she was to keep a man at her side, needed to develop other relationship and nurturing skills.

For women, attraction and bonding to a man was possibly, in the beginning, a natural transfer of the instinctive and pleasurable feelings she received from caring for and nurturing her infants. This love, a pleasurable emotion, may have made her prefer one man over another, but other reasons might have weighed more heavily. She needed a male who would: (1) help her survive by using his skill as a hunter and a protector; (2) be "good" with children; and (3) be able to give her sexual pleasure.

Also, those males who met all of the above requirements—good provider, good protector, good father and lover—were in far more demand than those men who didn't, just as they are today. And in securing one of these males, a woman's ability to nurture and love became a powerful charm. From the earliest times if she wanted a relationship with a particularly desirable man she learned to use not only her riveting sexuality but also the irresistible emotion of love. We say "irresistible" because, aside from the drive to survive, little else is as powerful for either sex as the innate desire to bond with another fellow human. As anthropologist Helen Fisher puts it, "Bonding is deeply engraved in the human psyche."[1] A woman's ability to love and nurture fostered, and still fosters, this bonding which in turn fostered her survival and that of her infants and her man.

THE POWER TO BOND

Women still bond with men in much the same way as they did in early times. This often means pleasing a man by satisfying all of his appetites. The woman learns to cook what he likes the way he likes it; she also admires him, takes care of his wounds, and nurses him in sickness; she provides him with children; she shares the tasks of living, the ups and downs, and the memories; and she lends a sympathetic ear to his concerns.

By meeting these needs a woman creates an atmosphere in which her man is comfortable and happy and to which he will return again and again. Since men often can't readily communicate the ways in which their needs can best be fulfilled, it has often been left up to women to figure it out for themselves. This need to "read" her man, as well as her children and the other women in her group whose cooperation helped her survive, encouraged women to increase their sensitivity and inner awareness. It was a skill that fostered the development of that "sixth sense" called *female intuition*, which then entered her arsenal as a central tool for survival, domestic peace, and happiness.

Fact #2: Women want to love and to be loved

"Love is such a big deal for women," says one young man. "Sometimes it seems that's all that's really important to them. Take my girlfriend. She is always snuggling up to me and wanting me to tell her I love her. And whenever anything goes wrong she'll say, 'You don't love me.' Women seem to measure things by love. If I do something really nice for her, she assumes I love her a lot. If I'm in a bad mood, she thinks I don't love her. Of course her career is important to her, but what seems really important to her has to do with love. She talks about it with her friends—about who loves whom and if they're going to get married or if they're breaking up and why. She even tells me about the love lives of her friends at work. Do I care if Molly is getting engaged to some guy who used to be engaged to the bookkeeper? I think women worry more about love than they do about anything else. Why is that?"

Apart from nurturing, there is hardly a trait more universal among women than their desire to love and to be loved.

This is due in part to women's strong predisposition to nurture and to the fact that they've been raised by their mothers to express and receive closeness both physically—through touching, holding, and cuddling—and emotionally—through sharing feelings, activities, and thoughts.

Love combines the physical and emotional nurturing into one, creating a bonding and blending with the beloved other whom most women value above nearly everything else in their lives.

Unlike men, who have been forced to develop an armor of separation and distance and an emotional anesthetic, women have had to develop neither. Instead, women remain open to love and closeness because they have never had to lose their emotional identification and attachment to their mothers, as boys are forced to do (see Chapter 2). They don't have to learn to anesthetize their emotions against the wrenching experience of detaching from mother or in preparation for war, as do boys. Instead a girl is permitted to retain, in essence, a psychological umbilical cord that encourages her to seek and give love her whole life long.

Girl babies retain and develop this attachment by sharing in their mothers' activities from a very early age. It is common, for instance, for a little girl to be Mommy's little helper, mimicking her mother's activities and, as she grows older, taking on more and more of a mothering role.

This role is assumed very directly in some cultures. In Mexico, for example, girls are called Mamita (little mother), giving them the message that they, too, will be mothers and will do as their mothers are doing.

In this way a girl learns that girlhood will lead to womanhood. Her life has continuity and, no matter how much a little girl may ultimately differ from her mother, she will always have the sense of a deep relationship with the one who produced her.

This sharing and this continuity, as de Castillejo says in her book, *Knowing Woman,*[2] lets a mother feel she can live again through her daughter and allows a little girl to feel she lives her mother's life.

Through this connection a woman extends backward into her mother and forward into her daughter, this participation and intermingling giving rise to a sense that her life is spread out over generations and that she is, in this sense, outside of time. In this way many women feel a broadened sense of identity, even of immortality. This lifelong connection creates in women a basic security, a powerful drive to bond and merge, and the drive to love and be loved in return remains with a woman more deeply than for a man. And it is this deep security and ability to give care, love, and nurture that plays such a large role in attracting men to women. She is the bridge to love and intimacy that for so much of history has been closed to him by his need to be ready for combat.

Fact #3: A woman is a man's bridge to the Inner World

"I hate to admit it, but I would be lost without Gina," said a New York businessman. "All day it's like a war out there, everybody shoving and competing. It's like playing no-rule football and everybody is after your ass! I have lunch with people who would smile at me even as they're calculating how to rip me off. And I sit next to people who ask about my health only to probe for a weakness. I can't trust any of them except to stab me in the back if they have the chance. Then I come home and there is Gina. It's such a relief. She's like an island of sanctuary in a sea of monsters. Somehow just being with her makes me feel human again. It's like returning to the most important part of myself."

This is what men are often looking for in women—a safe haven, a gentle touch, and a bridge back to their own inner peace. Because the woman has not had to think of herself as separate, she has not had to build the strong separate emotional boundaries to herself that men create for themselves, and therefore she is better able to connect with others on a deeper level.

Women also often have a profound sense of inherent self-worth from the simple knowledge that they are capable of bringing forth life.

All human life passes through women. This gives a woman a deep sense of connection to other women and a sense of completeness that is unavailable to the vast majority of men, who are told to find their completeness through work and success, which frequently lacks true depth, thus depriving men of the sense of completeness many women experience.

Because men lack this completeness and this connection, aside from their work-success search, they consciously and unconsciously look to women to create it for them. They also look to women to create a family and to connect them with love, with friends, and ultimately to that innocent part of themselves and to the emotions and feelings they lost through their combat-readiness training.

At the same time, because of their combat training, they fear the very reconnection they seek. They want to be close, just not *too* close. They want to love, but not too much or too deeply because these feelings make them vulnerable. A part of the man wants to be taken care of and nurtured, the other part wants to reject all of this as unmanly. This creates the push-pull between men and women that most couples have experienced, though few understand the reason for it and often blame each other for the frustration that results. But it isn't anyone's fault. It is the natural result of the rise of civilization and the struggle to survive in a violent world.

Many men are left with a desire to connect intimately, but they believe that the only manly way to do so is through sex.

Women, on the other hand, want to offer love and nurturing, to make a home and perhaps a family, but for a very good reason they are suspicious of men's sexual motivations. Does he love me? Does he want my love and nurturing? Does he want to be together with me for *me* and who *I* am? Or does he just want sex?

This, then, is another aspect of the battle of the sexes. She may feel comfortable attracting him through her sexuality, but she wants to connect emotionally through love *before* having sex.

He is afraid of loving, but he feels safe expressing love and intimacy through sex. But since she is afraid he doesn't love her and is just using her for sex, she is hesitant to have sex with him. As a result he doesn't get the sex he wants to make him feel good physically and to let him express his love and intimacy. He is therefore frustrated both sexually and emotionally.

But why are women so concerned about not being loved? Why do they often hesitate or flatly refuse to have sex just for fun, as men often want to do? Why do women say no to sex, even when they might really want to have sex?

Fact #4: Women often say no (to sex) when they'd like to say yes

"Why don't women know what they want?" says a construction worker in his late twenties. "First Angela is real sweet and gives me a kiss and wants to cuddle. She acts like she's all excited. But then when I start to get serious about having sex, she pulls away. We've been dating for months and I know she really has the hots for me, but she still keeps me at arm's length. She says it's because I like another woman named Lisa. I don't like her nearly as much as I like Angela, but I can't seem to convince her, and anyway she probably likes other guys, too. Anyway what does that have to do with the fact that Angela, I know, wants to do it with me, and I sure want to do it with her, but she keeps saying no."

"I used to think I understood my wife Sarah, but now I think I don't understand her at all," said a man in his thirties who has been married for five years. "When I met her she was so sexy and always wearing lacy things and wanting to make love and doing crazy kind of fun things that surprised me. Now everything's changed. She's still romantic, but now instead of making love, all she does is read about it in those pulp romance novels. She just eats them up. And it would seem that since she's reading all that sexy stuff she wants to have sex more, but now she just avoids me. Of course she always comes up with some kind of an excuse, but I can tell she's just not interested. Then last Tuesday I decided that if she was reading so much, I should get something to read, too, so I bought a copy of *Penthouse*. That night she was upstairs reading her sexy book, and I was by myself looking at naked girls. It was crazy. The weird thing is I know she can be so hot to make love. Why does she keep avoiding me?"

Most women don't say no to sex because they don't like sex or don't have the potential to be very sexually excited and receptive. It is interesting to note in fact that human females are the sexiest female creatures alive. Indeed, on a biological level, women are unique in the entire animal kingdom. Most female animals have sex only during "seasons"—short periods when they are fertile, but a woman can have sex any time—in season, out of season, and even during pregnancy. She can have sex night or day, for hours at a time. Some women can even have multiple orgasms. No other female animal can do this.

It is also interesting to note that, according to Dr. Helen Fisher of the Anthropology Section, New York Academy of Sciences, prehistoric women's sexuality evolved to its unique level of constant availability to keep men nearby. And once again the driving force behind this change was the presence of violence.

The period we are speaking about now was long before the peaceful Neolithic era we spoke about in Chapter 2. We are going millions of years back to the evolutionary period when human beings first left the relative safety of the trees and moved out onto the open plain.

At this early time, females had seasons, during which a fertile, sexually available female was the center of attention of the males. For example, when a sexually receptive female slept, the males gathered around her, and when she moved on, they moved on. They mated with her throughout the day, and during these interludes, her offspring were placed in the center of the group where predators could not grab them. Once these early human ancestors moved out on the plain, where they couldn't climb a tree, predators were suddenly a much bigger threat than they had been before. It became a matter of survival for females to have a male—at that time males were roughly twice the size of females— around for protection. This, then, became the key to females evolving their unique trait of being constantly sexually receptive. Now those females who were able to keep the attention of a male were more likely to survive.

Sex became a powerful tool of survival and women evolved into the most potentially sexy females alive, able to have sex at virtually any time.

This is still true of modern females. Women are, in fact, capable of having and enjoying sex far more often than they do in our culture. In Mangaia, in the South Pacific, for example—one of the very few cultures that are free of sexual taboos for females—women have sex several times a night and brag about the number of sexual partners they've had.

In our culture, however, the opposite is true, and it is valuable to see exactly why, because the answer sheds light on another aspect of the battle of the sexes. Why is it that women often say no when they'd like to say yes?

As we mentioned in Chapter 2, there was a period that ended six thousand years ago when women were not living in the open and were far less vulnerable than they've been at other times. Instead of being dependent on men, women were part of a team with men. It was also a time when women were given great respect for their dazzling ability to bring forth new life and nurture it.

Women held this position until the Kurgans and other violent hordes forced them to be dependent upon men for survival and therefore subject to men's will and laws.

Unfortunately for women, and ultimately for men, these laws also governed female sexuality, and women were forced into what biological anthropologist Irene Elia calls "the sexual contract." Elia bluntly describes this early situation of violence and female dependence on men where males in effect said to women, "Offer your fertility [sexuality] only to me;

become my slave, and I will be your ally. If you do not do this, I will not assist and protect you; I will not help nurture your infants or prevent other men from killing them and raping you afterward.'"[3]

This enforced subservience led to a whole new social organization.

Once male strength became the focus of all power and importance it became expedient to reduce the importance that women had received earlier. This meant that now, instead of seeing themselves as having been brought forth by the inherent female power to give birth, men now regarded women as child-bearing vessels. Men controlled these vessels and used them to exalt his status by demanding and receiving submission to his word, his law, and his idea of what women should do and be. This meant that women's new central role was to please the male protector and bear sons to increase the size and strength of the male force. A woman no longer governed her sexuality; it was owned by her man. And just as the new social order forced men to anesthetize their emotions in order to be combat-ready, this sexual enslavement forced the woman to anesthetize her sexual desires so that her sexuality could be given or reserved, depending not on her wishes, but on the wishes of her master. And, because women could no longer be independent, no woman could escape this new social order. Now women were "forced to buy protection with chastity, fidelity,"[4] and strict rules governing their sexuality.

Within this new social order a man could demand exclusive sexual rights to his woman or women. In other words, the woman was permitted to have sex with him and *only* him.

The woman was now his possession, and he had to have some assurance that he was the legitimate father of her sons. And sons were like gold in a fierce and dangerous world. Therefore, to enforce his will, the man set up rules and consequences that were driven by the struggle to survive.

These rules and consequences have varied from society to society and from time to time, but generally there were (and to a degree still are) two basic sexual rules for women and two for men which were to become primary building blocks for the battle of the sexes:

Men's Sexual Rule #1. Men were expected to want to have sex with any attractive woman. Generally, if he did have sex with a woman, however he might contrive to do so, it was a point in his favor, both as a virile male and as a man capable of taking and using another man's property and thus being able to dominate.

Men's Sexual Rule #2. A man was allowed to insist that his women be faithful to him and that his daughters remain untouched sexually. Their sexuality was his to give and control, not theirs. He was also allowed and in fact encouraged to punish any transgressions that were seen as a direct reflection on his honor.

Women's Sexual Rule #1. Brides were expected to be virgins, and wives expected to keep themselves solely for their husbands.

Women's Sexual Rule #2. Women who violated Rule #1 met with consequences that were serious or even fatal.

These rules did not take the feelings or natural desires of women into account, and they obviously set up opposing goals between men and women: men were to try to get sex any way they could; women were to try to give sex only to those who controlled them. This created the double standard that has been strictly, even brutally, enforced.

In some societies even the suspicion of a woman committing a sexual indiscretion could result in her being cast out of her family's protection or even put to death. Even in the last century a girl who was not a virgin was considered "ruined" and her chances of marriage greatly diminished; as recently as fifty years ago it was common for unmarried mothers to be openly shamed and scorned, and in some societies they still are.

This situation led to the development of two basic categories of women: women who followed Rule #1 were "good" girls or "respectable" women; women who violated the rules were considered "bad" and were regarded as prostitutes, call girls, whores, streetwalkers, tarts, tramps, harlots, sluts, trollops, or hookers.

"GOOD" GIRLS, "BAD" GIRLS

According to the male hierarchy in Western culture, "good" girls were those women considered honorable and available for sex only after making a commitment to marriage. "Bad" girls were those women who had been dishonored and were therefore available for sex without any future commitment. "Bad" girls deserved any bad consequence that happened to them; even today the rape or murder of a prostitute is not considered very serious.

Women, of course, found it expedient in most instances to remain in the "good" girl category. A woman could fall into the "bad" girl group if it was discovered, or in some cases even suspected, that she'd had sex with a

man who had not made a commitment to her. In many societies a woman
was scorned if her fiancé canceled his commitment to her.

Raphael Patai writes of Bedouin society, "Insofar as the main value of a
woman from the point of view of the group is her capacity as potential or
actual mother of male group members, if she commits a transgression
which makes her unfit for this supreme task of womanhood, she seals her
own fate: she must die."[5]

Women learned to control their sexuality!

This made a woman's brain her most important sex organ and the key
to triggering her desire. Instead of wanting sex for its own sake, as men
were encouraged to do, women learned to let their desire be triggered
only under safe circumstances. And because it was a matter of life and
death, women quickly learned which situations were safe and to pick up
any danger signals indicating unsafe circumstances.

A woman learned to ask herself not only "Do I want to have sex?" but
also "Is it safe to have sex?" She learned to filter her desires and feel them
primarily when she knew love and security were being offered, no matter
how much her physical passions, and the man in question, might be
urging her to have sex. She learned to separate herself from her own
passions and look for danger signals. Is this the wrong man? Does he only
want to use her? Or is he interested in making a commitment to love and
care for her? This difference in attitude and goal set up men and women
to engage in the battle we still see today.

If a woman has sex with a man who has not made a commitment
to her, he wins (he gets sex without having to make a commitment).
If a man makes a commitment to her before, or even after, having sex,
then she wins (she gives sex but in turn is given love and commitment).
This struggle over time became a central battleground for the war of the
sexes.

Indeed, this struggle remained unaltered through generations of men
and women until recently, when the women's movement called into
question the male hierarchy, the male and female sexual rules, and all
that followed from them. Women then received opportunities to escape
the male hierarchy by becoming independent of men. Some of the most
recent changes in society have centered on female sexuality, the attempt
to give women control of their sexuality, and the tendency to re-link
passion and sex, giving women permission to express their sexuality.

Still, women are more cautious sexually than men and are still, to a
certain degree, governed by the same rules that have always existed. In
Western culture most brides are no longer expected to be virgins, but

women are supposed to keep themselves solely for their husbands, and men are not allowed to kill their wives for a sexual indiscretion.

In essence there still remains a double standard and women still pay a higher price for sexual indiscretion than men do. And in spite of the sexual revolution women are still given strong signals from an early age that they should be very cautious regarding their sexuality.

For example, in a recent toddler play group for two- to three-year-olds sponsored by the San Diego schools, the instructor cautioned all the mothers to warn their children, particularly their girls, not to let *anyone* touch them, particularly their "private parts," defined as any part of them that a bathing suit would cover. They were further told that they should tell their mother immediately if anyone did try to touch their private parts.

This warning, so unfortunately necessary, is the first real message girls get about their sexuality: Don't let anyone touch. This message carries beyond childhood and into adult life. The woman, by this time, has internalized the warning and regulated her own defenses. Now she may let others besides Mommy touch her, but it must be someone who doesn't trigger any of the danger signals—someone who has made a commitment and who seems willing to continue this commitment into the future.

This is true even of women in relationships where there has been a commitment such as marriage. While a woman may know a man has made a commitment to her, she may still feel a danger signal if he does not give any recognizable indication that he loves her. Inside her head a sort of internal tape is asking her, "Are you being used for sex, or does he really love you?"

One big problem, as we have seen, is that the love cues that excite women, and that do not represent any danger signals to triggering women's defenses, are exactly those things that men usually don't understand because they go against men's own training for emotional and interpersonal distance.

This, then, is the problem for men: learning how to turn a woman on by giving her the love signals she wants and thus opening the way for her to be excited physically. A man must learn to make a woman feel that she is safe, that she isn't being used, and that he cares about her, not just about having sex with her. This is the difficult part for men, since a man often doesn't know how to express his feelings of caring and love to a woman. He may be a good lover physically, but he never gets the chance because he doesn't know how to be a good lover emotionally. This is a fact about women that most men don't understand and that most women don't communicate to their men, because they are so often uncertain about it themselves.

Once a man discovers how women work sexually (we'll give men specific how-to's in Chapter 5), he can release her natural sexual potential, bringing both himself and his woman greater emotional and physical satisfaction.

Fact #5: Women are attracted to powerful and successful men

It's sad perhaps but true that a man who is less "successful" is less likely to marry the woman of his choice than a man who is "successful." Statistics show that less successful men have less sex, marry less attractive women, and get less "love," than men who are more successful. While men pick women for traits such as physical attractiveness, many women consider being "a good provider" the most important characteristic in a husband.

This fact is certainly not meant to hurt the less successful man; it is simply another fact of life with a long history behind it. From earliest times, there is hardly a doubt that successful men were attractive to women. A hunter who could be relied upon to bring home meat was simply more desirable as a husband than the man who rarely brought home any meat. Particularly in her role as a nurturer of children, it just made sense for a woman to try to attract a successful man.

In violent times combat-readiness was prized by women as well as by men, because to "belong" to a combat-ready man meant that a woman stood a far better chance of surviving—no matter how difficult his combat-readiness made him to live with.

Historically, women have been regarded as either their father's property or their husband's. In many societies women were so clearly seen as property that a father was free to give his daughter in marriage to whatever husband he chose. In our own society the tradition of a father "giving the bride away" is a reminder of this time when marriage was viewed as a transfer of property from one owner to another.

Throughout history every generation has produced women who were unwilling to live by the male rules and who tried to live on their own. During most of history, however, the male rules have prevented most women from doing this with any real success.

Killing a woman for running away is still tolerated in many parts of the world. In parts of South America a wife who is said to have soiled a man's honor can be killed by him with little or no retribution. In other times and places women were further controlled by being forbidden to own property or to be employed. Even today a woman will often stay with her husband because she cannot support herself on her own.

There was one advantage to women being confined to their Inner World and prevented from entering the male Outer World: while this system was and often is still brutal and unfair, it did free women to be absorbed in mothering, and it did produce well-fed and well-protected children. Faced, however, with the inability to move beyond her role as mother and wife, a woman was forced instead to enter the world of men only vicariously through her husband and sons while passing her female traditions on to her daughters.

In the past, men might be politicians or merchants or sailors or soldiers, but women remained women and the caretakers of home, hearth, and children. A woman's only chance to increase her power or prominence was through a man. As a result, male power became synonymous with optimum survival, wealth, and importance.

Since women had to attain all of their status and power through men, it seems logical and inevitable that they developed a taste for powerful men and tried to choose their mates accordingly.

Of course, in very recent times some of this has changed. Women are no longer considered property and are permitted to be independent. More and more women choose to support themselves and live their lives on a far more equal basis. But even so, a successful male partner can make a woman's life and the lives of her children much easier. Therefore, women still value successful men, and being a good provider is still the number one trait most women look for in a husband.

The only problem is that men by and large still do the proposing, and so women must rely on their ability to attract a man if they hope to attain the most suitable husband.

Fact #6: *Every woman wants to be attractive, especially to the man she wants to love her*

Like it or not, as infuriating as some women find it, men's primary criterion for choosing a woman is her physical attractiveness. One survey found this to be true in all thirty-seven groups of men from thirty-three different societies throughout the world.[6] Therefore, women, if they are to compete for the most desirable men, are forced to do their best to be physically attractive.

But while women still use attractiveness to attract and keep a man, particularly the men they want to love them, women's need to be attractive has broadened to represent an attempt to attain power not only with men but with society in general.

Studies show that both men and women rate attractive people as brighter, friendlier, more competent, and as people they would want to know better.

Attractiveness for women, however, is often a complex undertaking, since women's standards require clothes that are complicated and makeup and hair arrangements that are time-consuming.

A couple we know lately reported having the age-old argument as they both prepared for a night out.

"Why is it taking you so long?" the irate husband demanded. "Why can't women get ready as fast as men?"

"Because we women are trying not to look like men," came her reply.

A woman wants to look attractive not only to attract a man, but also to increase her status among women. It is difficult for men to understand this fact and many others about women, which leads to the next truth.

Fact #7: *Women are frustrated in their relationships with men*

As we have seen, women need to be close to others, to love, and to relate in an intimate way. Men have been shaped by combat-readiness training, which keeps them emotionally distant and controlled.

At the same time, women have learned that optimum survival can be attained through a successful man and that powerful combat-ready men have, during most of history, tended to be successful. This means, then, that while a woman learned to pick a powerful combat-ready man, she also was doomed to be disappointed that this masculine hunk could not communicate or be intimate with her. He could not understand her emotions and often ridiculed them, and the very love, communication, and intimacy she valued were the things that turned him off and made him uncomfortable. Worse, once past the initial excitement stage of the relationship, he could not communicate the love she needed in order to trigger her sexuality. Instead, he focused on the physical side of sex, often to the exclusion of the emotional side, a fact that sooner or later would turn her off both to sex and to him.

Even today this problem remains. Indeed, while women have become more balanced and whole by developing both their Inner and Outer World expertise, the majority of men have remained masters only of the Outer World. Men have yet to develop an understanding of the Inner World and perhaps hardly recognize its existence or the advantages of having such understanding.

Women have come to expect this of men and often have trouble separating a man's highly desirable combat-readiness, which often still translates into competence and success, from his problematical armor and anesthesia, which translates into emotional distance and control. This has left women capable of relating to men in their Outer World but still unable to relate to them fully in the areas most important to them—love and intimacy.

Indeed, "98 percent of the women . . . said they would like more verbal closeness with the men they love; they want the men in their lives to talk more about their own personal thoughts, feelings, plans, and questions, and to ask them about theirs."[7]

And when this doesn't happen? Nowadays, "approximately 40 percent of married women initiate a divorce, when faced with the unequal patterns of the emotional contract. Another 42 percent of women create a double life for themselves, finding another primary relationship, whether it be with work, a lover, children or friends—yet 'staying' in the marriage.

"Thus, 82 percent of women 'leave' their relationships in some form; most express their regret and frustration over the insufficiency of emotional intimacy and equality, wishing that things could be different."[8]

Indeed, women are frustrated, and so the battle of the sexes continues. Women remain masters of their Inner World and now are able to relate to a man concerning his Outer World, but they are still waiting for a partner with whom to share what is most important to them.

Fact #8: *Women are in touch with their emotions, but avoid conflict and confrontation*

Women are much more in touch with their tender emotions than men are. Women are much more introspective, are much better able to identify what they are feeling, and value their feelings as valid and important.

Women are raised to feel sad, scared, loving, and happy, but they are schooled to avoid the primary male emotion—anger.

This is partly due to their style of survival through cooperation and harmony in relationships. Historically anger has not been tolerated in women, and women often had so little power to control events in a direct way that overt anger did not serve them. Therefore, women have very little experience with anger.

This means that, in a sense, men and women complement each other when it comes to emotions. They specialize in different feelings and together have a fuller range of emotion than either has alone. But instead of leading to harmony, this more often than not leads to conflict and poor communication.

For example, a woman wants to share her emotions, but the only emotion a man will readily display is anger, an emotion she may not feel comfortable with. Therefore, while a couple may together represent a fuller range of emotions, they have difficulty relating to each other's emotions and therefore to each other.

Also, besides avoiding such emotions as anger and situations that led to confrontation, women will often blame themselves rather than cause a fight.

For example, while men tend to blame someone else for relationship problems, women have been raised to blame themselves. A woman will also tend to assume that her husband's or boyfriend's bad mood has to do with something she's done. She often assumes blame even before it is given.

"When he comes home at night and he slams the door I always think, now what have I done?" says one woman. "I go over everything I said and did that morning and all the things my husband usually gets angry at. Sometimes I apologize before I know what it is he's mad about."

Of course much of the time a man's bad mood has nothing to do with his wife, but since women so readily accept blame and believe it must have something to do with them, many men begin to accept this pattern and blame their bad moods on their wives, however ill-placed this blame may be.

This is not to say that women don't experience anger. They experience anger, just as men experience fear and sadness and a whole range of emotions they avoid expressing. Women handle anger very differently from men. Instead of an outburst, women often withdraw love and tenderness. They don't actually *do* anything that can be identified and that they can be blamed for. Instead, they *don't* do things. Most women hope that their man will notice this, take the hint, and change whatever is causing the anger. Often men don't recognize this behavior as anger and simply think she is in a bad mood. Such misunderstandings often lead to even more anger, which women handle in various ways, including binges of shopping, eating, and other, often self-destructive, behavior. Only recently have women been given permission to be angry and learned constructive ways to express anger. In spite of the fact that women do repress some emotions such as anger, work more hours in the home, and deal with many other stresses, the truth is women are still healthier than men.

Fact #9: Women are healthier and live longer than men

Women are more attuned to their bodies than men, who have been trained to ignore discomfort and illness rather than seem weak by acknowledging them. Also, women are willing to seek help from physicians, psychologists, and other professionals more readily than men, and they are more likely to follow directions about their health. They are also more likely to be aware of stress symptoms and act to correct them, whereas men often ignore the problem and hope it will go away on its own.

It is also true that women tend to be healthier when they are less dependent on men, when they have friends and other relationships, as well as jobs.

The end result of it all is that on the average women live more than seven years longer than men.

Fact #10: Women are changing

Women have been actively changing for several decades. Many of these changes have had to do with making deeper and deeper inroads into the Outer World.

While this migration into the Outer World has brought tremendous benefits to millions of women, it has also brought tremendous confusion to relationships. Life used to be simpler. You got married and you stayed married, for better or worse, in sickness and in health, for richer or for poorer. Not anymore. About 10 percent of marriages ended in divorce in 1900. Today it's about 51 percent.[9]

We are simply no longer as legally and socially bound to stay together as we used to be. And while we are obviously affected by our society's past, women are entering the twenty-first century with a different blending and balancing of their Inner and Outer Worlds than has been possible in thousands of years.

NOTES, CHAPTER 3

1. Helen Fisher, *The Sex Contract: The Evolution of Human Behavior* (New York: Quill, 1983), p. 223.
2. Irene Claremont de Castillejo, *Knowing Woman: A Feminine Psychology* (New York: Harper & Row, 1974).
3. Irene Elia, *The Female Animal* (New York, Henry Holt, 1988), p. 255.
4. Elia, p. 255.
5. Raphael Patai, *The Arab Mind* (New York: Scribner's, 1983), p. 125.
6. *Newsweek*, March 13, 1989, p. 56.
7. Shere Hite, *Women and Love* (New York: St. Martin's Press, 1989), p. 27.
8. Hite, 439.
9. Francesca Cancian, *Love in America* (Cambridge, England: Cambridge University Press, 1987), p. 47.

4

Worlds in Collision

WHY MEN AND WOMEN STILL
DON'T UNDERSTAND EACH OTHER

As we've seen, the love-sex conflict between men and women is largely a result of war and violence. These two forces have kept alive a relationship between men and women that fosters survival, but also fosters the male-female conflict. The truth is, however, that now the social circumstances that supported a male-dominated, combat-ready society are fading. A new age is dawning that has made the old relationship between men and women no longer necessary or even workable.

In recent history a number of circumstances revolutionized our world—and the relationships between men and women. The central reasons for this social evolution include:

1. Wealth, leisure, and education in Western society created increasing equality between men and women, providing both sexes access to the ideas and information needed to master the new Outer World.

2. Modern technology created a need for a work force endowed with knowledge rather than physical strength. Our service-oriented economy needs workers who are able to relate well with others, a skill that is central to female training. This makes women highly desirable employees.

3. Modern technology and scientific advances gave women control of their reproductive system, allowing them to have more options about when or if they would bear a child and freeing them to work and therefore to gain financial independence. As a result, women now have greater freedom to express their sexuality than ever before.

4. Laws and institutions provided protection and independence. In other words, if a woman's house is on fire she isn't dependent on the brute force of her man and his combat-ready friends to put it out. She dials 911 and an organized team of men and women come to do the job, and she ultimately pays for their services with taxes from her paycheck, rather than with her earlier currency of her sexuality and nurturing.

5. The original reason for male armor and anesthesia has diminished as war, and particularly hand-to-hand combat, becomes far less likely.

6. Technology has created appliances, time-saving devices, house-keeping services, and surrogate mothers, making men less dependent on women.

Yes, our situation has changed, and society has changed, but our ability as human beings to assimilate these changes into our lives and our relationships lags behind these changes. There is no doubt that relationships between men and women are in a major evolutionary transition period. Circumstances have changed, inviting changes in relationships, but people are still confused about what this means to them. For example, these changes have opened the way for women to build careers and enter the Outer World, but people are still confused about how to combine a career with motherhood. On the other hand, these changes have made it possible for men to enter the Inner World, to be, for example, more overtly loving and closer to their families. Men, however, aren't sure how to open up to their feelings or if such feelings are truly acceptable. Also, reactions of both sexes to this new world and these new options vary widely.

Many women are disappointed and fed up. Many women we interviewed were disappointed and fed up with men, and some have given up on them altogether.

"I don't need a man, and now I don't even want one," says a career woman in her early forties. "I used to, but now I think they are simply more trouble than they are worth. Men don't really want a relationship; they want someone to do for them, and they want a convenient sex partner, that's all. Anyway, it's just too hard to be a wife and have a career, too, and I'm not cut out to be Superwoman, that's for sure. I mean that women work all the time and men just go to a job and come home and expect to be waited on. Women have changed a lot, but men haven't changed at all. I read that the women even say the same thing in the Soviet Union. Now a woman can have a career, but she is still responsible for everything in the home, too. My married friends are absolutely exhausted. Why do they want to be married? Not for sex. You can get sex married or not. They say it's because they want to be loved. But none of them seem satisfied with that, either. At this rate I'd rather save myself the trouble of having a man around and 'love' my cat. Thank heaven I can get a job and support myself so I don't have to be dependent on a man and have to take the load of shit that comes along with that dependency!"

Some women want to go back to the way things were. On the other side are the women who feel the changes taking place today between men and women are wrong and even dangerous. These women feel the traditional roles and relationships of men and women were correct and that changing them will bring disaster.

"The way things used to be between men and women worked just fine," says a housewife and mother of five in her early fifties, "and that's the good old-fashioned way my husband Dick and I have been together. Sure, I've had to compromise, and Dick has had the last word. But I run the house and he brings home the money, and that's how things work best. I firmly believe that, and I think that tampering with all this is wrong. I mean, women say they want equality, but just what is it getting them? Going out of the home to work just leaves kids without anyone to look after them. And look at all the drugs, crazy kids, music, and homosexuality. It seems all these new choices have just made people not know what they want or who they are. Things were better before. Anyway, I want my man the way he is and not wishy-washy like these young men seem to be. My man is a real man and I'm proud of him."

Most women like the change but are confused. The majority of women fit into an in-between category; they are glad for the changes that have freed women to pursue jobs, gain financial independence, and acquire an individual identity, but they are frustrated to some degree with men or with their man in particular. Like Julie and Bob, they want to work it out and learn to juggle a home life with careers and a love life. But that's hard to do, particularly when there are no role models or traditions to point the way.

"People say that women want it all, and I think we do," says a woman in her mid-thirties with six- and eight-year-old daughters and a job as an assistant manager in a department store. She's been married for ten years.

"The problem is how to get it and not have a nervous breakdown in the process. That takes real organization, cooperation, and endurance. Just keeping the wheels of a household turning is a major accomplishment, particularly if a woman has small children and is pursuing a career, too—and most couples I know need two paychecks. I mean, women are supposed to have choices about having a career or staying home with the kids, but for us and for lots of people, that option just doesn't exist, at least not right now. Things are just too expensive and if a couple ever wants to buy a house or send their kids to college, both people *have* to work. It's a lot of stress, and what makes it worse is that both Paul and I grew up in traditional families. Our mothers stayed home with us and our fathers worked. Both of us have in mind what our mothers did and expect me to do it all as a mom, in addition to my career. I'm beginning to wonder if it's possible. Women have changed, you know, but men haven't changed that much. Paul may help in the kitchen once in a while or entertain the girls on Saturdays when I have business calls to make, but it just isn't enough. I get really angry when I'm responsible for the kids and my job and he wants to be responsible for just his job and help me only when he's in the mood. He wants the same special treatment his father got from his mother, and he justifies his refusal to help me by reminding me that I make less money than he does. He sometimes points this out in subtle ways, as if he wants to make sure I know that he is still 'superior' and somehow smarter than I am. I'd just like to see him take on all of the work I'm doing, and then we'd see just how 'smart' he really is. Anyway, this attitude of his gets in our way. I want us to have a really loving, close relationship. I mean, what is the point of having a nice house and a nice life-style if we aren't good together? I guess what I'm saying is I wouldn't mind working so hard if he appreciated and valued my efforts. He says he does love me and does appreciate me, but that's not the message I'm getting from what he does. Why, for example, can't he be more loving and tender? At the end of the day that's what I want. But even though I say I want him to love me, he just acts like I'm saying I want to have sex. Then when I don't want to and try to tell him I want love, he just gets mad and insists he *does* love me. I guess I just don't know how to explain what I do want, or else he's simply incapable of understanding.

"Lately he's just been coming home at night and we watch TV or have friends over. But now I have more fun with friends than I have with him. It's easy to see how couples drift apart, and I know that's what's going to happen to us unless we find a better answer."

Many women have good relationships but are still confused. Still other women already have a smooth-running relationship. Some of these couples have worked the kinks out of two-career families; others don't have the extra pressure of kids. But even in these partnerships, the women find that their men aren't as romantic as they'd like or aren't able to show love in a satisfying way. In short, they know he could be the man of their dreams, but they aren't sure how to help him be that way.

"Oh, Dave," Pam says, rolling her eyes in mock ecstasy to express just how much in love she and her husband are even after six years of marriage. "He is such a sweetie. We do have our problems, though. I mean, we both really try, and we both have worked on our relationship. But we still have some problems. I mean, he's really terrific, but, well, he can still be such a 'man,' if you know what I mean. He can be dense when it comes to some things, like understanding what I'm feeling or when he's expressing himself. Sometimes he still acts as if I'm not quite as smart as he is, and he doesn't say he loves me nearly enough. I realize sometimes that even though we know each other so well, we still don't really understand each other. People say that's just how it is, but I know if we understood each other better we would have an even better relationship and avoid some of the problems we still have in spite of how much we love each other."

THE MEN'S HALF OF
THE STORY

Men have an equally wide range of reactions to the social changes that have taken place.

Some men are mad as hell. They are hostile, resentful, and suspicious of the changes that women have made and reject outright the changes that society is suggesting that men make.

"Sensitive!" a man in his early forties snorts, a foreman in a large construction firm. "Pussies—that's what they want us all to be, so they can push us round. To hell with that. Anyway, I give her what she needs and she knows I love her. I even gave her a new set of china for Christmas and took time off work to remodel the bathroom. She knows I love her, even if I don't act like some silly candy-ass wimp."

Some men have given up on women. "Women really just want a man for what he can give her," says a thirty-nine-year-old investment counselor who has been married twice. "My first wife wanted to retire from being my secretary. She took one look at my bank balance and fell in love. She made me think she really wanted me, that our life would be one big honeymoon. But after the third year of marriage all she was doing was playing tennis at the country club, getting her nails done, shopping, and having lunch with her friends. When I wanted sex, all she could say is that I was only in love with my business and was just using her. Using her? What did she think she was doing to me? We started fighting a lot, and she ran off with her tennis instructor. She said he understood her. Of course she went out and got the most aggressive shark of an attorney she could find and took me for everything she could get.

"We got divorced and I decided there'd be no more bloodsuckers like her in my life, so I married the other kind. Marjorie was a career woman who didn't want me for my money and had no intention of sitting around while I supported her. I didn't realize that she was just using me, too. She wanted my business contacts and needed someone more experienced to show her the real-life ball game of dealing with investments. She learned really quick. In two years she'd already moved on to someone else, a vice president of another company, and taken some of my key clients with her.

"Now I've decided that relationships with women just aren't worth the price. I'd rather just date a woman now and then when I really need to have sex or when I need someone on my arm for a social function. The rest of the time I just play racquetball with friends or clients. You know, a man doesn't really need a wife nowadays. I've got a dishwasher, a clothes washer, a microwave, and a dozen other appliances to do the things wives used to do. On Christmas I always have invitations to dinner, and as far as kids go, well, it would have been nice. But as I said, the price is too high. I can just enjoy my niece and nephew and let it go at that. Women have only screwed up my life."

Some men are confused. Other men, the majority, are interested in giving women what they want and even in (cautiously) exploring love and romance. Still, many a man isn't sure what she means when she says she wants him to be more romantic or more intimate or that she wants him to show his feelings. He knows she doesn't want him to be weak, and he isn't sure how to do what she wants and still maintain his self-respect and not look or feel foolish or unmasculine.

"I want her to know I love her, but it's difficult to know exactly what she means when she says I should be more romantic," said James, a twenty-seven-year-old architect. "I do send Bonnie flowers on her birthday, and I take her to dinner sometimes. She says I should talk to her more, but what does she want me to say? She says I should be more fun, but I take her wherever she wants to go. Isn't that fun? Then there is this stuff about being sensitive to her feelings. How am I supposed to know what she feels? Am I a mind reader? I just like to be together at the end of the day and have some peace, but she doesn't seem satisfied. I don't know what else to do for her."

Some men want change. Other men have seized the opportunity to explore the Inner World more openly, and the signs of this are everywhere. Men, for instance, are now participating more and more in the birth of their children. We have seen house husbands and Mr. Moms and even athletes and Presidents who feel they can show emotion and even shed a few tears in public. Men are taking charge of the house and kids more often, and more women report that their opinion is respected and taken into account rather than simply put down or put aside, as so often happened in the past. Many of the women we interviewed said that generally their man was trying harder to handle half of the burden. Many men are interested in actively exploring the Inner World of women, but these men are still a minority.

NOW WE HAVE A CHOICE

Our new world has offered us both benefits and drawbacks. Ironically, just as our modern society has made men and women far less essential to each other for physical survival, love and relationships are becoming ever more essential for our emotional and spiritual survival. The reason for this is that isolation has become a side effect of greater individual independence and self-development.

The extended family has broken down, and even the nuclear family is constantly threatened. Divorce and reconstructed families have created a generation of children who live with only one parent, with stepparents, or with no parents at all. The computer linkup is replacing emotional linkups. Family neighborhoods are breaking down and being replaced by isolating high-rises. The family farm is giving way to corporate agribusiness. Home care of children is being replaced by day care. And while one of these changes might not have a great effect on the family, together all of this creates one huge and unacceptable side effect: our society increasingly lacks basic human intimacy and love between people. This shift has made the relationships we do have all the more important.

Even longtime career women and men often say that while they love their careers, they miss the intimacy of a close relationship. Love seems harder to find, and yet commitment with intimacy is what people really need and want.

WHAT WOMEN REALLY WANT

A woman wants a deep relationship with a man who understands and accepts her and her feelings. She wants more intimacy, comprising affection, commitment, companionship, and respect for individual identity. She wants help in resolving relationship conflicts. She wants him to express his feelings—particularly his deeper feelings and his positive feelings about her—more often. She wants him to respect her intelligence and talent. She wants him to be romantic. And she wants to have good, satisfying lovemaking. But she wants sex within the context of a loving, committed, and intimate relationship with a strong, yet sensitive, man. Shere Hite found that "83 percent of women say they prefer sex with emotional involvement, sex with feelings."[1]

Unfortunately, most women are frustrated because what they have instead is a combat-ready male with anesthetized and armored emotions who has suppressed his Inner World, all of which prevents him from understanding the female viewpoint and the woman's needs.

Although she knows he wants sex, she is frustrated because this seems to be the only form of intimacy he is interested in with her.

WHAT MEN REALLY WANT

Men really want to love and be loved, but they want to give and receive love differently than women do. Because of their training, they are often uncomfortable expressing their emotions in nonsexual ways. Men are most comfortable expressing love through sex, through shared activities, through being a good provider, and through just being together, and they want women to accept these actions as love and not expect men to be different or to be like women.

A man feels frustrated and even angry when a woman doesn't perceive his version of love as "real love" or "good enough," when she isn't interested in sex—which is the primary way he knows how to express and accept intimacy—and wants him instead to be more romantic. He often doesn't understand romance, know how to express it, or feel comfortable with it.

Therefore, as much as he may be interested in solving this dilemma, he is usually confused about exactly how to treat this "new woman" and completely confused as to how to meet her needs, let alone how to get her to meet his need for physical intimacy and sex.

ILLUSIONS THAT CRIPPLE

This basic misunderstanding between men and women, created by their different worldviews, training, and expectations, creates another complication. This complication is a set of *illusions* men have about women and women have about men.

These illusions grew out of the historical roots discussed in Chapter 2 and have been maintained right up to the present day. The illusions play a highly significant role in relationships in that they prevent men and women from having more satisfying unions with each other. The fact is that society has opened the door to change, but the old illusions have not changed. This means that couples still do not understand each other and few are taking advantage of the opportunity to change. While things could be different, men still don't get enough sex and women still don't get enough love.

WHERE ILLUSIONS BEGIN

These illusions are usually introduced in informal sex education and are later reinforced by novels, ads, TV, movies, and magazines (X-rated and otherwise), male gossip about women, and female gossip about men. They are also often based on the erroneous notion that the sexes are far more similar to each other than in fact they are. Men still assume, for example, that women think and function much the same way they do—or at least they should. Women assume that men should be more like them—and could if they would only try.

We will deal with solving the problems these illusions cause in Chapters 5 and 6, but first let's examine the illusions that underlie the battle of the sexes.

MEN'S ILLUSIONS ABOUT WOMEN

Men's illusions about women are long on fantasy and short on reality and are often based on male-oriented published material such as the centerfolds in men's magazines, nude models cooing about "wanting it rough and hard," and fictional heroines such as the Harold Robbins women who nearly faint at the sight of an "angry erection" and who have multiple orgasms before entry. Another example is the cool, intimacy-avoiding James Bond girls who have sexy female bodies, but are strikingly male in their approach to sex. They are as readily aroused as men, even though they seem to know from the beginning that they'll be made love to and left.

These media stereotypes become the stuff of male fantasy, even though, as any woman knows, they bear little resemblance to the vast majority of real women either emotionally or sexually.

In spite of their inaccuracy, however, these stereotypes and exaggerated portrayals of women supply much of young men's practical male sex education. And because men receive so little information beyond fantasy women and male locker-room talk, they often apply what they've "learned" to women in general. They fill in the educational gaps with their own understanding of what works for them sexually.

Of course, the more experience a man has with women in the real world, the more clearly he realizes how inaccurate the media and locker-room stereotypes are. He continues to hold on to his illusions, however, because he lacks anything more reliable with which to replace them. And since the male culture generally won't permit a man to admit that he doesn't know how to relate to women—particularly how to make love to a woman—he isn't even free to ask for accurate information.

These illusions continue to be reinforced by the male culture, by society in general, and sometimes by women who lose track of their own needs and, for whatever reason, attempt to fulfill this male fantasy. These women, of course, often end up angry and frustrated because their needs go completely unmet.

Fortunately, these male illusions can be dispelled and replaced by an accurate and workable understanding of women that can make happiness and satisfaction possible for both sexes. But before we begin working to dispel these Illusions, let's look at what they are.

Male Illusion #1: Daily stresses shouldn't diminish her sexuality

"I work hard all day, and when I come home at night, I'm interested in being close with her. A lot of the time I'd like to make love with her, but she complains that she's too tired. It doesn't make any sense. I've worked hard all day, but I'm still interested in sex. If she really cared about me, she would want to make love, too.

"Instead, she pushes me away, and then if I'm frustrated or mad about it—what else does she expect?—she's hurt and says she wants us to be close. She's totally illogical. I want us to be close too, but she pushes me away. How can we be close if she's pushing me away?"

A man is often sexually aroused even when he's tired after a long workday, and he wants his partner to be ready, willing, and able to enjoy sex, too, regardless of how exhausted she might be. He isn't too tired to have sex. Why is she?

This problem is especially serious for couples who have young children or many children, and when the woman has a demanding career.

See Chapter 5, Step 1, for a discussion of this illusion.

Male illusion #2: Having sex is the best way to make us both feel good

"I feel good after we have sex, and a lot of times when we're both feeling bad about something, sex is a great way to feel really good. Particularly when we argue, the thing I want most of all is for us to make love so we can feel happy together again. Sex makes us forget the fight and puts it in the past. But a lot of the time, particularly after a fight, she gets even angrier if I want to make us feel better by making love. She says that sex isn't the point. But why isn't it? Why does she want to prolong the fight? I don't understand that at all."

Since sex is one of the few areas in which men are allowed to express emotion, it's often the first way a man will think of when he wants to express tenderness. It is also an easy way for him to feel good. Having an orgasm simply feels pleasant, and he assumes that having this simple physical release is the way to make her feel good as well. He is completely confused when he discovers that this physical sensation isn't what is most important to her. Making love after a fight doesn't solve the problem for her, even though it is one of the few ways that come to mind for a man who wants to kiss and make up. He doesn't understand why she doesn't feel the same way or why she seems determined to focus on emotions with which he may be uncomfortable.

See Chapter 5, Step 2, for the truth about this illusion.

Male illusion #3: Just being together should be enough for her, the way it is for me

"I care a lot about her, and I really like it when we're together. It's great when we're watching a ball game or a movie. I don't care if we go the whole night without saying a word. Maybe we read the paper together or watch the news or listen to music. Just being together in the same room is really satisfying. I have to listen to a lot of people talk all day at work, so I'm happy for us to be together without talking as long as we're watching the same game or show or just being together. Why isn't she just happy being with me?"

It's difficult for many men to relate verbally, and they feel awkward doing so. They satisfy their need for intimacy by simply being together in the same room, often without so much as a word being exchanged. He is surprised to learn that his woman thinks he doesn't care about her. He can't understand why she is dissatisfied with this arrangement, why she tries to get him to talk to her, and why she eventually abandons him for someone whom she can relate to more intimately.

See Chapter 5, Step 3, for the truth about this illusion.

Male Illusion #4: Women don't say what they mean

"Women never seem to say what they mean. Half the time they don't really get to the point, and the other half they are irrational and talk on and on without saying anything. Sometimes I don't ever figure out what it was she was trying to tell me. During an argument it's even worse. I try to be calm and stick to the facts, but that makes her even madder. Still, what can you do? That's just the way women are."

Since talking is simply a means of communicating information for most men, it's difficult for them to understand that talking for women is also a way of relating. Moreover, men and women often don't attribute the same meanings to many gestures and words. This sometimes leads men to assume that women are irrational and unable to communicate clearly.

See Chapter 5, Step 4, for the truth about this illusion.

Male Illusion #5: Women are often irrational and impossible to please

"No matter how much I try to show her I love her, it's never enough. I go to work, I bring home my paycheck, I don't run around with other women, I spend time with the kids, I remember her birthday, our anniversary, Valentine's Day, Christmas, and Mother's Day. I try to keep my bad moods to myself, and I don't hit her or the kids, even though I'm tempted to once in a while. What more does she want? I tell her I love her—at least, sometimes I tell her. I guess she'd like more hand-holding, but I'm not the hand-holding type of guy, you know what I mean? Anyway, no matter how much I do, she's not satisfied. Why doesn't anything please her?

"She says, 'Be sensitive,' but when I complain about how things are going, she says I'm being wimpy. Then she says she wants to be equal, but hey, I don't see her crawling under the car or emptying the mousetrap.

"She says, 'Be loving, be strong, be sensitive.' How can you be strong *and* sensitive—the two traits are incompatible. She says, 'Be playful,' then 'Be a good provider.' She's never satisfied with who I am."

This is an example of the erroneous belief that women are irrational, whimsical, unpredictable, and impossible to please. Little accurate information is available to men concerning what women really want from them, and so men operate under the influence of the old illusions. As a result, their efforts to satisfy women fail, and men conclude that women are never satisfied and are impossible to please.

See Chapter 5, Step 5, for the truth about this illusion.

Male Illusion #6: *Women are too emotional*

"Women are amazing; my wife will cry over anything. She cried when our little girl sang in a school play. She cried when her father sent her flowers. She even cries over the death of a character in a movie. Can you believe that? I could see her crying if one of her friends died, but a character on TV? And then there are her friends. They are always upset about what someone is doing, and they get all wound up and talk for hours about what someone said, or they carry on when one of them gets pregnant. I know my wife wants me to be emotional, too. I can just see it. I'll watch the news tonight and when I hear that the President vetoed a good bill I'll break down and cry, then call up one of my buddies and discuss it for an hour. She'd love that. She'd think I'd lost my mind. What is with her? Can't she get a grip on herself?"

Male training teaches men that emotions are generally bad and should not be expressed or even felt. Men therefore have a difficult time dealing with women's emotions and, in fact, do not even understand them. They often simply reject a woman's emotional life as strange and unattractive.

See Chapter 5, Step 6, for the truth about this illusion.

Male Illusion #7: *A straightforward approach to sex works best*

"My wife says I should come on slower, but I think what she really wants is for me to beg her for it like some kind of dog. She tells me to be subtle, but what am I supposed to do, play some kind of bullshit game with her? She probably wants me groveling at her feet. But I'll be damned if I'll be humiliated in order to get sex. I'm not that desperate."

This illusion is the result of men's general lack of subtlety where sex is concerned and of their unawareness of what sex means to women and what they are looking for when they make love.

Most men aren't sure what indirect sex cues are, let alone how to use them to be more attractive to women. A man who does know these cues is just dismissed by other men as having some magical charm, however mysterious it may seem.

See Chapter 5, Step 7, for the truth about this illusion.

Male Illusion #8: *A woman shouldn't need a lot of foreplay*

"If a woman is healthy she should be excited by being with her man, kissing him, and being touched in the right places. Sure, some women are slower to get going than others, but I'd say women ought to be turned on by a little holding and being touched. Then she should be ready to get down to business."

This is the false belief that women become sexually interested and aroused as easily as men do and that they are aroused by direct sexual contact. It is related to the false belief that the best way to excite a woman is to do it with her hot and hard and for as long as possible, as in porno movies.

See Chapter 5, Step 8, for the truth about this illusion.

Male Illusion #9: *Romance means sending her cards and flowers*

"Romance is the sexual excitement a man and a woman feel when they're really attracted to each other. Women like to know you still feel the same hot attraction to them, so that's why they like you to send cards and flowers and to remember birthdays and anniversaries and other holidays, because it reminds the woman that you love her and that she still turns you on."

Men have difficulty expressing tender emotions, and they usually know very little about what women truly find romantic, and so, for them, ritual expressions take the place of personal expression.

See Chapter 5, Step 9, for the truth about this illusion.

Male Illusion #10: If she looks sexy, she feels sexy

"I saw this great-looking girl in a cocktail lounge last night. She was dressed in a short black dress with some kind of a ruffle around it and had legs a guy would kill to get between. She was hot to go and every man in the place had his tongue hanging out. Then it was really too much when probably ten guys hit on to her and she turned them all down. Finally her girlfriend came in and they went into the restaurant and ate by themselves. None of the guys could believe it. What a tease! She's all hot to make it, we're all salivating like animals, and she has dinner with another woman. Who can figure it?"

"My wife and I went to a party last week. She spent the whole day getting fixed up and looked really terrific in this dress that showed everything she has was in all the right places. I had an erection for the last half of the party. But when we got home, she said she was exhausted, took off her makeup, and went to bed. How can women be so hot to go one minute and so cold the next?"

Many men believe that if a woman excites them sexually and looks sexy, she must be experiencing sexual feelings—in other words, if she looks sexy she must feel sexy; if she's exciting me, she must be excited, too. The man projects his own excitement onto the woman. Then, when she doesn't react the way he anticipates, he is confused or angry, as if she'd put a steak in front of a starving man and then refused to let him touch it. This doesn't make sense to him; it infuriates him and is a reason for much of the hostility men feel toward women. Since he has fallen for the bait, he feels he's been made a fool of.

See Chapter 5, Step 10, for the truth about this illusion.

FEMALE ILLUSIONS ABOUT MEN

Women just don't understand men.

When violence first became common, women were placed in a dependent position and kept there for thousands of years. This relationship distorted women's view of men. As a result, women still live with illusions that prevent them from getting what they want most of all—love and intimacy. These illusions also prevent women from understanding how to satisfy men's needs—and often keep them from even knowing what those needs are.

Women's illusions about men are reinforced by the media and by society, just as men's illusions are. Women, however, do try to understand their men, and unlike men, they discuss their relationships with each other, often at great length. Unfortunately, most women share the same illusions, so the discussions do little to change the situation. Also, women tend to assume the problems exist because men are "difficult," and they see women as blameless victims.

Like men, women have few sources of accurate information that takes into account both his point of view and hers. Even television—especially daytime TV—and self-help psychology books concentrate on the feminine viewpoint because women are the main consumers of this market.

Unfortunately, a woman can't even ask the man for help, because he doesn't understand the problem himself and can't tell her why he is the way he is.

We'll see in Chapter 6 how women can learn to see through these illusions to the reality about men, but first it's important to look at the illlusions themselves.

Female Illusion #1: A man who loves a woman will want to help her at home

"Sometimes I feel that he just thinks of me as a servant. I end up doing everything for everyone in the family, and a lot of the time I'm just exhausted. The thing that really makes me furious is that he keeps saying he doesn't understand what the problem is because I only work part-time while he works full-time. I feel so hurt and used and misunderstood. I work constantly, not just at the office, but at home, too. But when he comes home in the evening he just sits down and reads the paper in front of the TV, while I continue to work, waiting on him and the kids and taking care of a million details to keep the household running. Then he wonders why I don't have any energy to make love to him later. First of all, I'm so tired that it's difficult for me to feel anything, and second, I'm so mad at him that I just ask myself, 'Why should I do one more thing for him when he isn't helping me?' If he needs sex, let that be his problem. If he loved me he'd want to help me instead of just demanding more from me."

Women want help, particularly when they have young children or a career, or both. They don't understand why their husbands seem so reluctant to pitch in and help them run the household, particularly since many women are now bringing home some of the bacon. Most women feel it's only fair that he help out, and they feel resentful and used when he doesn't—to say nothing of being absolutely exhausted from bearing the double burden. As a result, the woman doesn't have the energy to make love, and her resentment undermines the loving feelings that would induce her to want to make love. She feels that, if he loved her, he would help her.

See Chapter 6, Step 1, for the truth about this illusion.

Female Illusion #2: Real men are strong enough not to need their egos fed

"A grown man ought to act like it and not constantly need attention and be told he's wonderful and clever and that everything that's good is his doing and everything that's bad is someone else's. A real man is self-confident and doesn't need anyone to bolster him up. If he does, he's just a phony, acting one way and really being another."

Since men act strong and independent, women feel that they should *be* that way, too. While women do want men to be more sensitive, they may also buy in to the stereotypes men themselves have created as to what a "real man" is. This is where one of the major double messages for men occurs. Women often seem to send out the message that they think real men should be tough, competent, strong, and in control, that they should not be vulnerable and should not need their egos fed, but women also want men to be sensitive, more human, and more aware of their own emotions and therefore of women's as well.

See Chapter 6, Step 2, for the truth about this illusion.

Female Illusion #3: A man wants to be with and talk to the woman he loves

"My husband is so wrapped up in his store and coaching his little league team that he doesn't have time for me. If he cared, he'd really want us to spend a lot of time together. All he ever does when we're together is just sit there. Sure, we might be in the same room at the same time, but what's the point of that? He'll say, 'Let's spend the evening together.' I used to really fall for that and be so happy he wanted to be with me. But then we'd sit down in front of television, and he'd just watch it and never say a word. That's his idea of being together, I guess, but it sure isn't mine. I think he just doesn't want to be with me, not really, so I get up after a while and call my daughter or my sister on the phone and we talk. The sad thing is that they're available to talk because their husbands are usually doing the same thing mine is. Then what do you know? He's upset because I'm talking on the phone! How can he be upset? He doesn't want to talk to me but he won't let me talk to anyone else, either. It's like the old story about the dog in the manger. The dog didn't want the hay, but he wouldn't let the horse have it. My husband doesn't really want to be with me."

When a man says he wants to spend time together, women assume that he means the same thing she would mean if she asked to be with him. She assumes that his way of expressing affection will mirror hers. When it doesn't, she is hurt and feels he doesn't love her.

See Chapter 6, Step 3, for the truth about this illusion.

Female Illusion #4: If a man loves a woman, he'll take the time to understand what she's saying

"If Jack loved me, he'd listen to me and understand what I'm trying to tell him. The problem is he just doesn't put in the effort. He doesn't really listen, and then he complains I don't make sense. All my friends understand me, so why doesn't he? It's just a matter of taking the time, but he doesn't. It's one more reason I'm mad at him so much and one more reason things have come to such a sorry pass between us."

A woman often assumes that when a man doesn't understand what she is saying, it's because he simply doesn't care about her enough to pay attention to what she is telling him.

See Chapter 6, Step 4, for the truth about this illusion.

Female Illusion #5: Men are impossible to satisfy

"I really do everything to try to make him happy, but he's *never* happy. For instance, he wanted me to help him with a report he was doing, so yesterday morning he insisted that I go into the den and start on this report. The next thing you know, I'm typing away and he bursts in to ask me why I'm not ready for a wedding we were going to. 'Okay,' I said, and went upstairs to get ready. The next thing you know, he asks me why I'm not getting lunch for the kids. I told him I could do that but it would take up more time and it would take me longer to get ready. That's when he blew up and accused me of taking forever to do anything and that he had to do everything. I was furious, but I didn't say anything. I hate going to parties when we're fighting. So I just stayed calm and fixed lunch and got dressed as fast as I could. When we got home he pointed out what a poor housekeeper I am because I'd left our bathroom a mess while I was trying to hurry. He also pointed out there was a typo on the report and that he had to make corrections. He fumed about that for two hours before we went to bed, saying he couldn't trust me to do anything. Then he wanted to make love. Out of the blue he says, 'Let's make up,' and grabs me. You know at that point I'd rather have made love to anyone else. Still, I did it to try to get him in a better mood. Then after it was over he said, 'Well, you sure didn't show much enthusiasm,' and rolled over and went to sleep. Obviously he had no intention of making up, he just wanted sex, and he even had to complain about that. I'm telling you, no matter what I do he's impossible to please, and from what I hear every man is just as impossible."

Just as men think women are impossible to please, the misunderstandings between men and women make women believe that men, too, are impossible to please.

See Chapter 6, Step 5, for the truth about this illusion.

Female Illusion #6: A man will share his inner feelings with the woman he loves

"I always ask him how his day went, and all I get is a litany of information—how the traffic was, how much he sold today, what he heard on the news. I never hear what's really important to him, what happened that day that made him happy or worried. I want him to really talk to me like a friend and a wife, but he just tells me things he could tell to anyone. If he really cared about me, he'd share himself more, but I guess he doesn't really care about me or trust me."

Women assume that if a man loves a woman he can and will share his intimate and personal feelings with her.

See Chapter 6, Step 6, for the truth about this illusion.

Female Illusion #7: When a man loves a woman, he knows what will excite and arouse her

"When a man really loves a woman, he wants to make her feel good, particularly when they're making love. I mean, maybe he doesn't know automatically, but he will figure it out and really take time with her—at least if he loves her he will. When a man doesn't do what excites her, that's a sign that he doesn't really love her and is just using her for his own pleasure and doesn't care about hers."

A woman may assume that a man who loves her will know how to excite her and will do things that will make her want to make love. If he doesn't, she feels he is using her.

See Chapter 6, Step 7, for the truth about this illusion.

Female Illusion #8: If he really loved me, he'd be more affectionate

"He knows I love it when we hug or when he puts his arm around me. It makes me feel good for us just to be close, like touching our arms against each other. It's silly, I know, but I like the way it feels when we're in contact like that. My husband isn't interested, though. He hardly ever looks at me or holds my hand. He doesn't want us to have that kind of closeness. He doesn't want anything to do with me except to have sex, and I know what that means—he doesn't really care as much as he says he does."

This illusion shows how clearly touching and feeling loved go together for so many women. When a man is not openly affectionate, the woman may falsely conclude that he doesn't really love her.

See Chapter 6, Step 8, for the truth about this illusion.

Female Illusion #9: A man wants to be romantic with the woman he loves

"His idea of romance is sending me a card on my birthday. That's supposed to show me that he loves me? Of course, I appreciate the card, but that's all he does, and it just isn't enough. I want him to do romantic things that show he's really thinking of me more of the time, not just during the two minutes it takes to buy a card. It's like he's bought a thing and that is also supposed to buy my love. It just isn't my idea of romance. I want to feel important to him and really cared about, the way I felt when we were first married. I'm never sure if he doesn't know how or just doesn't care enough to try. But romantic he isn't."

Many women want more romance from their partners than they receive, and they feel that a man in love knows how to be romantic. The fact that their partner isn't very romantic then makes them doubt the depth of his love.

See Chapter 6, Step 9, for the truth about this illusion.

Female Illusion #10: A man shouldn't need to be told how to make love

"We've been having sex for six years. Don't you think he'd get it right by now? I did try to tell him what was good for me in the beginning, but he just went his merry way, taking care of himself. Sure he was worried if I didn't have an orgasm; that injured his pride. He used to ask me if I had come and if I said no, he'd just keep slamming away until I did. Faking orgasms became a matter of self-defense. What else could I do? He doesn't do what I want, and then he's upset if I'm not satisfied. He forces me to lie, and sometimes I really hate him for it. Now I can never tell him the truth because he'll be so furious to find out that he isn't the great lover he thinks he's been all these years. And what if I told him what I want him to do? Even if he could do it, which I doubt at this point, he'd get mad and we'd have a fight because he'd think I was insulting him, saying he was a bad lover. He'd be really mad about that. He's convinced he knows what's good for me, that he's the one with experience. Besides, I'd be embarrassed to tell him."

A woman may feel that if a man really loves her he will understand her sexual needs. She is hurt, angry, frustrated, and often very unhappy when she ends up feeling he is only using her for his own pleasure and ego satisfaction.

See Chapter 6, Step 10, for the truth about this illusion.

REPLACING ILLUSIONS WITH TRUTH

These illusions men and women have about each other keep them from getting the love and satisfaction that it is possible to find in a relationship.

They are like a faulty treasure map directing men and women in the wrong direction so that no matter how carefully they follow the map, they don't reach the treasure.

This is the crux of the man-woman dilemma.

Men don't get enough sex and women don't get enough love because of the historical roots we discussed earlier and also because of our current culture's manifestation of these roots—these illusions. These illusions have given men and women an inaccurate view of the opposite sex and have kept them trying to relate to the illusions instead of the actual people behind these illusions. Hence, while men and women could understand each other far better, and while much more harmonious and satisfactory relationships are possible, men still aren't getting enough sex and women still aren't getting enough love.

We are suggesting simple step-by-step programs, one for men, one for women, that will offer men and women the truth about the opposite sex and show them how they can use this truth to create the kind of relationship they want and to leave all the frustration and misunderstanding behind. We are suggesting a new way of being together that will end these damaging illusions and instead foster understanding, love, and lovemaking. This brings us then to Part II, the Great Love, Great Sex program.

NOTES, CHAPTER 4

1. Shere Hite, *Women and Love* (New York: St. Martin's Press, 1989), p. 214.

GREAT LOVE, GREAT SEX

Introduction to
Part Two

In Part II, the Great Love, Great Sex program, we present our solution to the male-female conflict discussed in Part I. This is our plan to end the battle of the sexes, to help you make love, not war.

This program consists of ten steps for women and ten steps for men, designed to dispel the illusions outlined in Chapter 4 and to replace them with the truth.

This is what you and your partner need to do to create a more satisfying relationship that will allow both of you to fulfill your hopes and dreams.

This program will also help each individual understand his or her own needs and how more effectively to meet them, as well as the needs of her or his partner.

Before we present this program, however, we have a few basic suggestions for both men and women to keep in mind.

1. Work through the program whether your partner wants to or not.

Optimum results are more likely when both partners work on their programs together, but you will find it very worthwhile to do the man's or the woman's program on your own. Many individuals have created enormous positive changes in their relationships without their partners ever realizing they were using the Great Love, Great Sex program. Don't underestimate how much you can influence your partner once you know how.

Some couples may both want to participate in the program but at different speeds and with a minimum of discussion. This is also possible and workable, with each person doing each step to his or her own satisfaction before moving on.

2. Proceed at your own pace.

How long should you spend on each step? The answer depends on you. If you prefer to be flexible and let progress be your guide, just make certain that you stick with it.

If you like things structured, however, you might decide to spend one week, two weeks, or a month on each step, thus creating a time frame with which you feel comfortable. A time structure can keep you on track; otherwise the programs may die of neglect or get lost among the myriad responsibilities of your daily lives. Try this: Put up a beautiful calendar in your bedroom and use it as a reminder each day. Mark on your calendar which step you're working on each day, week, or month.

It's also important to remind each other in a helpful, positive manner to keep working: "Honey, I've been so busy lately I've neglected my woman's program. I want us to do great together, so I'm back on track as of right now."

An alternative might be to have a regular schedule—one step each week, for example—and to decide at the end of the week whether or not you need to spend another week on the same step. If your partner wants more time on the same step, it might be better for you to agree and to keep working together even though you may feel ready to move on.

3. Give each other a safety zone that is free of judgment and criticism.

Create a safety zone where each of you can feel safe while you're exploring new ways to act, feel, relate, and communicate. This is important to your success as a couple—both in using the Great Love, Great Sex program and in your life together. Do your best to make your home as much of a psychological safety zone as you can.

4. Reinforce each other's efforts.

Chances are you won't do everything right the first time. We're only human, we make mistakes, life is complicated, and we're not perfect. No one likes to feel like a beginner, yet many facets of the program may be new.

Keep the long run in mind. Persevere and keep encouraging each other: "I'm really glad you're trying to make things better. I love you even more for it." With encouragement and support you can continue to move through the program, making changes along the way that will benefit you both.

It may also be helpful for men to read the woman's program and for women to read the man's. This will help you understand what is expected of your partner.

Do your utmost to ensure that you both feel successful along the way.

5. Keep in mind the differences in the male and female styles.

Much of the success of this program can hinge on your understanding each other's view of the world.

For example, once Julie understood that Bob was not cold and unfeeling but was simply acting out his training and socialization as a man, it was easier for her to forgive him for past slights and problems. Similarly, once Bob understood more about women and saw why Julie was the way she was sexually, he was much less angry and more patient. Understanding each other better makes the program seem much easier.

If you haven't already done so, read Chapter 2 if you're a woman, and Chapter 3 if you're a man. This will help you better understand the opposite sex in general and your partner in particular.

6. Keep your strengths and your limitations in mind.

Julie knew that Bob needed to understand things thoroughly before he would make any changes. She saw this as both a strength (he really would act once something made sense to him) and a limitation (he had a hard time with her feelings as a result of his emphasis on thinking).

Bob realized that Julie valued his understanding of her feelings. He saw this as a strength (she was a very warm and loving person who got along well with nearly everyone) and a limitation (she would sometimes get so upset and already had warning signs of an ulcer).

They took each other's characteristics into account. Julie tried to explain herself in male-thinking language, and Bob tried to talk about feelings once he learned how to do so without upsetting her. Each realized that the other had strengths and limitations, and they tried to take them into account in dealing with each other.

7. Keep the long run in mind.

It's hard to bring about basic changes, and every one of us needs support, encouragement, and patience in order to persevere and be successful. Try to get an eagle's-eye view of life, seeing the overall movement of your life from where you were to where you want to be.

Expect to keep moving in the direction of your dreams, bringing them to fulfillment step by step and day by day. See your progress along the way and in so doing encourage yourselves to keep going.

8. Live by the Couple's Golden Rule.

Do unto your partner as you would have him or her do unto you. This is the Couple's Golden Rule. Differences in doing the program can mirror differences in your personal style and needs, and how you deal with these differences is a reflection of how you deal with each other in general. In other words, if you are impatient with your partner in other endeavors, you're likely to be impatient with him or her during this program.

Always keep in mind that you are trying to be on the same side, on the same team, pulling together in the same direction. Be mutually supportive and encouraging, even when you're impatient and frustrated.

Every step you take increases the chance of your having a relationship that is more satisfying to both of you. Perhaps we could say that each step adds 10 percent to the odds in your favor, and by going through all ten steps you increase the odds 100 percent toward achieving your personal goal.

The bottom line is to make the effort, to be loving and respectful of each other. You don't need to do everything perfectly all the time. But by continuing on and constantly aiming at the target, you will travel a long way toward a more satisfying relationship for both of you.

5

The Man's Program

This program is designed specifically for men.

It lays the man-woman situation on the line, and explains in frank and direct terms the things a man can do to get more of what he wants both from his relationships with women and from the world in general.

This program will help a man achieve his goals by balancing his mastery of the Outer World of work and money with a mastery of the Inner World that women understand so well. In essence, then, he becomes a warrior of the Inner World.

WHY BOTHER TO CHANGE?

"Dammit! Now I've really had it. It's divorce this time. I mean, it's really over!"

Bob was furious with Julie—and scared—when he came to his third therapy session.

"My ass is on the line now," he said. "Julie and I had this stupid fight over the weekend. She said I'd never get what I wanted from her unless I was able to give her what she wanted. She made it seem like I was supposed to be some goddam slave doing her bidding, like I'm supposed to lick her feet."

When he was asked what had happened, he said, "I couldn't help myself. I mean, I guess I could have refused to talk to Maggie—you know, the woman who owns the dress shop next to my store—but she started talking to me last Thursday after work. Well, actually I guess I started talking to her—what a mess, and I didn't even do anything.

"We were talking and before I knew it we were in her shop and then she asked me to go to her office and have some coffee, which was really nice of her, I thought. So nothing happened except we're in there laughing it up, and when I'm leaving she leans over, real friendly like, and gives me a hug and a kiss. Shit! I could see this in a movie maybe, but in real life—and why *my* real life?

"Just when she's being real lovey-dovey with me, in walks Julie's cousin Becky. Becky's eyes got as big as hubcaps, I swear. By the time I got home, Julie had already heard all about it, and boy, was she pissed.

"I told her I didn't do anything, but no way does she believe me. Not after my stupid comment about getting the sex I needed somewhere else. Why did I say that? Julie's been totally paranoid about my screwing around ever since I said that."

Julie had told Bob she'd had it. She said she couldn't go on the way they were and wanted to move out.

Bob said he was "freaked out" because he'd read an article in the paper that said 62 percent of divorces were brought about by wives, that having children raised the number to 66 percent, and that cooperative no-fault divorce accounted for only 6 percent of divorces.[1]

"Do you know what this means?" Bob asked. "I always thought women were the ones who wanted to be married. I know my mother would have died before divorcing my father. But now it's different. Women are the ones who want out, and I can tell Julie is really serious. She even told me if I want Maggie, I'm welcome to her and that she knows a divorce lawyer who helped one of her friends. Great! Now she's about to have a damned lawyer interfering and making things worse. Before it's over, I'm not only going to lose Julie, I'm going to lose everything I've worked for, and all because we can't seem to get this problem straight between us. So I told her I'd try to make things better, though I'm telling you honestly, I don't know what I'm supposed to do to make it better. Still, she says it's the only way we're going to make it together. If I want her I've got to figure out how to show her I really love her. If I don't, our marriage is going to be over and I'm going to have to start all over. What a frigging mess! And all because I can't figure out what the hell that woman really wants!"

Bob was scared and angry, as well as confused. Even though he wasn't happy with the amount of sex he was getting and Julie wasn't happy with the amount of love she was getting, he hadn't anticipated the situation would come to a head so quickly. Before he could get a handle on the problem, he was facing a divorce.

"Give me the answer," he pleaded. "What am I supposed to do? What does Julie want from me? I don't even know the first step. But whatever it is, I'm going to give it a real shot. I've got to, or else. Besides, I married the woman for a reason. It wasn't like I was stuck without another choice. I really do care about her a lot, but I guess I've never stopped in all these years to think about how much she really means to me and how important all this love stuff might be to her. I guess it's time. Give it to me straight, Doc," he finished, hanging his head like a man ready to go to the gallows. "I'm ready."

Bob was in for a surprise. The solution was actually going to be fun, and best of all, he would end up having more sex. Of course this meant he would have to change, and that would be hard work. But his chances of making his relationship with Julie a success seemed excellent *if* he was willing to put out the effort. If he wasn't prepared to persevere, there was little chance of avoiding a divorce, and worse, the same problem he was having with Julie would probably crop up in his next relationship and cause the same problems all over again.

LOVE OR WAR

You may be saying right now, "Why try to change? It's too hard."

We're all creatures of habit and few of us want to alter how we act and think. We're willing to do so only if we have a truly compelling reason.

Unfortunately, some people—and we hope you're not one of them—have convinced themselves that basic changes cannot take place: "Tigers can't change their stripes" and "You can't teach an old dog new tricks."

Nonsense. Human beings are neither dogs nor tigers and are tremendously flexible. It is in our nature to be loving and peaceful, or we can be warlike and combative. We can love each other or we can follow the traditional path of domination, misunderstanding, resentment, and frustration. We can choose: Do we want to make love or make war?

COLD WAR ON
THE HOME FRONT

Most men are living in the midst of a cold war and don't even realize it.

Only a small percentage of men truly understand women and know how to have a woman enjoy giving them exactly what they want sexually and otherwise.

Most men don't know how to get what they want from their women in a positive way, and when they try to get it in the wrong way, the result is an undercurrent of tension and resentment that sours and poisons their relationships. For example, a man may demand what he wants, get it, and that's all there is to it for him. He doesn't think very much beyond this because most men value career success much more than relationship success, and he divides his energies accordingly. Unfortunately, that's not all there is to it for her. He doesn't realize how much she resents giving in to his demands—and what a high cost is attached.

For example, many women engage in sex out of the desire to avoid a problem with their men. Many feel financially dependent or physically vulnerable and know they *must* make their man happy or else.

Therefore, a man might feel satisfied with his relationship, without realizing how resentful his wife is or how, over time, this situation will erode her caring for him and contribute to separation, divorce, or a cold war on the home front. (As we mentioned, 62 percent of divorce petitions are initiated by women).

That's not to say that men don't care about their home life. They do care, but male standards are very different from women's expectations. It may be easy to ignore the woman's expectations, but typically, if a man does this, he is suffering for it in one way or another.

Often such a man is bewildered and amazed to wake up one day to find himself in a tension-filled relationship, in marital coma, or to find that his wife is leaving them and getting a divorce. "But our marriage was just fine," these men say. "Of course she complained sometimes, but doesn't everyone get unhappy once in a while? I didn't think anything of it. I never knew she was so unhappy."

Many men don't have what they want, don't know how to get it, don't know how to satisfy their women, and their relationships are already suffering for it.

MEET HER HALFWAY

What lies ahead is a no-bullshit approach to having a better relationship with your woman. If you want her to be more interested in sex, then you've got to meet her halfway.

Here is what you have to look forward to if you fail to meet your partner halfway:

1. A deterioration of a good, loving atmosphere at home.
2. A partner who is not fully engaged in sharing your life together.
3. A poor or nonexistent sex life.
4. Marital coma.
5. A partner who is more interested in other activities and other people than she is in you.
6. Affairs, separation, and divorce.
7. The loss of income and Outer World success and a lower standard of living.
8. More health problems and a shorter life.
9. Having to find someone else and start over again, with the same or similar problems cropping up again.
10. Never understanding the Inner World of women or benefiting from its power.

And here is what you have to look forward to if you meet your woman halfway:

1. A more peaceful, calmer, and more loving home environment, more fun, and a happier life. When you come home everyone will be happy to see you and glad you are there.
2. A partner who is actively engaged in sharing your life together, and who is truly interested in who you are, in making you happy, and in trying to help you in every way she can.
3. A more satisfying sex life in which she will be more interested more often because she finds you so exciting and romantic.
4. A relationship that maintains its positive energy and continues to grow, with the feelings between the two of you deepening instead of stagnating, with your feelings becoming more profound instead of slowly evaporating.
5. A certainty that you are the one who counts the most with her and that you have a partner with whom you can share a lifetime of love and memories in a secure relationship in which there is trust and fulfillment.
6. Freedom from the traps that lead to divorce.
7. Greater likelihood of maintaining or increasing your income, success, and standard of living, since your home life renews your energy and because you and your partner are pulling together as one.
8. Better health and a longer life.

9. Solving problems as they arise instead of letting them fester and hurt the relationship, because each of you understands what the other needs and you can be clear about giving it to each other. Also, a loving and trusting relationship can weather storms far better than an unstable one.
10. An understanding of women's Inner World and benefiting from its enormous power.

REASONS TO CHANGE

There are many reasons for you to change. You might want to have a better sex life, a happier and more loving home life, avoid the emotional and financial costs of separation and divorce, have a longer and healthier life through less stress and more support at home, or be more successful in your career, since success at home fosters success at work.

Think about your reasons for putting out the necessary effort to complete the man's program. If you're not willing to put in the work, then forget the program and live with the status quo. If you are willing to put in the work, then keep your personal motivating forces in mind and go for it.

Only you can decide how much effort you are willing to put in and how willing you are to do things differently in order to make your life and hers better. Every man must decide for himself. For some men it will be easy, while for others it will be more difficult. Change, however, is possible and worth it.

Also, in our view, there is less and less choice for men. The truth is that the new woman has already emerged. Women are going to be beside us, shoulder to shoulder, briefcase to briefcase, and there is no going back to the way things were. As more women gain more power in the Outer World, they will no longer be financially dependent on men and stuck in marriages that don't satisfy them. Women no longer have to tolerate men they cannot relate to. Now they have a way out and many are taking it.

This puts men in a position they have not been in for sixty or seventy centuries—that of needing to take more responsibility for the relationship because they have just as much or more to lose from dissolving it. Women now want, need, and in some cases demand a new kind of relationship with a new kind of man, a man who is not just a warrior of the Outer World, but a partner who can relate to her Inner World as well. In essence, she is looking for an intimate warrior.

The ten steps that follow are designed to help you become an intimate warrior. The program begins by helping you dispel the illusions men have about women and replace them with reality. Then you will be taken step by step into a program that will show you how to get what you want from your relationship and have your woman love giving it to you.

STEP 1: FINDING YOUR WHITE HORSE

The first male illusion about women is that daily stress shouldn't diminish her sexuality any more than it does yours.

What's the Problem?

Daily stress may not diminish most men's sexuality, but this is untrue for millions of women. We know how intensely men are focused on sexuality and we now know how women have been forced to suppress their natural sexuality, except under certain circumstances. So the result is that there is almost certain to be a difference between your interest in sex and hers, and the impact of daily stress is probably significantly greater on her than on you.

What's the Truth?

Millions of women are more heavily burdened than men, even though men may not think this is true. Men are often so consumed by their Outer World drive for success and so drained by their own heavy burden that they may not take a careful look at the load their women are carrying. We feel it's important for you to make this assessment.

Therefore, for the next week, when you go home, be aware of what both of you are doing during the evening. Chances are you've both already put in a full day.

Even if a woman doesn't have a job outside the home, she may put in just as hard a day as you do, especially if she has small children to look after. If you don't think so, take care of the kids by yourself some Saturday and see how difficult her job is.

Pay attention to what she does in the evening. Are you taking time off while she is still working? Are you, for example, unwinding in front of the TV while she continues with chores?

Mentally make a list of everything she is doing. Even if she's on the phone, notice what kind of call it is. Is it truly a social call or is she making plans for the following day, setting up appointments for children, arranging for someone to fix the dishwasher, making work appointments.

It's been estimated that women put in as many as twenty more hours of chores a week than men. At the same time we know that if a woman is to feel sexually receptive, she must feel loved and cared about. Love and caring are not conveyed by being overburdened.

If she is still working even into the night, there is every reason for her to be not only exhausted but also resentful. Neither state is conducive to sexual receptivity.

What Can You Do?

We saw that the male style of love includes offering practical help, but all too often the help that a man offers is the help he wants to offer when he wants to offer it, rather than the help she actually needs when she needs it.

She's stuck with whatever chores have to be done when they have to be done and probably has little choice in the matter. This means there's a big discrepancy between his offers to assist her and her ultimate responsibility for all of the work.

If he wants to make her feel more loved and cared about, which is one step along the way to her being more sexually receptive, then he needs to be more helpful on a regular basis—for life.

This is not a one-shot deal that temporarily placates her and leaves him feeling he's the hero of the day. Sure, she wants him to come to her rescue, but not just today. She needs help every day.

When a man does help out at home, the woman not only appreciates the help, but feels less tired and less resentful. This adds to the likelihood that she will want to have sex.

In essence, you scratch her back and she'll be more likely to scratch yours in return.

1. Find the Caregiver in You Who Wants to Help

Even though you, too, are tired after work, find the loving caregiver in you who is willing to care for the most important person in your life, your partner. Find the part of yourself that truly loves and cares for her and focus on this as you come home. Try to set aside the day's aggravations and remember: this is also in your own best interests in that it is likely to benefit your whole relationship. It will enhance your own maturity, your ability to love, your health, and your sex life.

Keep your basic attitude in mind: you love her, you want to help her be less burdened, and you're on the same team pulling in the same direction.

You don't need to do all the following things today or on any given day, but you must consistently from now on do one or more of these things, or similar things, each day. If you want an improved home life, you have to show her consistently day after day that you want to help and look after her because you genuinely love and care about her happiness and well-being.

2. Ask Her to Make a List

Ask her to make a list of five or more items that you can do to help her and to demonstrate that you care about her. Ask her to include things that you can do on a regular basis. They should be specific, not vague or general, and they should be things that will actually make her feel good and will not create a conflict between you. Here are some examples:

Asking her how her day went and listening to her answer
Filling her car with gas
Giving her a back rub
Giving her a hug
Squeezing her some orange juice
Trying to get home from the office by seven rather than seven-thirty
Eating dinner together without TV
Picking up your socks from the floor
Bringing her a small surprise
Bringing dinner home from a take-out restaurant
Cleaning up the kitchen after dinner
Calling her during the day to tell her you care
Putting on some music she enjoys
Unloading the groceries from the car
Giving the kids a bath
Putting the kids to bed
Making sure that the kids do their homework
Feeding the dog

Taking out the trash
Assigning chores to the kids and seeing they get done

She may amend her list at any time, adding items or taking away.

3. Do One or More of the Items
from Her List Each Day

You have to show her consistently day after day that your attitude, goals, and actions are designed to help and care for her because you genuinely love and care about her. And you're willing to do this for life in order to have a happier relationship in which you both get what you want insofar as it is possible.

4. Post Her List

You may find it valuable to post her list in a conspicuous place—on the refrigerator, perhaps, or on the bathroom mirror—and jot down the dates you do each item as a way to remind and encourage yourself until you become accustomed to your new habit of taking on more responsibility at home. Writing what you did on her list only takes a moment, and it greatly increases the likelihood that you will follow through and keep at it. It also serves as evidence of your efforts to show caring in ways she says she wants.

5. Look for Other Ways to Help and
Show You Care About Her

Look around your home with an eye toward finding what needs to be done that you can do instead of her, or with which you can help without having to be asked. If you want to help with a particular chore but don't know how, tell her you want to help but need some basic instructions and ask her to be patient until you get more expert at chores that are new to you. Do things that show you care.

Ask her, "What can I do to help? What can I do to lighten your load? What can I handle that will make things easier for you?"

Encourage her to take some time to relax, take a bath, read, meditate, talk to a relative or friend on the phone, or just have time alone to regroup.

Tell other people nice things about her in front of her.

Fix her something refreshing such as juice, coffee, tea, soda, water, lemonade—something she'll enjoy and that will make her feel that you're looking after her and caring about her.

Ask her how her day went and listen to her answer.

Suggest that she do less cooking. Maybe you could prepare dinner one or more nights a week. Encourage your older children to help out more, just as you are doing. Perhaps you could bring home dinner from a take-out restaurant or order food to be brought in, or have frozen dinners and you make a salad and bring home dessert. Or you could cook a pot of spaghetti sauce on the weekend and freeze it for meals during the week, letting her know that you're trying to be of help to relieve her burden.

Help with the cleaning. If the vacuuming is especially hard on her back, you could take over that job on a regular basis. Or maybe you could take over the bill paying or the dish washing or the laundry. Sure you have a lot to do, but look at her workload. It's nearly endless. If your budget can handle it, maybe you could have a cleaning person come in every week or two. If money is tight, offer to give something up in order to do this: "Honey, I've decided to give up lunches out on Friday and use the money I'll save to pay for someone to come and do all the heavy cleaning; that will save you a lot of time and effort and make your life a lot easier."

George found that Rita most of all appreciated being taken out to eat once a week, even if it was just to a local fast food place. She said this gave her a break from the usual routine and gave her and George a chance to talk.

Bob found that Julie loved fresh-squeezed lemonade, and he also started experimenting with coffees and teas as a way of doing something nice for her.

Allen, a psychiatrist who came for help with his marriage, found that he could take his shirts and Carole's dresses to the laundry, thus saving her the time and effort of laundering them. He was surprised at the result: "I never thought that my shirts were a burden to her, but it was really a big deal. She's told me over and over what a help this is because the million little things add up to a lot. It really counts with her when I do anything that relieves her burden."

PUTTING IT ON THE LINE

Men are used to favored treatment in ways that they may not realize. This is not to say that men have an easy row to hoe. On the contrary, most men carry an enormous weight of responsibility and put up with tremendous pressures. When wars come it's the men who go and put their lives on the line, and it's men who bear the primary financial burden for the family. Nevertheless, most men are used to having a lot of power in the relationship, and to suggest that they voluntarily give up some of their privileged status makes them uncomfortable. Some men feel demeaned or even foolish when they do more work at home.

Try to find the adult caretaker inside you who's looking out for your partner. This can be hard because men are used to doing whatever they want to do at home. They expect their partner to be the mom and nurse and cook and maid and shopper and errand runner and laundress and on and on. Men expect favored treatment, even demand it. Many men desire it, they're attached to it, they even manipulate to keep it. Many men use intimidation to get power and privilege and throw tantrums to hang on to it. If a man is used to being treated like a king or a pampered child at home, this can be a difficult change to make, but it will be worth the effort. The benefits will be greater than the cost.

Men have had the upper hand in relationships for six thousand years. It's time to create more equality—it's coming, ready or not—and the partnership will work better in the long run, sexually and otherwise. You'll have a little more work at home, but you're likely to have a happier partner, a better relationship, and an improved sex life.

Think of the changes as a test of your manhood. Bite the bullet and become the knight who saves his damsel in distress. A warrior who understands the Inner World of women will find his white horse and ride to the rescue. He helps his woman be relieved of stress, and he helps her feel better about herself. As he grows in power and strength, he feels better about himself and becomes more and more appealing to her.

STEP 2: COUNTING THE WAYS

The second male illusion about women is the belief that having sex will make both partners feel good.

What's the Problem?

It is quite true that sex makes men feel good under almost any circumstances, but this is not necessarily true for women. Many women say they would rather cuddle and have a sensual experience than have intercourse. We've seen how historically women learned to arouse their sexuality most fully only in the context of a safe and loving relationship, and that if love is absent, sex in and of itself is typically not as satisfying for her as it is for him. In fact, it may be dissatisfying if she feels she's having sex only out of obligation or to avoid a problem.

What's the Truth?

She wants to feel good about herself *before* making love. Sure, sex may make her feel good physically, but women are not focused on this the way men often are. Women want to feel good emotionally. This is the key, the turn-on, to making them feel good physically. If they don't feel good emotionally, then it is more difficult, perhaps even impossible, to make them feel good physically no matter what sexual techniques a man uses or how good a lover he is.

Remember, a woman's brain is her primary sex organ. Her thoughts and her emotions need stimulation first, not her breasts, not her butt, not her vagina. She needs to feel that he loves her, admires her. He thinks she's gorgeous. He wants her because of his love for her. He isn't using her for his own selfish satisfaction; he cares about hers and he will be here for her and is willing to make a commitment to her. Now she's more receptive!

So take another step toward arousing her sexuality by knowing how to make her feel good about herself. Most men know how to do this, but don't take the time because they don't realize how important it is. Yet how she thinks you feel about her has an enormous effect on how she feels about herself and, more particularly, about you.

For example, if you're critical of her, that's how she'll feel about herself and, unfortunately, about you, too. Your obvious choice here is to make her feel good about herself. Say something nice to her that makes her feel good and she'll be more likely to feel closer to you and more likely to be interested in having sex with you.

What Can You Do?

How do you do it? As Elizabeth Barrett Browning wrote, "How do I love thee, let me count the ways."

In order to say nice things you have to know what you think and feel. A lot of men aren't sure what they think or feel about their woman and therefore don't know what to say.

DIRECTIONS

Read through the following traits, circling the ones you honestly feel your woman possesses.

PHYSICAL traits that I especially like, love, value or admire include her hair, face, eyes, eyebrows, eyelashes, cheeks, chin, forehead, ears, skin, teeth, nose, lips, mouth, smile, laugh, neck, back, shoulders, breasts, arms, hands, stomach, waist, thighs, buttocks, legs, knees, height, weight, feet, vagina, athletic skills, physical coordination, physical health, posture, looks good in certain clothing, jewelry, makeup.

MENTAL traits that I especially like, love, value or admire in her. She is: abstract, artistic, bright, creative, good at problem-solving, alert, aware, astute, bold, original, clever, complex, able to concentrate, curious, detail-oriented, honest, imaginative, ingenious, innovative, inventive, knowledgeable, musical, objective, observant, open-minded, perceptive, practical, precise, reasonable, reflective, sensible, thoughtful, understanding.

EMOTIONAL traits that I especially like, love, value, or admire in her. She is: accepting, agreeable, balanced, calm, carefree, caring, cheerful, controlled, cool, dreamy, easygoing, gentle, happy, hot, intense, intuitive, jovial, loving, patient, playful, powerful, relaxed, sensitive, shy, sincere, stable, strong, sweet, vulnerable, warm.

SOCIAL traits that I especially like, love, value or admire in her. She is: candid, caring, committed, community-minded, considerate, cooperative, diplomatic, expressive, fair, friendly, generous, loyal, well-mannered, a good mother, motivating, an organizer, respectful, sensitive to others, willing to share credit, sociable, supportive, tactful, a good teacher, well-liked, a good wife.

BEHAVIORAL traits that I especially like, love, value or admire about her. She is: adaptable, adventurous, ambitious, assertive, authoritative, capable, competent, a good cook, cooperative, courageous, decisive, good at decorating, dependable, disciplined, dynamic, efficient, energetic, enthusiastic, expressive, willing to follow through, freely giving, a good housekeeper, independent, industrious, good at mechanics, neat, orderly, organized, an outdoor person, able to perform under stress, persistent, playful, polite, good at problem-solving, punctual, quick, quiet, reliable, responsible, resourceful, risk-taking, spontaneous, success-oriented, successful, a gardener, a sport, zestful.

EGO traits I especially like, love, value or admire in her. She is: authentic, balanced, confident, determined, dignified, extroverted, firm, flexible, generous, capable of good judgment, growing, healthy, honorable, idealistic, introverted, mature, modest, mystical, normal, optimistic, poised, principled, progressive, proud, realistic, resourceful, self-accepting, self-aware, self-reliant, serious, spiritual, spontaneous, stable, strong, tenacious, thorough, trustworthy, unassuming, versatile, wise, witty, youthful.

After circling the descriptions above, read through the ones you circled, picking out those you consider most important to you and the ones that are probably most important to her.

Look especially for those about which she has the most insecurity or self-doubts, because then you are caring for her in a way that builds her up in the areas most in need of strengthening.

For example, she may have beautiful eyes and be confident about her eyes, but not about her hair or how bright she is or how good a mom she is. She would like to hear you tell her she has beautiful blue eyes, but she hungers to hear how much you love her silky smooth hair, her quick, clever mind, and her ability to be a loving mother. She may even say no in a tone that says "Do you really mean it?" Then you know you've hit the bull's-eye—a sore spot in need of healing words.

On the lines below, write down the traits that are the most important to you and those that are probably most important to her. Put one trait on each line:

_____

_____

_____

_____

_____

_____

_____

_____

_____

_____

_____

_____

_____

Now add specific details to each trait to make your positive feelings about her concrete and uniquely applicable to her. For example, if you listed "hair," you might add "reddish brown," or "silky smooth," or "smells good." Notice that each of these details refers to the way her hair appeals to one of the senses: sight, touch, smell. Keep thinking in terms of the senses, and don't forget taste, as in the taste of her cooking, and sound, as in the sound of her voice. This gives you a way to be specific about physical attributes.

If you listed "patient" as one of her traits, you might add such specifics as "with the kids," "with the money crunch we're in," "with my trying to be more loving."

Here are a few top items from some sample lists.

Bob's list about Julie:

Confident at work
Great at handling money
Sexy smile
Beautiful green eyes
Silky, golden skin that's wonderful to touch
Hard, conscientious worker
Imaginative problem-solver

George's list about Rita:

A great cook
A patient teacher
The memory expert of the year
Super in dealing with people

Makes others feel good about themselves
A very religious person
A great gardener with a green thumb

Allen's list about Carole:

A great and clear mind
An extremely effective human being
A loving, warm, and liberated romantic
Multitalented
A patient, helpful wife and mom
A loyal, trustworthy friend
A beautiful, sexy lover with sky blue eyes
A wonderful horsewoman with great hands
My best friend

Give her one a day. You now have fabulous emotional nourishment to feed her each day, and you'll come up with more as you go through life if you keep your radar attuned to her good points. Keep this information about her handy. This is the source of tremendous power that can carry you forward through the rest of the steps. Refer to it over and over to refresh your memory about all the nice things you can say to her, and in so doing you will also feel more love for her.

The big key from here on is to *express* to her your appreciation of these traits, giving her the nurturing praise you've just come up with. It does her little good if you do this exercise and fail to follow through in action, though thinking good things about her is always valuable.

Tell her—in words, writing, music—so she gets the full impact. Convey to her the positives you sincerely feel about her. Do this at least once each day. And do it for the rest of your lives.

Once, or once in a while, is not enough. If you want someone to remember something it's a good rule to repeat it five times. If you want her to remember she's truly special and loved, or that she's appreciated for something about which she has self-doubts, you need to repeat it over and over and over again.

At first this can be tough to do. Don't wimp out. Get past beginner's jitters.

This was a big problem for George, the divorce attorney we discussed earlier. George said he wasn't used to "being soft and mushy," that he was more comfortable going "balls to the wall" with people, battling things out. Nevertheless he was determined to change his relationship with Rita. "The last thing in the world I want is to have to hire a lawyer for myself and go through a divorce." When George tried to "count the ways" he loved Rita, he was very uncomfortable at first: "I felt like a real jerk, like I was back in high school tripping over my tongue." George found that he was more comfortable telling her nice things in writing and on the phone, which is exactly how he started. He left her little notes when he went to work in the morning and made a point of calling her and telling her the nice things he genuinely felt about her. He said he could do it if he said them quickly and then went on to other topics. It didn't take very long before he felt comfortable telling her in person what he felt, and after a while he no longer needed to race through his nice words to Rita.

At first you too might feel uncomfortable or awkward or weird. It's okay to have these reactions. In time you'll get more comfortable.

HAVE THE RIGHT ATTITUDE TOWARD HER

You want to make her feel good about herself. You care about her, you love her, and she deserves to feel good about herself because she's a special person. She's your friend, and you want her to know the things you like, love, value, and admire about her.

TELL A FRIEND ABOUT HER

Tell other people nice things about her, too. Tell your family, friends, neighbors, and others things you like, love, respect, and admire about your woman. Imagine how good it would make her feel to have some really nice compliments get back to her. Imagine how golden that would make you look in her eyes. Imagine how that might be returned to you.

Continue with Step 1 at the same time you're concentrating on making her feel good about herself. This means that each day you're looking for ways to help relieve her stress and ease her daily burden, and at the same time you're finding ways to build her esteem and good feelings about herself. The combination is powerful and will be returned in a positive way. At first this may seem like a lot, but it's mostly a matter of changing your daily patterns, gaining new experiences, and forming new habits.

Helping your partner feel good about herself will lead you to your next goal—having fun together.

STEP 3: FRIENDS AT PLAY

The third male illusion about women is that being together is really satisfying.

What's the Problem?

While men want emotional closeness, their male training has taught them to avoid emotional closeness because it is a sign of weakness. As a result, most men substitute physical closeness for emotional closeness.

A man may want to be in the same room with his woman, for example, watching television, but he won't want to relate to her verbally or show emotional intimacy. In other words, he might come in and sit down with her. He may impart what he considers important information: "The children's bicycles are in the driveway again," or "Someone is coming to trim the trees on Saturday," or "I bought two new front tires for your car." He may say, "How was your day?" but he won't want a long answer.

This does not mean that the man doesn't care how his partner feels or that he doesn't love her deeply. This is simply a male style.

The problem is that this kind of relating is much too distant for most women. They find it frustrating and may take it as a sign that their man doesn't really want to be with them.

This female frustration and need to interact is at the base of what usually follows in this situation. The woman often decides to do something else or talk to someone else, and the man often feels abandoned and thinks she just doesn't want to be with him.

"Why does she complain that I don't want to do anything with her?" said one male interviewee. "She's the one who leaves and wants to do something else. She just doesn't find being with me good enough."

What's the Truth?

The truth is that you may love your woman deeply but your male style takes the vitality from your relationship and is a sexual turn-off to her.

This style may satisfy your needs to be together, but it probably doesn't do that for her. As a result, she becomes increasingly frustrated and turned off both emotionally and sexually.

"He just doesn't care about me," said one woman interviewee. "He has nothing to say to me and doesn't want to do anything but look at the tube. So I get busy doing something else, and then he seems to resent it. I never understand that. He doesn't want to be with me, but he doesn't want me to do anything else, either. Then later he wants to have sex. But why should I want to have sex with him when he doesn't even want to talk to me?"

In one study, 98 percent of the women said they wanted their men to talk more personally more often. [2]

It is common for couples with sexual problems to spend little time talking and having fun together.

Remember, the last thing a woman wants is to have sex when she feels that you don't care about her or, worse, that you're just using her for sex. You love her and want her to just know this, but remember that women need you to show that you truly care. You must relate to her in a way she identifies as loving, and then her awareness of being loved will overflow into her level of sexual interest.

What Can You Do?

One large survey asked women what they wanted in a lover. Their answer was that they wanted a companion who was fun, sensitive, supportive, a good listener, tender, and playful. [3]

We'll deal with the other aspects of what women want in other parts of this program. What we want to address here is the need to be playful.

We know what you're thinking: "What the hell does she mean by 'playful'?" Right?

The fact is, she doesn't want to just be together in the same room. She wants to relate more fully and she wants to play.

It will be helpful for you to find the happy kid part of yourself and let him out to play and have a good time. It will not only produce a much better relationship, but it will also give you a break from the routines that the typical male style so often lets you fall into.

It's fortunate that most men have had a childhood with the emphasis on fun. This means that even if you haven't focused on fun very much in your adult life, at least you do have some past experience to draw on. You can use your childhood memories to help bring out that spirit of play once again. Your woman will appreciate it, and it is likely to pay off not only in a more fun, but in a better sex life as well.

Make this a couple's project in which you jointly discuss the possibilities and make something new and fun happen. Consider several options you both would enjoy.

Look at it as a fun equation: *Shared fun = time + activity + positive emotional atmosphere.*

Coming up with ideas that fit the fun equation can in itself be fun. It will mean taking some *time* together. It will mean you will have an *activity* to share, and it will create a *positive emotional atmosphere* because you will be discussing the things you both like to do and thus sharing ideas and feelings. This in itself creates an atmosphere of playfulness and a nurturing experience that helps you both relax. It is also likely to make her feel cared for, and in so doing, it is likely to increase her sexual desire for you.

Your mission will require you to take several measures:

1. Initiate the Subject

Let her know what you want to accomplish and engage her in a positive search for shared fun activities. Figure out when you'll be able to do it and how much time you realistically will have. This can have a very big affect on what you will do, if you're short on common time together alone.

Talk it over with her and see what she would like to do. See if she'd rather do something else that would also be enjoyable for you.

Avoid situations that won't be pleasant for her. George decided that a good change would be to take Rita fishing. For some women this might have been perfect, but Rita hates the water and hates fish. His suggestion made matters worse because, from her viewpoint, it showed that, once again, George had been insensitive to what she was interested in doing and seemed to be interested only in pleasing himself. The key is to keep both your interests in mind, thinking about it from her point of view as well as your own.

2. Track Down Ideas

Look through the Sunday newspaper's entertainment section, seek out other sources of entertainment information, or ask friends for ideas.

Think about your hobbies and hers.

Think about things that you both enjoy: dancing, crafts, picnics, cooking together, making up stories, planning your next vacation, walking or other forms of exercise, doing puzzles, playing cards, going for a drive, hiking, doing volunteer work, reading aloud to each other.

Think about movies, plays, aerobics groups, music, the circus, dance groups, spectator sports, participating sports, boating, taking classes.

Think about natural places where you can go for a walk or just to see the beauty of the trees, the hills, the sunset or sunrise, the flowers, or the water. This can give you both a lift and an emotional cleansing.

Some couples sit down and make a list of possible activities and put them in a box, later drawing out one and doing it, thus adding an element of surprise and excitement to their outings. This obviously requires several or many possible activities and only works if you can generate enough good ideas.

Other couples make a calendar of things they could do together and plan when they will do them.

Others try to make more of an event of small things. For example, instead of just going out to get ice cream or yogurt at night, they stay out and walk around the shopping center, eat the ice cream in the shop instead of taking it home, or drive somewhere nice and eat it there. This gives them a chance to talk outside the house and away from everyday distractions.

One couple played the What If We Were Tourists game, looking at their community as if they were visitors and going to see the sights. Often there are great things to do in town, but unless you look for them, you don't find them.

Some couples find that the richest rewards come from creating a project to work on together, something they can discuss with each other.

This step opened up a whole new life for Pam and Brad. Instead of watching television together as they had been doing for years, they set up a workshop in an unused garage on their property. Brad was great with his hands and Pam was a really good designer. Together they renovated the garage into a charming studio apartment, which they rented out, thus creating a second income. They had so much fun they soon began finding old houses to fix up and sell at a handsome profit.

Sometimes couples find that it is best to do exactly the opposite of what they do all day. One couple, for example, both had physical jobs: Dan was a construction foreman; Sandy assembled jewelry in a small factory. At night they found stimulation from reading the newspaper together. Later they took a series of classes together on world affairs.

Another couple had desk jobs: Jack was a loan officer at a bank, and Andrea was an accountant. At night they found they had a wonderful time with colored pens and some of the beautiful new coloring books for all ages that are now available. They also set up a Ping-Pong table in the house, put a badminton court in their back yard, and had a great time playing each other, as well as playing doubles against friends and neighbors.

For every couple this step will be different and should evolve and change over time as interests vary and change. The most important thing is to get busy and make it happen.

3. Make It Happen

After you've figured out one or more possibilities for having fun together, arrange for the two of you to do it. Make it happen; be the leader-organizer. Or the two of you could share the leadership responsibility, each of you taking on some aspect to make the fun happen. The best criterion to use in choosing an activity is whether or not it happens and how it makes you both feel. Whatever leaves you both feeling regenerated and provides you with a good time is what counts.

Take responsibility for at least some of the leadership so that you're doing your part.

4. Keep Sharing Fun Activities on a Regular Basis

Women often complain that their man will occasionally do something really nice, and then months go by and nothing happens. They feel let down and disappointed, and these feelings interfere with women's sense of closeness and therefore their sexual desire.

Try to do something together on a regular basis. Exercising together can serve several purposes. Mild or moderate exercise is good for both of you, it's a way for you to intereact, and it enhances sexuality. Exercise, then, is a great option. Even if one of you must modify your pace to enable the other to keep up, it is well worth the effort.

Jackie was not in very good shape, and Bill was an exercise nut. He said she was out of shape and lazy, which hurt her and made her mad. She said she *was* out of shape, but she *wasn't* lazy; she was simply caught in the inertia of inactivity—all habits perpetuate themselves—and she didn't know how to get started.

Bill wanted to help, and Jackie agreed, with the one condition that he take her present out-of-shape condition into account and engineer the activities so she would feel successful. They started going to a low-impact dance-exercise class that Jackie said was much easier and more fun than she'd imagined, and she loved going with Bill.

Bill said he loved it: "I was one of three men in a room of fifty women all dressed in tight leotards lying on their backs with their legs spread in the air." He decided he could spend an hour doing that *any time*. And Jackie loved it because she liked watching herself get into shape and noticed how much better she felt and looked.

Find things you can do on a regular basis and take responsibility to make it happen. If you get past being a beginner, you will find that as your experience develops and your interest increases, your shared activity will grow a life of its own and carry you forward to having more fun.

STEP 4: DOING IT WITH WORDS

The fourth male illusion about women is that women have difficulty saying what they mean and are often hard to understand.

What's the Problem?

While there are many situations in which couples do understand each other, a man feels extremely confused when he can't understand his partner and she doesn't understand him. As George once said of Rita, "I can do anything but understand her."

Because men often don't understand women, they often assume that women are irrational, don't communicate well, and are difficult to understand. Women, in turn, assume that men are impossible. Both end up not communicating, often fighting, or not talking at all, particularly about certain subjects.

What Is the Truth?

We've seen how men's and women's worlds evolved side by side, but with very different, often opposite priorities and responsibilities. These differences can often be the basis of misunderstandings that generate bad feelings and exacerbate any problems the couple already has.

One result is that even though men and women speak the same words, they may mean different things. It's as if they actually speak different languages. It's as if he speaks MaleSpeak and she speaks FemSpeak.

Take a conversation concerning sex, for example:

She says: Honey, I love you.

She means: I feel close to you. We have a good life together. I want you to put your arms around me and say, "I love you, too!"

He hears: Great, she loves me, maybe she's in the mood to have sex.

He says: That's wonderful, sweetheart (and reaches under her blouse to unhook her bra).

She says: What are you doing? I said I love you.

He says: Right. So let's make love.

She says: You don't care about me at all. You're just interested in sex. Forget it.

Now he feels she's just teasing, and he doesn't understand why she's angry, or why she's turning him down. Still, he has been trained to keep his emotions under control and may not express his anger or frustration. Instead, he stores it inside to build up into more bad feeling that will no doubt be released another day, perhaps at a time when she—and he—least expects it.

Even if he knows he missed something in the conversation, he won't know what it is. For him this is simply more reinforcement for the illusion about women not being able to communicate. He will assume that women are simply irrational, can't make up their minds, and are often impossible to understand.

She feels deflated. She tried to reach out to him and have a nice exchange, and he ruined it once again. Sex is all that's on his mind. Reaching out to him has only caused a problem, and next time she'll remember not to even try. But she'll resent it, and while she might not say so—women generally try to avoid conflict—she'll store it up as another example of why she can't reach out to him and why she is dissatisfied and he is insensitive.

A *Redbook* study found that the strongest indicator of sexual satisfaction was the woman's ability to discuss sex with her husband. The more often they discussed sex the higher they rated their sex lives, their marriages, and their happiness in general. [4]

A common trait among couples with sexual difficulties is that they don't take time to talk—about sex or anything else.

Remember, women want to communicate by expressing feelings of love and having these feelings expressed in return. In fact, "the half-hour a week that married couples spend in conversation is not nearly enough for most women, who tend to get involved with extramarital lovers more out of a desire for communication than a desire for sex."[5] Most women want love far more than they want sex.

Every misunderstanding adds another emotional brick to the wall in between them, a wall that can ultimately lead to a sense of hopelessness about ever being able to resolve their conflicts—sexual and otherwise.

Another common misunderstanding involving communication is that men believe that women talk and talk but aren't really saying anything important, and therefore their talking should be ignored. Some men actually find women's talking painful and see it as a sign that women are less intelligent and not to be taken seriously.

This attitude has long infuriated women and has added tremendously to the battle between the sexes. It is actually a misunderstanding of what conversation means to her and an assumption that the male view is the only "real" and valid view.

Men have been trained to use few words and get to the point. This is certainly a valuable and valid use of language. Some men use many words, but instead of providing the closeness women seek, the words are often another form of armor. These men keep distance through words.

Women, on the other hand, use words and conversation as social glue to relate to and develop relationships with others by sharing feelings, reactions, problems, insights, and solutions as well as information, both vital and not so vital.

A good conversation gives a woman a sense of warmth and friendship and understanding. It also has other uses that men don't take into account. Men depend on women to be a bridge to the rest of the world and to use that bridge to benefit them. That means that while you may think your partner's conversation with a neighbor is frivolous, the relationship she is nurturing through conversation may actually be of great value to you.

For example, it may mean that the other woman, because of the relationship, will watch the children on Sunday while you go to the baseball game, thus freeing you from any child care responsibilities; or the neighbor's husband may help you move a big piece of machinery or lend you some tools. These things benefit you directly, but they wouldn't have happened without the seemingly frivolous conversation on the telephone.

The subjects of men's and women's conversations differ tremendously. Men usually enjoy talking primarily about their Outer World—sports, work and career, money, and politics.

Women also enjoy talking about the Outer World and about their Inner World of relationships, emotions, personal problems, children, other family members, and friends. These topics are usually given more time and a higher priority.

Your partner may consider your Outer World talk interesting to a point, but it doesn't touch her emotionally and it keeps you at a distance from her. On the other hand, you may find Inner World talk boring, confusing, or annoying. You may feel that she's spending all her free time talking on the phone and never giving you the attention you want. You may feel annoyed, left out, and ignored. If you withdraw, she's annoyed, and if you speak up in anger, she's upset, so you try to put up with the situation.

Finally, you get angry. If there's no outlet for your pent-up emotion, it may come out as feeling more distant from her, feeling angry at her, and it may lead to sexual or romantic involvement with other women. This can lead to an even more damaging situation. But it need not be this way.

What Can You Do?

1. Learn to Speak Her Language—FemSpeak

If you're going to progress toward a more fully excited woman through a better relationship and more emotional intensity, you've got to learn to speak her language—FemSpeak—and to increase the quantity and quality of your conversation.

If you want to understand her—which is the only way you're going to get what you want from her, like it or not—you need to realize she often means different things than you think she does, especially when it comes to sex.

Once again, remember that the message she doesn't want to hear is that you just want to have sex for its own sake. She wants to hear that you love her and that's why you want to have sex with her. You love her, meaning that you are committed to her well-being and that you want her specifically, not that you're just interested in having sex.

Consider whatever you say in this light. Ask yourself how she will hear it, and if necessary rephrase it with this in mind. Jackie got angry and hurt when Bill said she was lazy, but she admitted she was out of shape. Bill explained that he was simply talking MaleSpeak. He said he didn't mean any harm and that that's simply how he would "talk to another guy." He said guys tease each other and egg each other on by name-calling and throwing out challenges. He thought she was being overly sensitive.

Jackie said that was a perfect example of MaleSpeak and that if he wanted to talk her language he could have said something like "I love you so much I want you to have good health; I worry about you and exercise will help you be around for longer so we can be together longer." She said that would mean something to her in FemSpeak and would have gotten him a lot further with her.

Bill pointed out that he did get where he wanted by speaking Male, since she did start exercising. But Jackie pointed out that she decided to exercise in spite of his comments, not because of them, and that the main result of his name-calling was that she pulled further away from him, not closer, which is what he supposedly wanted. Bill said he was starting to get the point and that he would try to understand FemSpeak if she tried to understand MaleSpeak. She said (also getting the point), "I bet I can learn Male faster than you can learn Fem."

"How much faster?" he asked, taking up the challenge, then added, "I love you when you speak Male."

Remember that a woman's brain is her most powerful sex organ and you can communicate with her brain through words.

So do it with words. Learn to talk FemSpeak.

2. Talk About Your Own Inner World and Listen to Her Talk About Hers

As much as you are able, tell her about your own Inner World. Talk about what you need, what you feel, what you hope for, and what your dreams are for the future.

Let yourself be more personal than you're used to being. Get to know her Inner World more fully.

This practice violates the boundaries most men have erected, but you have to cross those boundaries sometimes so you can be closer to her. Remember, you don't have to do this with the whole world, just with your woman, your closest partner.

You can see how this is done by listening in on her conversations with women. See how she reveals more of herself to her friends than you and other men normally reveal. See how she shows her feelings and intimate thoughts. Try doing this with her. Let down your guard a little more with her. Maybe even let her know that you want to do this. Tell her you feel a bit uncomfortable with this experience at first, but keep at it and you will be more comfortable in time. Tell her what's important to you and why you care.

For example, let her know when you're having a problem at work that you'd usually keep to yourself. Instead of bearing the whole load alone, try talking to her about it. If this is new for you, be as patient with yourself—and with her—as you can. Even if she doesn't fully understand the problem, even if she has a hard time grasping why it matters so much to you, you will still be creating closeness—and maybe you'll feel less weighted down and alone with your problem.

Allen, the psychiatrist mentioned earlier, said that he was used to shouldering his work stress alone and didn't want to burden his wife with what he heard from his patients. When he thought about it more deeply, he realized that he didn't need to go into the details about others' problems with Carole. He just needed to talk with her about the effect his work had on him. She had told him that she was interested in how he was doing, but he was so used to being the listener rather than the talker that he had a hard time in the beginning telling her about his feelings. Yet he started anyway and began by briefly telling her if he was saddened by his patients' problems or angered by the hospital bureaucracy. And soon he was eager to tell Carole how his day had really gone, rather than giving her the phony non-answer that everything was fine.

Let her know how sensitive you are about the things that are important to you. For example, you might say, "You know, when you're on the phone so much with Sarah I begin to think you don't want to be with me. I know you want to talk to her, but I need to be with you, too."

If you say this to her, at least she will understand that even if you aren't saying very much to her when you're together, you very much want and need to be with her. This will create better understanding between you and better feelings.

As another example you could say, "You know, when you don't want to make love, I feel as though you don't really care about me or love me, and that hurts."

She may say that she feels as though you just want sex and that hurts *her* so much that she doesn't want sex or anything else. This will give you a chance to bring this issue out in the open. You may suspect this is the case even if she won't admit it. This is an opportunity for you to ask her: "Are you angry or are you avoiding having sex because you think I just want to have sex with you and that I don't really love you?"

Asking this question shows her that you understand her perspective and that you want to understand her. It also says that indeed you do care about her or you wouldn't be taking the time to reassure her about your feelings for her. It also says something about your courage in directly discussing such a sensitive matter.

If this is done without a show of anger, if you can just discuss your needs and feelings with her and understand hers, you're taking a big step to building communication between the two of you and getting past some of your frustrations with each other.

Another topic you might discuss is how she felt when she read Chapter 3 of this book and how it relates to her. You might ask her if she feels frustrated by how history and circumstances have shaped us, or how the chapter related or didn't relate to her. These questions show your concern for her feelings and let her know that you are sensitive to them.

Or pick other subjects. You can talk about something you saw on the news, how it moved you, and how it made you feel. You can express anger here as long as it isn't directed at her. Or you can talk about your work and how exciting it was to have your proposal accepted and appreciated. The topic is not important. What counts is that you discuss it in a personally meaningful manner and in a way she can share. For example, if she asks, "What happened at work today?" don't just give her the facts, tell her also how you felt about what happened. The point is to get into the habit of letting her know how you feel, telling her what's going on inside you. This is speaking in language she understands.

A man who knows FemSpeak might say, "I need more of your time than I'm getting. I love you and it makes me feel good to be with you. I'm glad you have a lot of friends, and I understand you need time with them. I'm also glad you dress nicely, and I realize you need time to shop so you have nice things. I don't begrudge you time for yourself, either. But I feel ignored and sad and lonely when I don't get enough time with you. How could we work it out so that we have more time together?"

3. Tell Her That You Care

Make an effort to truly understand what she means when she talks. Find out what's important to her and how she sees things.

1. Ask her to tell you what she wishes you would say to her, the things that would really tell her that you care about her.

2. Try to express in words to her the things she wants to hear at least once each day.

3. Let her know when you are looking after her best interests. Tell her when you come home at night after you've worked especially hard that you did it for her as well as yourself. Say, "I want to be successful for us, honey. I want you to be proud of me and help build a great future for us." When you have success that she should share in be sure to let her know and give her credit for her contribution: "I couldn't have done it without all your support and help."

4. If you haven't already done so, read Chapters 3 and 4, so you have a better understanding of what she wants and needs, and how she sees the world.

5. Strive to increase the number of words the two of you exchange each day.

6. Ask her each day how she's feeling or how her day is going. And listen to her answer.

7. Tell her one thing each day—something you would ordinarily keep to yourself—that you find funny, interesting, unusual, or important. Let her know how you felt about it. She wants to know what's going on inside you, so be sure to tell her if something mattered to you or bothered you.

8. Tell her when you feel upset about work, when you're disappointed or frustrated or feel that you've been stabbed in the back. Let her know you're trying to be more open and you want her to know what happened, why it matters to you, and how it makes you feel. If you're not sure how you feel about it, ask her how she would feel in the same situation. She might feel differently, but you're still accomplishing the goal of relating to her on a more intimate level through words.

9. Tell her about the things that are important to you, like work or sports or politics or your hobby. Put your own interests into her language. Describe the thrill of seeing a diving catch by a shortstop or the beauty of a wide receiver flying to grab a football out of the air. Talk about how it makes you feel to have your team win a game or to go to the World Series or Super Bowl or NBA finals. Tell her what matters to you and how it affects you. This

addresses one of the chief complaints women express in their relationships with men. They often say men fail to discuss things that are important with them, making women feel shut out of the world of men. So let her into your world.

10. Turn your gripes into solutions. Instead of calling her a nag, tell her that you don't mind being reminded sometimes, but it bothers you to have her tell you over and over again. Then get the pipes fixed so she won't *have* to nag. Instead of calling her unaffectionate or unsexual, work on ways to draw her closer to you so she'll want to be affectionate and sexual. Instead of being angry at her for spending so much money, work with her to find a solution. Make it a mutual problem-solving process. Do it together and keep working on the gripe until you've jointly turned it into a mutually satisfying solution.

11. Convey more directly to her your emotional needs that aren't being met. For example, the following is a conversation in which he speaks MaleSpeak and she speaks FemSpeak.

HE: Another bill from the department store! Haven't you got enough shoes yet? Do I look like I'm made of money?

SHE: Well, I know you want me to look nice when we go to your office party, and I just thought—

HE: You thought it was a great excuse to buy another pair of shoes. Haven't you got any self-control?

SHE: You don't care about anything I do. I just wanted to look good, because if I don't, you'll be mad about that. You're mad no matter what I do.

Here's how the conversation might go if he spoke her language:

HE: The bill came for some shoes you bought. I'm under a lot of pressure from the bills, and this upset me because I didn't expect it.

SHE: I'm sorry, honey, but I did let you know that I was buying the shoes for the office party, and you did agree that it was a good idea. Is there a money problem this month?

HE: There sure is. Once again we're right at the limit, and the pressure of having to go through this every month is killing me. I can't stand it. It makes me really irritable.

SHE: I know it. It's upsetting for me, too. Let's think about ways we can handle the problem. One thing would be if I helped handle the bill-paying. Maybe we could do it together. And maybe we need to really work out that budget we're always talking about so we can cut back on our spending.

HE: Those are great ideas, honey. Anything you can do to help me be under less pressure will help out. I'm glad we're in this together, because it's sure hard when I feel like I've got all the money stress alone. I love you.

The tone and mood are different when he speaks FemSpeak. In the first conversation he's angry and she's hurt, she feels misunderstood and reacts defensively to his angry attack. In the second he expresses the underlying reason for his anger (the pressure), and she reacts with closeness and offers of help. The creation of this better atmosphere between the two of you is your aim in learning FemSpeak.

12. Keep track of your progress in communicating with her by speaking her language. Each night get out your list of nice items about her and write down what you said to her that day. Put down the date, too.

   Doing this is a way of igniting sparks in her and between the two of you. At some point the sparks will burst into flame and then you'll be ready to turn up the heat and help her get fully turned on.

STEP 5: THE FOUR INNER MEN

The fifth male illusion is the belief that women are impossible to please.

What's the Problem?

The problem is that men are so confused about what women want that they regard women as endlessly vacillating and irrational beings who are impossible to please.

What's the Truth?

The truth is that most women really want a relationship with four different men or, more precisely, they want one man who can fill four different roles. These four roles are the hero, the playmate, the friend, and the lover. Let's look at each of those roles:

The hero is the traditional strong and capable male protector who will look after and take care of his woman and make her feel less vulnerable to the dangers of the world. He offers commitment and security. He is the mature protector a woman can rely on to help and rescue her. He is successful in dealing with the Outer World in ways that cause her to admire and respect him, thus making any love he sends her very valuable. He is usually serious and often seems to be the strong, silent type.

The problem is that the hero is often *too* serious and silent. Women also want a playmate to balance the hero in her man.

The playmate is a lot of fun. He likes to have a good time with his woman. He's lighthearted. He likes to laugh and play. He is spontaneous and often unpredictable. He offers a diversion from everyday problems and is able to simply laugh at them. He has a lovable boyish quality.

The Chinese philosopher Meng Tse wrote over two thousand years ago, "The great man is he who does not lose his child's heart." The playmate is just such a man. He knows how to have fun and enjoy life. He is strong enough to be vulnerable and open. He still has his child's heart.

Having fun is important, but sometimes a woman also needs an equal partner, a friend.

This friend is an equal. He works side by side with his woman to achieve their goals. He can both offer and take advice. He can talk about his problems and listen to hers. He is a valuable confidant and ally. It takes a courageous and confident man to be a good friend.

This brotherly-sisterly relationship with the friend is wonderful, but a woman also wants a lover.

The lover is passionate and romantic. He makes love to her both emotionally and physically. He expresses his love and passion and is sensitive to hers. He often tells her she is a highly desirable woman. He lets her know that he desires her and only her, causing her to feel excited and romantic. He strives to master the art of sensual lovemaking that merges the emotional and the physical.

What Can You Do?

Imagine that you have four men within you, each one representing a separate part of your personality. Your goal is to develop all of their differing talents, handling their responsibilities in the ways that suit you.

This won't be hard to do, because, like all men, you already have these four components blended together within you in various proportions.

Some men find that the hero role comes most naturally to them and that the playmate role is more difficult. A very combat-ready man, for instance, may tend to be a hero rather than a playmate.

Women also vary in their need for a man to fill each of these roles. Some women want their partner to be a friend first and foremost while the other roles are less important. Other women want a lover more than the other roles. Your goal is to understand how much of each your partner wants and then learn how to emphasize certain parts of yourself so you can give her what she wants.

This may seem lopsided in terms of effort, but soon you're going to have a chance to tell her what roles you want her to emphasize or deemphasize.

FOUR INNER MEN ASSESSMENT

Rate yourself on where you are now and on where you would like to be: 1=rarely or very little; 2=sometimes or moderate; 3=usually or very much

	Where I Am Now	Where I Want to Be
AS A HERO		
She can depend on me		
I'm a good problem-solver		
I look after her		
I'm a good provider		
I'm worthy of respect		
TOTAL AS A HERO		
AS A PLAYMATE		
I like to have a good time		
I enjoy laughing and playing		
There is a happy kid in me		

	Where I Am Now	Where I Want to Be
I can be lighthearted	_____	_____
I can enjoy life even when it's not going well	_____	_____
TOTAL AS A PLAYMATE	_____	_____

AS A FRIEND

	Where I Am Now	Where I Want to Be
We're good buddies	_____	_____
I see her as my equal	_____	_____
We share life's ups and downs	_____	_____
I can offer and take advice	_____	_____
We understand each other	_____	_____
TOTAL AS A FRIEND	_____	_____

AS A LOVER

	Where I Am Now	Where I Want to Be
I know how to please her	_____	_____
I enjoy sensuality	_____	_____
I like physical affection	_____	_____
I know how to make her feel desirable	_____	_____
Passion and romance are an important aspect of our lovemaking	_____	_____
TOTAL AS A LOVER	_____	_____

If you are doing the program with your woman, or if you can enlist her help, have her rate you below so you can understand her view of how well you fill the four roles in your relationship with her and how she would like you to improve. This will help you decide what changes you could be working on to make her feel more satisfied and happy—which will result in your getting more love and better sex.

1=rarely or very little;   2=sometimes or moderate;   3=usually
or very much

	Where I See Him Now	Where I Would Like Him to Be
AS A HERO		
I can depend on him	_____	_____
He's a good problem-solver	_____	_____
He looks after me	_____	_____
He's a good provider	_____	_____
He's worthy of respect	_____	_____
TOTAL AS A HERO	_____	_____
AS A PLAYMATE		
He likes to have a good time	_____	_____
He enjoys laughing and playing	_____	_____
There is a happy kid in him	_____	_____
He can be light-hearted	_____	_____
He can enjoy life even when it's not going well	_____	_____
TOTAL AS A PLAYMATE	_____	_____
AS A FRIEND		
We're good buddies	_____	_____
He sees me as an equal	_____	_____
We share life's ups and downs	_____	_____
He can offer and take advice	_____	_____
We understand each other	_____	_____
TOTAL AS A FRIEND	_____	_____

	Where I See Him Now	Where I Would Like Him to Be

AS A LOVER

He knows how to please me

He enjoys sensuality

He likes physical affection

He knows how to make me feel desirable

Passion and romance are an important aspect of our lovemaking

TOTAL AS A LOVER

Now it's time to compare the four ratings to see how they match up and to help you decide what you could be trying to change.

Transfer your totals to this chart.

	Where I Am Now	Where She Sees Me Now	Where I Want to Be	Where She Would Like Me to Be
HERO				
PLAYMATE				
FRIEND				
LOVER				

Couples get along if the partners are well matched in these areas. In other words, if a man is very high in his rating as a playmate and his woman wants a man who is weighted heavily in this area, then they are compatible in this area.

On the other hand, if a woman wants very much to have a hero and her partner is rated very high as a playmate and low as a hero, there is likely to be a problem. She will be like the interviewee who said, "I just wish Jay would grow up and start acting responsible. He doesn't take anything seriously and I end up having to handle all of life's problems alone. He says I worry too much. But he doesn't worry at all."

The aim of this step is to help you understand what she wants from you and to help you better match her idea of what she wants in her man.

From the profile you can decide what roles you need to work on. Use the information below to steer yourself toward the actions you need to take to become the kind of mate your wife is seeking. If the steps you need to take lie ahead in the program, work your way toward them, keeping the area you need to work on in mind.

If she wants you to be more of a hero than you now are, work hard to be more responsible as a provider and protector who is competent and strong, whom she can rely on and even look up to. Try to live up to your standards and your moral principles so you will be worthy of respect and admiration. Show more confidence and self-esteem, and use your ability to solve problems and handle life's daily chores and crises calmly. Be strong in your dealings with the outside world, but don't forget to be sensitive and caring in your intimate life together.

If she wants you to be more of a playmate than you are now, try to find the playful kid in you. Bring him out and let him lead the way to having a good time together.

If she wants you to be more of a friend than you are now, work at being more of an equal partner with her. Be there for her so she knows you're her buddy who's reliable and who genuinely values and cares about her. Ride along with her on the roller coaster of daily life; stick together through all the ups and downs with a long-term connection and commitment to each other.

If she wants you to be more of a lover, learn to convey your feelings of love in words and actions. Express them physically both sexually and nonsexually, clearly taking into account her likes and dislikes.

A common difficulty with this step is discovering that the man and woman are mismatched in such a way that it is difficult to balance them. This was particularly true of one couple in their twenties. They had no children, and at twenty-three years of age, Laura wanted her husband, Robby, to settle down and be a good provider. According to his ratings, they both saw him as playmate—he said he was a 14; she saw him as a 12. His lowest score was as a hero—he saw himself as a 10; she thought he deserved a 5. Laura wanted him to be a 7 as a playmate and a 12 as a hero; he wanted to change very little.

Like many couples, Robby and Laura had emphasized the fun part of their relationship before they were married, but in Laura's view, circumstances had now changed. She was thinking about children and wanted to start planning ahead, saving money, and creating more security. Robby felt unwilling to change as much as she wanted him to, and he felt angry that she expected so much of a change from him so soon. Laura explained her concerns about the future, and Robby explained that he was not ready to settle down. He knew he'd be stuck with responsibility for the rest of his life and felt that they should enjoy life while they were still young. They agreed to compromise for the near future, and Robby agreed to modify his style and aim at being a 10 both as a playmate and as a hero.

A couple in their forties had just the opposite problem. The man, Jim, had spent the last twenty-five years being a great provider but had always had trouble relaxing and having a good time. His wife, Jan, said that it was time to slow down and enjoy the rewards he'd earned. They both saw him as a 6 on the playmate scale. She wanted him to be a 12; he said maybe he could be a 7 or 8. They both agreed that any change would be valuable to both of them, and they would aim at whatever improvement they could create.

So while Robby struggled to grow into more of a responsible hero, Jim had to work at being a more relaxed, fun-loving playmate. Robby found that part of his problem was that he had few work goals and had never thought about what he wanted to do with his life. Jim had never developed any hobbies or interests outside of "slaving away at work."

One of the first things Robby and Jim needed to do was to find a target at which they could aim. Then they could take action to hit their bull's-eye. Laura encouraged Robby to go through a career assessment with a vocational specialist to help clarify his work interests, while Jim and Jan spent weeks exploring all the enjoyable ways he could be using his free time.

Robby came to the conclusion that computer repair and installation would be perfect for his interests and talents. He enrolled in a technical school to "get my act together," as he put it. After six months Laura said that she could hardly believe the change in Robby. She said, "Since Robby enrolled in the computer program he seems like a new man—as if he's grown about ten years." He was more responsible and more of a hero to her than she'd ever thought possible.

Jim's hobby search finally paid off when he discovered a class on the Navajo Indians in a local college bulletin. He had always been interested in Native Americans and had often joked that he must have been an Indian in a past life. He lived in the southwestern United States where the Navajo had lived for so many generations, and he wanted to explore their world and try to uncover artifacts. Jan said this was great for her, since she loved to travel and be outdoors. They started taking classes together on Indian culture and went on digs with different university and college archaeology classes. Now that Jim had discovered a new passion, Jan said their relationship had never been better—or more fun.

STEP 6: DOING IT WITH FEELING

The sixth male illusion says that women are too emotional.

What's the Problem?

The difficulty with this illusion is that it has given rise to the notion that because women are too emotional, they are irrational. To some, this has meant, among other things, that women are poor decision-makers who can't be counted on and must have a man to take care of them and make their decisions for them.

Men's view of women's emotions is due to male training that has caused men to devalue and distrust emotion. The reason for this is easy to see. Imagine again how the world has been for men. In times of war they had to walk into battle; in times of peace they were the hunters, killing animals for their meat and cutting it up to be eaten. They were always out there competing in the dangerous, difficult, often shark-infested outside world where the strongest survived and succeeded.

As a result, men long ago learned to harden themselves against emotion. Emotion would have made them vulnerable and given the competing males an edge. In the heat of battle emotion might have made a soldier less effective as a fighter and a decision-maker and thus a threat to himself and his fellow combatants. To men, emotion itself seemed dangerous and was therefore eyed with caution if not outright rejection.

One result is that men learned to generalize their emotional control so that they sometimes even rejected feelings in others to keep the feeling from infecting them.

One of men's chief complaints about women is that they are too moody. Women value and are in touch with emotions, and they complain that men are too emotionally constricted. The result is that both men and women are dissatisfied.

If a man is to fully arouse his woman, he must become aware of, comfortable with, and understanding of his own emotions so that he need not reject hers. In fact, understanding one's own emotions allows us, male and female alike, to be far stronger than we are when we hide from our feelings.

Most men, however, think just the reverse—that to be in touch with their emotions will make them weak and that this is what women are asking them to do. Nothing could be further from the truth. No one, least of all women, want men to be weak.

The problem is that many men are not just controlling their emotions; they've suppressed them to such a degree that they no longer know they are there. George was an example of this phenomenon. In a therapy session, when Rita asked him how he felt about a particular issue, George responded in perfect seriousness: "I didn't know I was supposed to have feelings until you told me, and I'm not sure I have any."

The fact that a man's feelings are repressed doesn't mean they don't affect him, however. Just the opposite is true. Without understanding his own feelings, a man can't hope to control their expression or use their power, let alone deal successfully with women. Therefore, in a broader sense, his emotions control him.

Repression of emotion, then, not only keeps a man from better communicating with and understanding women; it also robs him of strength.

It's as if men's minds are houses. Inside each house is a full range of potential feelings and emotions. They are living with a staff of servants who are there to regulate how these emotions are felt and expressed. These servants represent our experience, are governed by years of male training, and act in compliance with who we feel we are and how we must act.

So how do these servants serve you? Let's say you are suddenly confronted by emotional pain of some kind. Perhaps you've been demoted at work or find yourself suddenly facing a financial crisis. Because you don't want to feel this pain and all the attendant emotions— fear, grief, rage, hurt, embarrassment—you call for one of your trusted servants to anesthetize you.

This servant dulls your pain while urging you to get busy with some activity to try to distract yourself. For some men this can mean drinking or screwing around. For others it means working even harder. Others react by watching more TV. Whatever it is, it gets your mind off the problem.

Now you don't feel the pain as much, but another problem can arise when you allow this process to tie up a servant's energy. This can be okay if this is the only emotion you're suppressing. But if you're suppressing a lot of emotions, as most men do, you're expending the energy of many of your servants, thus using up an enormous amount of your psychological strength and power. Your strength and power are tied up with these servants keeping the cap on your emotions. You therefore don't have as much energy available for other things. You're being weakened by your unmastered, unacknowledged emotions whether you realize it or not. This often causes a sense of exhaustion or depression. You feel out of sorts, irritable, stressed, and overwhelmed.

In addition, those suppressed emotions may become so powerful that the servant won't be able to keep them out of your awareness any longer and they will erupt at another time, perhaps over another issue.

We've all experienced this to one degree or another. For example, a man might be frustrated over how his boss is treating him, or he may feel that his wife has him by the balls and isn't having enough sex with him. He feels annoyed, but it makes sense to shut up and tell the feeling to go away. Maybe he forgets this even happened. Or maybe he just refuses to feel this emotion. But the feeling doesn't go away. Instead, it bursts forth later over another issue, and he finds himself being suddenly and disproportionately furious at someone cutting him off in traffic, or at the children for not picking up their toys.

Women, as well as men, often fail to acknowledge feelings and find themselves depressed or overreacting to unrelated issues. Women will often not acknowledge anger, while men hesitate to acknowledge more tender emotions for fear of looking or feeling weak. Yet this very style of dealing with emotions does, in itself, weaken men and women who fail to master their feelings, robbing them of the personal power they might have had available to be more effective in their daily lives. One can truly master the Outer World only after becoming master of one's emotional world.

What's the Truth?

The truth is that it actually requires more bravery to feel emotion than to repress it.

For example, if you acknowledge being angry at your boss, you have to decide what to do with that anger. Perhaps you should confront him, find a new job, admit you were wrong, or learn how to live with his incompetence, if no other job is available right now.

Making these choices is difficult. It's easier to repress the anger than to make the choice of what to do with it.

The fact is, however, that it is usually far healthier and more empowering to deal head on with our emotions. Research shows that we may protect our health by ignoring our feelings when we are in a hopeless situation where we are upset and can do nothing to change our situation; but otherwise our physical health is better served if we are aware of our feelings and able to handle them effectively.

Once you learn to deal effectively with your own feelings, you will also be better able to handle your woman's feelings and emotions. This is especially important in the context of this book since, as Helen Singer Kaplan writes, "any of the so-called emergency emotions—fear, anger, guilty fear and guilty anger"—can inhibit sexual desire. "Anger at the partner for any reason is probably the most common cause of inhibited sexual desire. It is difficult to desire a person with whom one is furious, or to allow oneself to be vulnerable in a relationship devoid of trust."[6] Thus, it is in your sexual best interests to effectively deal with your woman's emotions so as to have a better relationship both emotionally and sexually.

Emotion normally flows like a river, sometimes smooth and manageable, other times rough and bumpy like white-water rapids. Feelings are changeable, and we may have several seemingly contradictory feelings at the same time. This makes it quite a challenge to learn to deal with emotions. It can be done, however. Put on your life vest. We're going for a ride.

What Can You Do?

Your goal here is not only to put yourself in touch with your own emotions but also to help you feel more comfortable with your woman's emotions.

Men sometimes find themselves in a no-win bind: they have to keep their distance from others and control their emotions in order to comply with the rules of manhood. Men are rewarded by other men and by women for being successful in the Outer World. Then they're criticized by women for being emotionally armored and anesthetized so thoroughly that they can't meet women's needs for closeness, love, and sensuality. That's why so many men feel damned no matter what they do. Heads they lose, tails they lose. If they're not emotionally armored and anesthetized enough to be successful, they fail to get the most desirable women. If they are armored and anesthetized enough to succeed and to win the woman of their dreams, they are faulted for not being sensitive and close.

But today the situation is different; now men *can* have less armor and anesthesia because conditions in the Outer World have changed, enabling men to develop a deeper awareness of their own internal world and thus a greater awareness of the Inner World of women and love and lovemaking. What is needed today is a new kind of warrior, one who is competent not only in the Outer World of success but also in the Inner World.

A good way to begin to understand your own internal or Inner World is to see how armored and anesthetized you are now, and how far you have to go to be a warrior of the Inner World. Let's try to assess these two powerful keys that unlock Inner World power—closeness and feeling.

ARMOR SCALE

Rate yourself as honestly as you can on how close or distant you are from your woman.

1. How much of your free time each week do you spend with your partner?

   0 – 25% 2
   25 – 75% 1
   75 – 100% 0

2. When you think about your partner do you have

   Few feelings 2
   Good feelings 1
   Warm, positive, loving feelings 0

3. Do you confide in your partner and share your intimate thoughts? Do you tell her when something is really bothering you? Do you let her know when you need to be held or helped?

   Rarely 2
   Sometimes 1
   Nearly always 0

4. Do you really listen when your partner tells you something important to her? Do you go out of your way to try to understand what she's saying?

   Not usually 2
   Usually 1
   Nearly always 0

5. Do you show your partner physical affection (hugs, kisses, hand holding, back rubs) on a daily or weekly basis? Do you feel good enough about her to want to show her physical affection?

   Not really 2
   Usually 1
   Nearly always 0

6. If you knew you were going to spend the day or evening totally alone with your partner, would you

   Want to avoid it 2
   Feel okay about it 1
   Eagerly look forward to it 0

7. When something is really important to you (a problem with your health, a disappointment at work, a success of which you feel proud), are you most likely to

   Not tell my partner 2
   Possibly tell her 1
   Definitely tell her 0

8. If your partner is obviously upset about something, are you most likely to

   Not really care 2
   Be interested 1
   Definitely want to know 0

9. Do you consider your partner to be your best friend?

   Almost never 2
   Sometimes 1
   Definitely 0

10. Do you clearly let your partner know your tender feelings or in some way clearly demonstrate your love on a daily or weekly basis?

    Not really 2
    Sometimes 1
    Definitely 0

TOTAL SCORE _____
Put an X on the line below to indicate your score.

ARMOR SCALE

20	10	0
Fully armored (very distant from her)	Shielded (arm's length)	Without armor (very close to her)

You can see from your rating where you are now in terms of closeness to or distance from your partner and you can make a decision about your goal.

Put an X where you would like to be in your relationship with your woman. Keep in mind that the less armor you wear the more you release her natural sexual potential and at the same time her love for you.

ANESTHESIA SCALE

Rate yourself as accurately as you can on how close or distant you are from your feelings.

1. When you have a success at work, do you feel happy and satisfied?
   Definitely 2
   Sometimes 1
   Rarely 0

2. When you are with your wife, children, or best friend, do you feel love and caring?
   Definitely 2
   Sometimes 1
   Not really 0

3. Are you aware when something makes you angry or do you find yourself more likely to have bad moods and be irritable and grumpy?
   Definitely aware of anger 2
   Somewhat aware of anger but moody, too 1
   Not really aware of anger, a lot of irritability 0

4. When something is really scaring you (you have to speak in front of a big group, you're afraid for your future, you're seriously concerned about money matters), do you
   Definitely know I'm scared 2
   Feel somewhat aware of being worried 1

Try not to think about it 0

5. When you lose something (your pet dies, you give up on achieving a long-standing goal), are you aware of feeling sad and blue?
Definitely; I cry if I need to 2
Somewhat aware; I feel sad sometimes 1
No way; I don't lose control 0

6. When you have strong feelings, are you
Definitely trying to be aware, understand,
and learn from them .2
Somewhat attuned to emotion, but
it's not a top priority 1
Not really interested; I don't think
about my emotions .0

7. When a person you are close to is crying and feeling upset, are you most likely to
Try to be with the person and help 2
Feel somewhat upset by it all, but ask what's wrong 1
Avoid the whole thing 0

8. When your woman shows you love and affection, are you likely to
Definitely show her love and affection in return 2
Feel pretty good about it 1
Not have much response 0

TOTAL SCORE _____
Put an X on the line below to indicate your score.

ANESTHESIA SCALE

0	8	16
Emotionally anesthetized	Somewhat emotionally aware	Emotionally alert and alive

You can see from your rating where you are now in terms of emotional awareness and comfort, and you can make a decision about your goal. Put an X where you would like to be in your emotional alertness and remember that the more expert and comfortable you are with your own feelings and your woman's, the more you are likely to release her natural sexuality.

FEELINGS AS INFORMATION

Our emotions give us information about our life. If we are frustrated with a situation because we want something different, we may feel irritated; if someone we love dies, we feel the sadness that comes with a loss. Irritation tells us we want something different; sadness tells us we've lost someone important.

Let's begin to understand our emotions by looking at five basic feelings—anger, sadness, fear, happiness, and love—and some of the normal reasons people experience them.

Anger can come from sexual frustration, from feeling your woman has power over you, from wanting to go at your own speed but waiting for her to deal with her clothes, hair, or makeup. Anger can also be caused by daily hassles and pressures such as money problems or difficulties at work. Anger can come from being irritated by physical pain or poor health or being out of shape physically. Anger can come from going through a major life change—beginning career, marriage, fatherhood, midlife, retirement—with the confusion and uncertainty that usually follow such transitions. Anger can also be caused by any other emotion that is blocked. For example, if a man is not comfortable experiencing fear, he may experience the fear as anger.

Sadness can result from disappointment at not being able to achieve a financial or career goal. A death or the loss of friends or family can be saddening. Sadness can also come from saying good-bye when moving, or from looking back on one's childhood with fond memories, or from thinking about something you want but will never get. Sadness can also come from the normal boyhood woundedness of feeling alone, from the bumps and bruises felt while growing into adult manhood, and from the bumps and bruises of being a man.

Fear can come from any threat, real or imagined—fear of failure in your business or career, for example. Fear can also come from concern over not achieving your goals; fear can come from closeness and intimacy if you're not used to this. You might fear being embarrassed in front of others. You may experience the elemental fear of losing the people you depend on and care about, and you may also fear illness and death.

Happiness can arise out of satisfaction and contentment with your life, being with people you love, achieving your goals; it can come from seeing beauty in nature or from taking part in activities you enjoy. Joy can come simply because it is a part of your basic nature.

Love can spring from feeling close with your woman, your children, pets, or feelings of spiritual oneness with life. You can feel a sense of love from great beauty, natural and otherwise. And you can find a deep intimate love that is there for no reason at all except that it is a part of our inherent nature.

WHAT DO I FEEL?

Information is often hidden within our feelings. This information tells us, for example, if we need to take action and make a change, if we need to have more fun, or if we need to confront someone or some problem.

To know what information needs decoding and handling, you must first know what you feel. What emotions are you generally aware of having? Which ones do you never have or avoid? Which ones can you comfortably hear your woman talk about? Which ones make you uncomfortable hearing her discuss?

This step is much more important than many men realize.

1. Read through each of the mild, medium, and strong forms of the five emotions below. Underline the ones you feel at least once a month. Circle the ones you experience daily or weekly.

   ANGER
        Mild: You feel bothered, upset, put off, uneasy, displeased.
        Medium: You feel annoyed, aggravated, frustrated, irritated, grouchy, provoked, distressed.
        Strong: You feel furious, fed up, irate, indignant, disgusted, bitter, exasperated, cheated, distraught, mad, livid.

   SADNESS
        Mild: You feel low, glum, apathetic, blue, disheartened, moody, disappointed, disillusioned, listless.
        Medium: You feel down, unhappy, hollow, sorry.
        Strong: You feel miserable, hopeless, wounded, lonely, rejected,

empty, depressed, lost, crushed, beaten down, devastated, despairing, grieving.

FEAR

Mild: You feel uneasy, concerned, uptight, rattled, flustered, confused, on edge, jumpy.

Medium: You feel anxious, alarmed, frightened, worried, nervous, apprehensive, insecure, rattled, harassed, stressed.

Strong: You feel terrified, petrified, panicky, helpless, distraught, afraid, horrified, intimidated, overwhelmed.

HAPPINESS

Mild: You feel hopeful, encouraged, satisfied, content, peaceful, comfortable, relaxed, calm, grateful.

Medium: You feel good, pleased, relieved, lucky, happy, optimistic.

Strong: You feel thrilled, eager, excited, exhilarated, overjoyed, moved, glowing, delighted, marvelous, proud, energetic, great, ecstatic.

LOVE

Mild: You enjoy, are fond of, like, prefer, favor, or wish for someone.

Medium: You desire, want to be with, or have a crush on someone.

Strong: You are infatuated, have deep feelings for, yearn for, are passionate about, long for, are dying to be with, feel devoted, adoring, ardent, or enchanted with someone.

2. Now list the feelings you're aware of having.

Feelings I'm aware of having on a daily or weekly basis (those you circled): _____

_____

_____

_____

Feelings I'm aware of having on a monthly basis (those you underlined): _____

_____

_____

_____

3. Feelings I'm unaware of having. List the feelings you neither underlined nor circled: _____

_____

_____

_____

_____

Now let's take a look at how we can handle our feelings.

START SMALL

From the exercises just completed you should have a good idea which feelings you experience and which you don't. Begin working on this by being aware of how you feel as you go through your day. You don't have to act on your feelings yet, just tune in to what is there.

Emotions serve a purpose and are neither good nor bad in and of themselves. They are a problem only if they are ignored, or if a person goes to the extreme of wallowing in a certain feeling. They are of value to you if you can find a middle ground in which you are aware of the feeling, understand its message, take effective actions, and then release it.

Start small. Look for minor instances of feeling, especially if you are trying to become aware of an emotion you don't ordinarily notice. Ask yourself if you are having any of the mild forms of the five emotions. You can keep a feelings journal if you enjoy writing. In it you will identify emotions as they arise in your daily life.

You can also practice alone in your car. Be aware of your anger at other drivers, or think about any sadness, fear, happiness, or love you feel. Or find time to be alone in your office or den to focus on how you feel. Or talk about your feelings with your woman. Let her know exactly what you are trying to do and ask her to help you tune in to the whole range of feelings.

Don't expect too much too soon. Be aware of your feeling and then let it go. There is no need to dive deep into your feelings; just tune in to a feeling and then release it. This lets you get comfortable with emotion, keeps you from feeling overwhelmed, and makes it easier for you to tune in to the feeling the next time it arises, since you now know that you can manage it.

Getting in touch with long repressed feelings is something that usually comes slowly, so let yourself work at this with the expectation that you simply need to persevere over time.

This starting-small method is very valuable, since anger can be hot and explosive; sadness, fear, and hurt can be uncomfortable; love and happiness can be unfamiliar. By starting small you can learn to master each of these emotions so that when they are stronger you will be more experienced and comfortable with them.

As you become more aware of the whole range of emotion, you may want to transform your feelings into action.

THE ALCHEMY OF EMOTION

If you are to transform your emotions into a better relationship and sex life, you must become aware of your feelings and deal with them in a positive way.

We talked above about feelings as a source of information. Once you're aware of how you feel, you will have access to valuable information to help yourself be more powerful and effective with your woman as well as in life in general.

Once you're aware of your feelings you can translate them into information, then you can transform the information into positive action. Let's say, for example, that you're angry at your woman, and you realize the anger is caused by the fact that you want more sex. Instead of saying, "You bitch, you never want to do it," simply venting the anger, consider strategies for turning her on. Take effective action that addresses the root of the feeling. Tell her something you love about her, have some fun together, or touch her in ways that will arouse her, bring you closer to her, and make her more likely to be sexual with you.

Perhaps, on another day, you'll feel defeated and sad about your work situation. Instead of burying yourself in the job and feeling down, tell your woman that you're really dissatisfied with your work, that it's really getting to you and making you feel rotten, and you need some help to work on how to handle it. Maybe she can help you find a way to change your work problem into an asset, or come up with a new idea for a way out of your current job and into a new one that will make you happier. By seeking her help, you're opening up your Inner World to her, and she feels closer to you as a result.

You become aware that you're nervous around your secretary, and the nervousness tells you she's doing something that makes you uneasy. Listen to your feeling of uneasiness to see what it's telling you. You may suddenly realize that you dislike the way your secretary is talking with your clients on the phone. Now you can transform your feeling into positive action by taking an appropriate measure: the next time you hear her speaking nicely to someone on the phone, tell her you really like it when she's considerate and patient with your clients.

By looking at emotion as a source of information and by transforming the information into action, you can harness the emotion's power to gain more control and be more effective in your daily life.

HANDLING RESENTMENT

In nearly every relationship there are problems that create pain, difficulty, distrust, anger, and thus, resentment.

Part of learning to understand feelings is accepting that you do feel resentful, that resentment is normal, and that it can be dealt with in a positive way. Unless you get past the resentment and forgive your partner, it will be difficult to move the relationship forward.

What can you do about resentment?

One technique you can try, if both you and your partner agree, is to sit face to face and say five things you resent about your partner (no response allowed), followed by five acknowledgments of something you love or appreciate about her. She then gets to do the same—five things she resents, without your responding, followed by five good things about you. This can be a very powerful cleansing experience as long as you both resist the temptation to defend yourselves when the resentments are expressed.

Another technique you can try is to use your imagination. Let yourself have whatever angry thoughts you want, being careful not to turn them into actions. In this way you can safely release your resentments.

Forgiveness is an essential ingredient in every successful relationship. Learn to heal past wounds caused by frustration and anger; then let them fade into the past. Practice this with small things. Become aware of them and allow your feelings to come to the surface; then let them go. Be careful not to short-circuit the feeling; let yourself be angry and then be done with it. Think of the resentments as bubbles that rise to the surface and then burst and disappear into the air. If you have a large storehouse of resentment you will need to allow this process time until all of the feelings have been released. Over and over, allow the bubbling and letting go to take place.

COMMUNICATING ABOUT FEELINGS

As we have seen, nearly every woman wants her man to communicate with her in more personal terms. She wants you to let her know how you feel and to listen to her feelings in ways that are constructive. How can you do this? Here are ten suggestions.

1. *Talk about feelings.* Try to use at least one "feeling word" each day when you talk to your partner. Use the list in the "What do I feel?" exercise, above, as a source of feeling words, and put them into your vocabulary with your woman. Even if this seems artificial at first, it is still valuable to do so. Like anything new it will seem awkward in the beginning, but as you get more familiar with the words you will also get more familiar with the feelings they represent.

2. *Think before you speak.* Decide what you want to convey to her before you sit down to talk with her about feelings. Keep two things in mind: she wants to hear how you feel, and she wants you to express yourself without seeming to attack her.

   Perhaps you want to talk about your sex life and how you want her to be more open to variety with you. You can tell her that you feel frustrated and even that you sometimes get angry, even though you still love and care for her. Use feeling words to describe your position: sexually frustrated, wanting to feel close with her, being happy with her, feeling sad that you can't seem to resolve this dilemma, loving her, feeling great about being with her. You could tell her that just looking at her gets you really excited and that you want your sex life to be adventurous and satisfying to both of you.

Try to anticipate her reaction to your words. She may feel defensive, or she may feel this means you want to find more exciting sex with another woman. Reassure her of your love and commitment to her. Then use the emotions you've identified with her to help you solve the problem together.

3. *Sit down together or take a walk by the ocean or a drive in the country when you have set time aside for each other.* Stay focused on the discussion at hand. Also, keep in mind that people can more readily digest something negative if it's sandwiched between two positives. If you're going to express anger or criticism, be sure to start with something positive and end with something positive.

4. *Use "I," not "you."* Put things in terms of yourself. Instead of saying, "You never take care of me the way I want," or "You're uptight," say, "I feel weighted down by the financial responsibilities I have to shoulder, and I want relief from all the tension when I get home by feeling cared about by you. One of the things that would help me is making love more often to express how we care about each other. I wish we could experiment and have more fun and variety. Sometimes I feel angry that we don't make love more often. Maybe I shouldn't be angry, but that's how I feel. This is important to me."

Remember that the word *you* will put her on the defensive and make her feel attacked. Imagine how you would feel if she said these things to you. By using *I*, you put things in terms of yourself, and it's much easier for your partner to get your message since she doesn't feel she has to defend herself.

Instead of "Why don't you leave me alone; can't you see I just got home from work," try saying, "When I come home at night from work I feel so tired and irritable that I sometimes snap at you and the kids. I'm sorry about that, but it would really help if I could go in the bedroom and get cleaned up and have five or ten minutes to myself before being with anyone."

5. *Try to be concise.* When you're talking with your woman about feelings and problems, get to the point as quickly as possible. Stick to the topic at hand and work at resolving only one dilemma. Save other issues for other talks. Avoid digressions that

can complicate things. Avoid lectures. Remember that your goal is to come up with a mutually satisfying solution.

6. *Give her a chance to talk.* Listen to what she has to say. Maybe she's afraid of being hurt if you try another sexual position, or maybe she was taught that "nice girls" don't do certain things. Hear her out, and then work together to find compromises that will satisfy both of you.

   Respect her feelings. Let's say she's feeling upset and insecure about experimenting sexually. Tell her you understand her concern and are sensitive to it. Perhaps she only needs you to hear what she's feeling. Don't push her feeling away or try to talk her out of her emotion. Ask yourself if you're uncomfortable with her point of view simply because it prevents you from getting what you want. Value what she's going through. You don't have to hear it as a problem you're supposed to solve for her. Hear what she's feeling. Hear what *she* wants from you. Maybe she just needs to express the emotion. In so doing, she may feel a sense of release from it. She needs to feel that you value her emotions. Telling her so will create the closeness she wants from you and will go a long way toward solving problems between you.

7. *Turn your gripe into a solution.* Turn the discussion into something positive by presenting the problem as something that both of you are facing. One way to keep the discussion positive is to tell her the things you *do* like sexually with her. Sex is a sensitive subject, and when you bring up something you're dissatisfied with, she may feel that you're dissatisfied with everything about her. So be sure she understands there are many positive things about her that you do love. Even though you are working on this one problem right now, many other things are not a problem and are very enjoyable.

   Tell her you love the feel of her silky smooth skin, or the smell of her hair. Tell her it feels good to hold her close to you and just lie there for a little while. These nice things make her feel that not everything is a problem. This will help both of you see things in perspective and will encourage you to work to end your sexual boredom and frustration. If you can turn your gripe into a solution, you'll be taking a major step in the direction of the kind of sex and home life you'd really like.

8. *Engage in a mutual problem-solving process.* First define the problem: how can you get more sexual variety while making sure that she feels comfortable?

   Next, brainstorm until you come up with ideas that will satisfy her concerns and needs as well as yours. You might suggest bathing or showering together as part of your lovemaking. Or you could make love with the lights on if you usually do so in the dark. Instead of using the bed, you might try the sofa or the floor. You could use a mirror to watch yourselves or find a safe, private outdoor place and make love there at an unusual time. Perhaps you could bring a glass of wine or a nice meal to bed to enhance the experience, or add music, candles, or incense. You could first give each other massages, tell each other a fantasy that would be exciting, or try a vibrator. Maybe you could pretend you've never seen her before and pick her up at a local bar and head for a motel. Use your imagination to find ways of satisfying both yourself and your partner.

9. *Act on the results of your discussion.* Put the proposed solutions into action. If you've agreed to experiment by having sex in different locations, go ahead and set things up so it will work out successfully. Don't just leave it as an idea. Make it happen. Make it fun.

10. *Tell her your feelings along the way.* Convey to her your feelings about her cooperation and effort to satisfy you sexually. You love her and appreciate what she is doing. She's special to you and you feel good that you can talk about problems, facing them rather than avoiding them, as so many other couples do. You feel happy that the two of you are together and you're glad when you can feel close and work together to make each other happy.

BREATHE AND RELAX

Most men fail to master the world of emotions, and one result is that they are rendered incapable of harnessing their full power. Fortunately, power loss and power suppression can be recovered and reversed. And it's not as hard as you might think. Most power suppression takes place in your body, in the form of shallow breathing. Most people breathe shallowly and often hold in their breath. They get inadequate oxygen to their blood system and their brain. They lose more power and the cycle pulls like gravity. Then they feel uptight, literally and figuratively, when they hold in their chest muscles.

Try a brief experiment. Take ten normal breaths and pay careful attention to all ten. Are you breathing with only a small portion of your breathing capacity?

Now breathe slowly and deeply ten times.

Close your eyes and allow yourself to do ten more slow, deep breaths, ten breaths with awareness.

Breathe and relax, breathe and feel your present emotion. Breathe, bubble up, and let it go. Don't worry about it. Breathe and relax. Loosen any tightness in your chest or head or neck or stomach or groin. Relax your whole body and feel the life force rushing through you, feel your basic aliveness.

If someone angers you, breathe slow and deep, feel the anger, and let it go.

If something saddens you, breathe slow and deep, feel the sadness, and let it go.

If something makes you scared, breathe slow and deep, feel the fear, and let it go.

If you're happy about something, breathe slow and deep, feel happy, and let it go.

If you love someone, breathe slow and deep, feel love in your heart, and let it go.

PRACTICE LOVE

Practice caring about the object of your love. It's not that difficult once you know how. Think about who or what you love—your woman or your kids or your football team or your car or your favorite fishing hole. Then close your eyes and feel good about her, them, or it.

Stay with this good feeling as long as you can, and return to it whenever you have a chance. This is a way to practice caring and loving.

Maybe you're at home and the kids are playing on the floor. Your woman is cooking in the kitchen, and you're reading this book trying to recover from your day at work. Look at your loved ones. Think about what you love and like and respect about them. Be aware of your good feelings for them. Think about your woman and how hard she works and about why you married her. Think about the things you wrote about her in Step 2. Then close your eyes and let yourself care. Let yourself feel your pride or warmth or respect or appreciation for her. Realize how lonely you'd be without her. Think about the wonderful times you've had together in the past, about how you felt toward her when you first met and fell in love. Let that feeling come back to you. Let your heart be filled by your caring—and if tears come to your eyes, it shows you're alive.

PRACTICE CLOSENESS

One thing women universally want from men is more emotional closeness, yet one thing men learn to do is to keep their distance and not allow anyone to be close to them. You measured your closeness or distance in the Armor Scale. Now practice relating on a closer level, allowing others to be more important.

You may want to start with your pet or children. (Many men find it is easier to be close to a pet or a child than to another adult.) Bring your dog or cat into the room with you. Care about your pet and let yourself feel how much you care. Touch it and let yourself feel your love for the animal. Let it be important to you.

If you have young children try playing Puppies and Tigers. Get on your hands and knees with your young son or daughter and pretend to be a puppy or a tiger. Try letting the kids win when it gets to be a tiger battle or a puppy tug-of-war. This is a comfortable way to show your feelings. You can purr or be a pile of puppies or you can growl at each other. You can have contact in a playful way, enjoy the physical contact, and get used to this kind of closeness.

Once you've gotten comfortable with your pets and children, you may find it to be a natural transition to be close and feeling with your woman. Hold her in your arms and feel your caring for her. Let her be important to you and learn to open your emotions to yourself and to her. Even more crucial, learn to value and listen to her emotions and let her know you love her.

When you've achieved greater mastery of your emotions, you will feel a deeper sense of strength and power than ever before, not a power of domination or aggression, but the power of your warrior spirit put into the service of life and love. And when you achieve this, you'll notice your woman getting more excited by you, especially as you learn to be romantic.

STEP 7: THE WARRIOR'S HEART

The seventh male illusion about women is that romance means sending her cards and flowers.

What's the Problem?

Men think that romance means the same thing to women as it does to men. In fact, it means something quite different to most women. Men often think of romance as a sexual feeling that makes them crave physical intimacy with someone they find attractive; for women, romance is much more of a desire for an emotional intimacy in which his attention is focused on her and only her. This is quite different from the card-and-flowers routine practiced by so many men two or three times a year.

At some point in a relationship most women will say, "Be more romantic." Eventually, however, they give up asking because most men don't have any idea how to be romantic and most women don't know how to explain it to them. Anyway, as several women we interviewed explained, "If you have to tell him what to do, then whatever he does seems to lose a lot of its romance."

Consequently, men continue to give women flowers and cards or gifts on special occasions because that's all they know how to do, and women remain frustrated because they aren't getting what they want.

What's the Truth?

Actually, there are four basic truths.

Being romantic is giving your partner your full attention and conveying your intimate feelings of closeness and love for her and only her.

Being romantic means taking her needs and feelings into account and acting accordingly to look after her, to protect her, and to make her feel cared for.

Being romantic is demonstrating your desire to make her feel good about herself and safe in the knowledge that you truly, genuinely consider her special and valuable.

Being romantic can also be doing the unpredictable, the spontaneous, the surprising, or the daring.

What Can You Do?

Most important, keep in mind your genuine feelings of love and affection
for her. Then use this love as the power behind your romantic actions.

But what can a man actually do to be romantic? What actions can he
take?

1. Sweep Her Away

Being swept away is one of the most romantic of all situations. It has been
played out over and over again in every kind of romantic novel and
movie: the hero takes the heroine into his power and care, sweeping her
out of her ordinary world into one where he is in control, where the
burden of responsibility is shifted to him, and where she need only relax
and enjoy his amorous attentions.

It is romantic for a woman to feel wanted for herself and to be the focus
of the man's attention. Women find it seductive to be taken into the care
of a strong man and whisked away from the cares of everyday life—at
least for a time, at least once in a while.

Doing this in real life can turn an ordinary man into a heroic figure.
The possibilities for sweeping a woman away are endless and can fit any
budget.

If you can bundle her off to an exciting weekend in a beautiful vacation
spot, that's wonderful. But this romantic interlude can still be carried out
much less expensively. You, the man, must make all of the plans and
relieve her of all responsibility. She must be able to relax, enjoy herself,
and rely on you.

David, who wanted to make his marriage stronger, was urged to sweep
his wife away. The following weekend he awakened Jane early, asked her
to be ready in an hour for a surprise, and suggested that she wear
comfortable clothes.

"I've sent the kids to the movies with Bonnie and now I'm going to take
you away from all this," he told her. When Jane was ready, David
blindfolded her to enhance the surprise, then treated her to a sunrise ride
in a hot air balloon.

Later Jane said how exciting it had been. "It was so romantic, and
David was wonderful," Jane said in the next session. "I felt like I was being
carried off into something magical. Then on the way home we stopped at
a hotel and made love. It's as if something in us was revived. We've both
been so absorbed in work, the kids, and just surviving that we haven't

been spending time with each other. But now we're going to change all that for good!"

This is a classic example of how, by stimulating a woman's emotions, both partners receive more of what they want, and their relationship is infused with positive, loving feelings.

You might try a swept-away interlude as simple and inexpensive as a picnic. The real fun of this is the spontaneity of it for the woman, the man's taking control, making arrangements, and sweeping her away from it all. A picnic can be great fun, if you both enjoy this type of outing. Try waking her up with a kiss and a "Surprise! You're coming with me today. I'm taking you away—a day for just the two of us, and everything's been arranged."

Given most women's burden of responsibilities, you may have to assure her that you've anticipated and taken care of everything. If it is possible, clear her schedule for her. If it isn't, you'll have to ask her in advance to clear a certain day. For some women the anticipation can actually add a wonderful dimension to the time preceding the date. Keep the outing a surprise as much as possible. Don't tell her any details about what you've planned. Just say it's going to be romantic.

George ran into a problem when he tried doing this with Rita. He called several of Rita's women friends with whom she had dates on the Saturday he wanted to spring a surprise. Somehow word got back to her that something was up, and George got really angry that his romantic surprise "was totally ruined." Rita said, "Nonsense, I think it sounds wonderful!" But George took it as a sign that their efforts to change were failing.

"He's turned the whole program into a failure because this one thing didn't go the way he wanted. It's ridiculous," Rita said sharply.

George felt that she didn't understand his side; he just wanted things to go well, and the setback worried him. He added that he'd been trying to tell her his feelings, as requested.

Rita said it wasn't a setback, and we talked about measuring progress from the starting place before working on their programs, seeing the difference now compared to the way things were between them before.

As George put it, "According to that measuring yardstick, we're doing great, but compared to how I wanted my surprise to go, it was a setback." Once he felt his reaction was justified and understood, he agreed to let it go and get on with the romantic fantasy—an elegant steamboat ride around the bay, complete with dinner.

On the appointed day, take her away to a lovely secluded spot at the beach, the mountains, the river, the lake, or a park. Maybe you could go back to the spot where you met or to some favorite place you both love. Bring a lunch and maybe some chilled champagne or some other favorite food or drink.

Once you are alone together, keep the conversation positive. Stay away from topics you've been arguing about. If a disagreement comes up, just say, "Let's not talk about it now. Let's have a nice time together today, and maybe we can talk about it tomorrow in a positive and understanding way."

Now is the time for the two of you to enjoy yourselves away from the everyday drudgery and problems. Focus instead on things you both enjoy—pleasant memories, dreams about the future, or good things in the present. It is a day to be swept away from the everyday worries and responsibilities. Remind her how much you have together that's good. All of this will take her mind away from the difficulties and put her attention on the good parts of your relationship. The fact that you cared enough to arrange the outing will surely touch her heart, and touching her feelings will make her more receptive to feeling and, of course, to making love. You may even be able to make love in the place where you have your picnic, or you may want to postpone love-making; this will depend on the state of your relationship, the situation at home, the location of the outing, and how she responds to your advances.

If your relationship is already good and just needs some enlivening, you are likely to find her generally more sexually receptive for days to come. If, on the other hand, you have become estranged, the last thing you want her to think is that this was just a performance for the sole purpose of getting more sex. In this case, it is better to back off, knowing that by showing how you care about her, a healing will take place that will bring you closer emotionally and make lovemaking a better possibility in the near future.

Also, if your relationship is very new, no matter how romantic or swept away she feels, she may not be ready for sex. So don't expect an immediate sexual response. Just keep your eye on the goal of building a strong and loving relationship. Do this and good sex will follow.

In any of these situations, you might carry things further by some pleasurable touching, to the extent that she seems comfortable and interested. You could begin by holding hands, putting your arm around her, or touching her shoulder. Always remember that touching bare skin usually suggests more intimacy than touching clothed skin. In other words, it is sexier to run a finger along a bare wrist than to touch a clothed shoulder.

At this point a woman will give you a signal that she likes what you are doing or that she does not. If her signals are encouraging, you can move on to more intimate touching. A massage is a wonderful place to start. There are many books on massage, but even the uninitiated can give pleasure by gently rubbing the neck and shoulders and by asking her what she does and does not like. Almost everyone finds this pleasant, and for those who tend to store tension in these areas such touching can be pure ecstasy.

Ask her what she likes you to do that is romantic and loving. Have her come up with a list of romantic things you could do.

Try to accommodate her wishes. You could concentrate on her favorite nonsexual place to be touched. Then watch for signs that she is ready to go further. If so, you may consider removing some of her clothes and continuing the pleasurable touching. Particularly in a new relationship, you may want to give assurances that you don't want to go any further than she wants to go. Then be sure to honor this commitment. If you do, she will be able to relax far more with you the next time, and you will be building trust with her, one of the primary foundation blocks of any relationship.

Keep the long run in mind, being aware that you want to have a good loving and sexual relationship in the future as well as in the present, and act accordingly. Anyway, as the most seductive men know, if you leave her wanting more, you can be sure the relationship will continue to progress toward greater intimacy.

In any case, backs, necks, calves, feet, hands, arms, scalps, and shoulders can all be nonthreatening and very sensual places to begin touching. The secret is to listen to her likes and dislikes as she reveals them in words or physical responses.

Every situation must be taken into account individually, and no one but the two of you can decide when it's best to have sex. However, a swept-away interlude will go a long way toward creating the right mood to make love in the present and to prepare the way for a loving and sexual relationship in the future.

2. Something Special Just for You

Another way to convey romance to your woman is to give her a gift of love. Romantic gifts are always appreciated—gifts that convey your love for her, gifts that show you thought about her and what she would like rather than what you want her to like.

Don't wait for a holiday to give her a gift of love. Gifts are expected on holidays, and it's certainly nice to receive them, but a gift takes on more romance and meaning if it comes at an unexpected moment.

Don't think that romantic gifts have to be costly. The important thing is not cost, but feeling and thought. A romantic gift conveys your love for her and tells her that you've been thinking about her and about what she would like.

Your time and effort will also be appreciated. The fact that you took the time to think about her and get something to convey your love for her is one of the vital elements in making a gift truly romantic.

Think about her and her interests. Does she love flowers? Crystal? Dolls? Does she have a collection of ceramic cats or stuffed animals? Pay attention to her hobbies and interests and choose a gift to suit her. This conveys your appreciation of her as a unique person, and shows her that you chose the gift from her own point of view.

Does she love fruit? Stop at a specialty store and buy her some out-of-season fruits as a small surprise. It will convey the message that you thought about her likes and went out of your way especially to make her feel good. That's romantic, especially when the ripe peach in December comes with a long look into her eyes and a loving kiss.

Perhaps she loves silver spoons. Why not find a beautiful one, have her initials engraved on it, and give it to her with a note telling her she's the best.

Maybe you could put together a photo album of her favorite people from all those loose pictures in the photo drawer. Or put together an album of photos of the two of you over the years.

Write a love note that tells her how special she is to you and how much you admire her and tuck it into her underwear drawer. Or write her a loving card—"Honey, my life is happier because of you" or "Sweetheart, I'm the luckiest guy in the world to have you for my wife"—and hide it among her lace panties and bras. Or put a little bottle of perfume in with her stockings as a nice surprise.

You can use her purse or briefcase the same way, but be careful what you put in there. One of our friends was eager to try out this suggestion and put a pair of black lace panties and stockings in his wife's briefcase, only to have her open it at a high-level business meeting in full view of her company's top brass—who no doubt will never again see her as the conservative and traditional woman they once knew.

3. A New Lover in the Bedroom

When your relationship first began, it was new and probably very exciting. You didn't know each other well, and part of the fun of being together was the newness and surprise and mystery about this new person and what you would learn about her.

Another part of the excitement was the exclusive attention you gave each other and how special and cared about that made both of you feel.

Unfortunately, the surprise and mystery and attention fade over time—if you let it. The good news is that it's not necessary to let it fade. You can keep the mystery alive. All these feelings can be re-created with a little time and effort and interest in making it happen.

One of the easiest and most fun ways to do this is by acting out a fantasy we think of as "A New Lover in the Bedroom." In this fantasy, you can re-create the surprise, mystery, and attention so many couples lose after the early stages of their relationship.

First, pick a time when you will have some privacy. You can arrange for other family members to be out of the house, or you and your partner can go to a hotel.

Second, find out when your partner will be coming home and make sure that you get there earlier to prepare.

Third, write her a note and place it where she'll find it when she comes in. It could say, for example, "Prepare yourself for an evening of surprise and pleasure. Begin by taking off your clothes and putting on the robe provided. Then come upstairs to the bathroom." In the bathroom there might be a bath already run and filled with bubbles or scented with oil. The note here might say, "I love you. You are the most important treasure in my life. Enjoy this bath knowing that this is true. Then put on the clothes provided and come into the dining room."

Obviously, there is room for variation here, particularly in the clothes you might have provided for her. This is going to depend on her and your relationship. It could be something you've picked out of her closet. It could be something new. It could be a relatively modest dress, or it could be wild and racy. You decide what's right and what she would be most comfortable with.

The next step is up to you. You may order a dinner to be brought in, buy something that's already prepared, or prepare a meal ahead of time so you need only put the finishing touches on it while she's in the bath. Your choice will depend on your budget and your talent in the kitchen.

When she arrives in the dining room she is already going to be feeling loved and cared for and probably surprised and very pleased that you have gone to so much trouble for the two of you to have such a romantic evening. She will also feel a sense of mystery and suspense, wondering exactly what you might do next, a sense that replicates the feelings most couples have early in their relationship.

You might have a candlelight dinner; you might have wine. Make it something easy to serve, if you like. Certainly try to make it something easy to clean up. Everything depends on your own taste. Fondues can be fun and can create a lot of interaction over the pot. If you do this, try cooking something for her yourself, feeding it to her, and dabbing off her mouth with a napkin or with your own mouth. This can be very sensual and a great way to express love and caring.

Remember to keep the conversation pleasant. Tell her the reasons you admire her. Talk about things you love to share with her. Talk about the happiest moments of your life together. *Avoid anything unpleasant.* This is no time to have a fight.

Depending on the relationship, the evening might end without making love, or you might prolong the fun by giving her a dessert plate and leaving the room. Under the plate or hidden in the dessert is another note. This one could invite her to the bedroom, to an evening out, or to another entertainment, which could conclude with another note on what to do next.

It's most important to keep things mysterious, not to tell her what is happening next, and to keep an air of mystery about the evening. Remember it is a time of surprises. Use your imagination.

If your relationship is ready for you to make love, of course this becomes a part of the evening.

4. Bath and Game Time

Another romantic interlude we call "Bath and Game Time." So much can happen around a bath that is sensual and results in giving a woman time to warm up both physically and emotionally. Drawing her bath and putting in bubble bath or fragrant oils can be very exciting. Scrubbing her back, giving her a massage, drying her off in a sensitive way, can all be very sensual.

These romantic games make a woman feel more intimate, and a man can learn to further excite a woman by paying attention to the subtle cues that turn her on.

STEP 8: TURNING HER ON

The eighth male illusion is the notion that the best way to approach a woman sexually is straightforward.

What's the Problem?

The fact is that while many men realize there are subtle cues or romantic gestures that attract women, the majority of men don't have any idea what those cues are. They don't know how to figure them out, and they can't get much help from other men, who are equally in the dark. The natural course of action would seem to be the straightforward approach.

And since most men are so focused on sex, so readily aroused, and so short-term in their impulses, the straightforward approach seems to be the natural option.

The result of the straightforward approach, however, is unsatisfactory. Far from exciting most women, it is a turn-off. This is true not only when a man and woman are first getting acquainted, but even when they have known each other well or have been married for years.

In a new relationship, a woman may be insulted and angry. Men may accept anger from a new partner, but they have difficulty understanding it in a wife or girlfriend of long standing. They often fail to understand why she is not turned on the way he wishes she would be—and the way he would be if their positions were reversed.

This is often the result of a misguided notion that a man must court a woman initially, but once she has been won, it is unnecessary ever to court her again. Many men know they should be seductive during courtship, but they feel that once the relationship has been established, the need for seduction is past.

The concept of winning a woman is taught over and over in the media and in folk tales. Winning thus has less to do with interacting in a personal or intimate manner than with the man's demonstrating his success and dominance. In many fairy tales, the man wins the princess by slaying the dragon or fighting his way through a thorn hedge. Aladdin, for instance, must perform a series of dangerous tasks. Even the new stories are little different. In the most recent of cartoons for children, the hero does not woo the woman directly, but somehow subdues the Outer World through strength or cunning, making her world safe and prosperous.

Most women value a man's success in the Outer World and may be drawn to him as a result of it. But when it comes to fully arousing her natural sexuality, the slaying of a dragon does not have the seductive power of a loving look in his eyes.

What Can You Do?

1. Make Eye Contact

The eyes are the most powerful and primary source of body language and therefore have tremendous potential as a tool for closeness and seduction. Be sure to look into her eyes when you're talking to her, especially when she's talking and you want her to know you're listening to what she has to say.

Looking at her, but not staring, will convey the feeling that you care. Most people are comfortable being looked at for about five seconds out of every thirty. This shows interest without making her feel uncomfortable. You can judge how you're doing by her response.

Nothing reveals people's thoughts and feelings more than their eyes. A man can be completely solemn, without a hint of mirth, yet if his eyes dance and twinkle, we know he is laughing inside. Conversely, a man's smile can take on a sinister quality if his eyes are angry or aggressive.

Eye contact is one of the first ways we know someone is attracted to us. As mentioned, most of us unconsciously make direct and continuous eye contact for about five seconds out of every thirty before looking away, then moments later returning to look again. But people who are attracted to each other hold this eye contact longer, for perhaps a full fifteen or twenty seconds out of each half-minute. This longer look is a signal we instinctively receive, even if we don't know why. It says things like "I like you," "You're important to me," "I'd like to get to know you better," "Let's keep talking," or "Let's break away from the others and have our own private conversation."

Both men and women know when they have attracted someone and the signals continue. If the woman looks away or won't maintain eye contact, she is possibly saying, "I don't know you and I'm shy," "I feel uncomfortable," "You're moving too fast," or "I wish you'd go away—I don't want to know you any better." Not acknowledging someone's look or looking away is a direct signal to turn off or turn down communication.

These signals affect us even when we're not paying close attention. They are a part of the unconscious communication that takes place between acquaintances, friends, and lovers, and they are invaluable when it comes to seduction.

Lovers look at each other all the time in a way that shows they can't get enough of each other. It's as if they are drinking each other in through their eyes. Unfortunately, too many couples who have known each other for a period of time hardly look at each other at all. There are countless examples of husbands shaving off their mustaches or wives cutting their hair without their spouse noticing for hours or even days.

Couples especially fail to see each other when they harbor bad feelings for each other or are being dishonest with each other in some way. The bad feeling or the deceit is kept hidden through the absence of eye contact. It's been said that the eyes are the windows to the soul, and one way to keep one's soul from being seen is to keep the windows hidden.

Thus, when two people are angry at each other, they tend to avoid looking at each other. This can be a signal that something is bothering one or the other without anything being said in words.

There is also a lack of eye contact when a man and woman are dishonest with each other, as when one or the other has had a secret affair. This also happens when they fail to confide in or trust each other.

There is also the ritual hello kiss, a quick peck often made with no eye contact at all, and hence no feeling. This seems especially true of couples in marital coma. Even if the couple hasn't yet reached a coma state, this is a sign of a complacent relationship where the excitement is surely on the wane.

Women are at least as aware of body language cues as men. If a woman's husband or boyfriend doesn't look at her, it triggers the same feeling of rejection as in any social situation. Not looking says, "I don't want to relate, don't talk to me, I don't want to be close to you," or perhaps "I'm angry at you."

If a woman is given this signal—not being looked at—continuously, she is not being prepared to make love; quite the opposite: she is being given an unspoken message of rejection. It's no wonder that a woman feels her partner doesn't find her attractive or interesting and is simply using her, when he spends the entire evening without looking at her until they get into bed and he wants sex.

She may even feel angry or used and may say something like, "You don't care about me at all and now you want to make love." This may utterly confuse the man because he may have spent the entire day and evening working to be a good provider, paying bills, running errands, fixing a leaky faucet—all things that to him expressed his caring for her and the family. Now his wife is not only unresponsive to his need and his show of caring, she's downright hostile for what seems to be no apparent reason.

Once again, he thinks to himself, "Women! Who can figure them out?" as he rolls over, feeling angry and rejected and confused, and goes to sleep hoping the whole thing will somehow get sorted out, but not knowing what to do.

Yet with very little effort, and without saying a word, he could have evoked an entirely different response simply by making eye contact. Instead of the ritual hello kiss, he could have looked her directly in the eye with warmth and affection. Then having her attention, he could have let his eyes roam leisurely over her features with a warm, appreciative expression, as if he liked what he saw.

This simple act alone makes a woman pause, makes her keenly aware of the man, and makes her aware of herself as a woman. He is focused on her. She has his concern, his interest, his attention. All these things are very seductive, because none of us get very much of this focused attention. She feels special and important. If he didn't value her, he wouldn't take the time to gaze at her in this way.

Consider the smoldering looks movie stars give each other on screen. The right look can say much more than words. Words are no match for a truly loving look, since the right look taps directly into the emotions of the moviegoer or, in real life, the person being looked at in this way. Dialogue is unnecessary at such a time; the look will touch her heart.

To add real dynamite to this look, combine it with a smile, a gentle, affectionate touch to her cheek, and then a kiss that expresses love and real affection.

Suddenly she sees you, feels your presence, and experiences the emotional rush that comes with knowing she's attractive to you, feeling loved, and knowing she's a woman. These powerful reactions excite her, add a touch of romance, and help a man be more seductive.

2. Be Aware of Your Facial Expressions

You show your feelings with your facial expressions. People draw conclusions about what you are feeling from your expressions and take you at "face value."

Because the male training urges men not to show feeling, particularly soft, affectionate, or loving feelings, many men don't show these feelings on their faces at all. Rather, they adopt a neutral or even a tough or hostile expression much of the time. Ask yourself if you do this. Do you convey your true feelings to your woman through your facial expression? Look in the mirror and put on your usual expressions. What would you think of the fellow you're seeing?

When she asks you if something's wrong or if you're angry at her, she may be taking her cue from your face. Perhaps without realizing it you are sneering or looking bored when you may actually be feeling contented. Or maybe similar questions from others can give you food for thought about your mood; something may be bothering you without your fully realizing it—and it's showing on your face for others to read.

When you look at her and want to convey a message that you care about her and like her, be sure your expression matches your intimate feelings.

Smiling at her is the most obvious and direct nonverbal way to tell her you care about her and like her, and a smile, if it's genuine, makes you look friendly and approachable and welcoming. All of these traits are important in drawing her closer to you, which is what you want if your sex life is to be invigorated.

3. Posture and Position Are Important

You may or may not be a terrific-looking man, but just improving your posture gives out a number of attractive nonverbal messages to your woman and to the world.

If you stand up straight and hold your head up, you look stronger, more powerful, and worthy of admiration and respect. Sagging posture and a protruding stomach give the appearance of weakness and laziness, and those traits are anything but seductive. No one expects you to stand at attention all the time, but remember, if you want to appear more attractive, this is an important part of doing so.

Position is also important. Physical closeness is another way of saying, "I like you, I want to be near you, you are special to me." It is more seductive to position yourself close to her than it is to position yourself farther away. Most women feel good about this, particularly if you combine it with other cues like a warm smile.

You should avoid getting too close, however, if she doesn't seem ready for it. If you are new to each other, if you have been fighting, or if you have some other reason to believe she won't feel good about you being too near, then avoid getting close until you are closer emotionally. Remember that her brain is her most receptive sex organ. You must be accepted emotionally before you're likely to be fully accepted physically.

A good way to determine whether she is ready for you to be closer is to see if she smiles at you or touches you casually, even on the arm or shoulder. These are signals that a woman is ready for you to be nearer.

If you're not certain, you can try getting closer and see her reaction. When you get closer, does she smile? Is her expression welcoming? Does she seem comfortable or does she move away? If she doesn't seem comfortable, the best thing to do is move away. Getting closer than she wants you to get can create a number of negative reactions in women, from discomfort to downright alarm, anxiety, and rejection.

Being able to read her nonverbal signals is another important reason for you to get in touch with your own feelings. Once you are more sensitive to yourself and your own inner workings, you will be better able to read her.

4. Be Aware of Your Voice

Your voice makes a strong statement about you to others. If you mumble or have a nasty tone, it gives your woman a signal to keep her distance from you. If it's high or whining, it acts as a turn-off to others. If your voice is monotonous and boring, it can make her feel bored and dull with you. And peculiarities of speech such as nervous laughter or frequent unfinished sentences or hesitations can all act as barriers to closeness by irritating or frustrating your listener or making you sound immature or timid, even if you're not.

If you're not sure about your voice, try turning on a tape recorder while you're in the midst of a normal conversation with your partner. Later on, listen to the tape and ask yourself how you would react to the voice you hear. You can also ask her how she reacts to your voice—or to any of the other cues we're discussing.

5. Pay Attention to Her

Most women agree that seductive cues are simply those signals that indicate to a woman that you are concerned about and focused on her. Giving her your close attention is a tried-and-true cue. Let her see you looking at her as she walks across a room or when you are out in a crowd. Men who are excited by women look at them. You should be particularly attentive if she is wearing a new dress or something else special or unusual. There are few things more frustrating to a woman than to spend time, money, and effort getting ready for an occasion only to have her man give a noncommittal grunt or a bland, token compliment: "You look fine, dear." The woman asks herself why she bothered, vows not to care so much the next time, and is likely to feel used when he wants sex later on, after not even noticing what she looked like.

Also she needs to see you are listening to her when she is talking. If you're not a good listener, try to avoid situations where conversation is the main mode; do something together that doesn't require a lot of talk. Better yet, learn to be a better listener. Tell her that you have a limited ability to concentrate, but that you want to get better at it. Then try to really listen as long as you can. When you can't concentrate any longer, let her know in a nice way that you want to pick up on what she's saying another time so you can really hear what she has to say. In other words, you care about her.

When she is talking, respond to what she has to say with a nod or smile or verbal response, and look at her. This is one of the most effective and seductive of all the things you can do. Try it and you'll see.

6. Use Small Seductive Cues

Do things for your woman to make her feel special and cherished. Here are some possibilities that women we interviewed found exciting and seductive:

- After helping her on with her coat, wrap your arms around her and give her a big hug.
- Cut out the most delicate portion of a steak or a melon or any other kind of food you might be eating and give it to her. This can even be the center bite of a sandwich.
- Feed her like a small child.
- After zipping up her dress, kiss her back at the top of the zipper.

Hold her hand when she doesn't expect it.

Write her a note. It can be just a few words of affection left somewhere where she'll find it.

After you make love, tuck her in bed as if she were a small child.

Give her a brief gentle shoulder massage. Do this away from the bed and let her know it won't lead to sex.

Put lotion on her after a bath.

Comb her hair.

Do other small things to let her know you're not just interested in having sex; you care about her apart from wanting to have sex.

When Bob tried monitoring his facial expressions and posture with Julie, he said he felt ridiculous. It made him feel self-conscious at first, but he quickly became aware of a slight sneer on his face, his head thrust forward, and his avoidance of eye contact with her. "I felt stupid when I really looked at myself in the mirror, and I was sorry I had looked so carefully," he said. "But now when I look in the mirror a month later I like what I see a lot better. I'm standing up straighter, my face looks happier, and I'm really seeing Julie much more than before. I think part of the reason I didn't look at her before was that I was mad at her a lot of the time and I didn't want to let her see it. But things have gotten so much better between us that I'm not really mad at her very often now, and I can look at her in a way I couldn't do before."

It's common for people to feel self-conscious and self-critical when they first take a hard, objective look at themselves, but awareness is the route to change and improvement. Like Bob, if you have the courage to face facts about yourself, you will soon understand the Inner World—the key to releasing your woman's natural sexuality.

STEP 9: HEATING THINGS UP

The ninth male illusion is the belief that a woman shouldn't need a lot of foreplay.

What's the Problem?

This illusion is based on what men want to believe rather than on reality.

As we saw in Chapter 3, women have been forced to suppress their sexuality in order to survive in the male-dominated world of the past six thousand years. Women do not want a hard, thrusting, big penis; that's not the way things work for most women. Long before she's interested in intercourse a woman needs to feel close emotionally and interested physically. This warm-up can be accomplished through indirect nonsexual means.

A man might become immediately aroused if a woman's first action was to put her hand on his penis. A woman, however, is more likely to be repulsed than aroused if a man's initial action is to put his hand on her breast or genitals. This kind of a turn-off is exactly what a man needs to avoid because it strikes at the heart of a basic female insecurity: "He just wants me for sex." This is not only a turn-off for this sexual experience, it can severely damage your entire relationship.

Woman after woman that we interviewed had a strong reaction to this particular illusion. "My husband doesn't know how to warm up to anything, particularly sex. He just gets in bed and grabs me. Not a kiss, not even a hello, how are you. Then he expects me to be turned on." Women voiced this view over and over again, sometimes with resignation, often with anger. As one woman put it, "All he wants is to stick it in, and he doesn't care that much what he sticks it into as long as it moves. It's almost like he's playing a game and just wants to score."

THE BASEBALL PHILOSOPHY OF LOVE

The problem for most men is that they were raised on the baseball philosophy of love: touching her breast is like getting to first base; second base is getting her bra off; getting in her panties is a triple; intercourse is a home run. The aim is not to enjoy the game, but to run as many bases as possible. This view turns sex into a competitive game that feeds the man's ego with a victory—or starves it with a defeat—and puts him on the opposite team from his woman, setting up a win-or-lose situation. This game philosophy that men find exciting and normal is a turn-off to most women and is exactly the wrong approach. It is not seductive or exciting, and it will not arouse her sexuality.

What's the Truth?

A man feels good as a *result* of having sex, but a woman has to feel good *before* having sex, and her emotions must be aroused before her body can be fully aroused. Remember that her brain is her primary sex organ.

Any long-term relationship, including marriage, is a team sport. You're on the same side, trying to win the game of life. You win by pulling together, helping each other along the way. You may not always get the big hit you'd like—this is the big league, and real life throws a lot of curves and sinkers—but you can increase your batting average as a couple if you work together as a tight team. You win by what you gain through your closeness. If you achieve greater intimacy, you will arouse her emotions. If you succeed in arousing her emotions, she will be more interested in being warmed up physically. If circumstances have prevented you from arousing her emotions before you go to bed together, this warm-up becomes even more important. Remember that what she hopes to get from lovemaking is not so much the pleasure of intercourse as the pleasure of intimacy.

The biggest sexual complaint that women have about men is that they focus too much on genitals and too little on sensuality. It's been said that "Women make love in order to touch; men touch in order to make love."[7] Women prefer a more sensual sexual experience with more touching all over their bodies. This, for them, is the way to greater sexuality.

Some of the men interviewed said that when they try to be physically affectionate with their wives they find the women pulling away, as if they don't really want nonsexual touching. They *do* want it. The problem is that the supposed nonsexual touching is nearly always a prelude to intercourse, so the women are saying no to physical affection as a way of avoiding sex. As one woman put it, "As soon as he tries to get touchy-feely with me I know where we're headed—right into the bedroom. So even though I'd like him to just touch and hold me, if I do this I'm obligated to have intercourse. If we touch and don't have sex, he gets mad at me for teasing him. I wish we could touch without it being sexual, but I don't know if that's even possible."

To many women, intimacy is more important than sex. Many women say they'd just as soon be held and cuddled, and sex is second best. No man we interviewed ever said or even suggested any such an idea.

A study of men and women found that the number one way people indicate interest in sexuality is through touch: 100 percent of the women and 95 percent of the men said that touching—snuggling, kissing, and so on—was the most common way to indicate interest in sex.[8] Other methods included using familiar code words, playing games and rough-housing, using suggestive body movements, changing appearance or clothing, creating the right atmosphere with lighting and music, allowing the hands to wander, offering compliments, asking directly, making eye contact, changing the voice, and talking indirectly about sex.

Women are much more sensually oriented and more whole-body oriented than most men, who often simply try to hit a home run as quickly as possible. If she wants a pleasurable experience that warms her up and makes her feel loved and valued, while he is focused on sports competition centered around her breasts and vagina, this arrangement is guaranteed to prevent maximum sexual sharing and fulfillment: "Without intimacy, the spark goes out of the relationship, eventually seriously affecting sexual desire. Any feelings of disappointment over any of the aspects of intimacy can eventually produce [diminished] sexual desire."[9]

Stress also inhibits arousal and vaginal lubrication. If you do anything that makes her feel anxious, pressured, or afraid, she will automatically pull away from you sexually. If you can help her to relax and feel comfortable and safe, both emotionally and physically, you will be better able to turn on her sexuality.

What Can You Do?

1. Initiate Foreplay

Turn up the heat through emotional and physical foreplay. Start by taking your temperature with the foreplay thermometer. Where are you now and where would you like to be?

THE FOREPLAY THERMOMETER

FROZEN	COLD	COOL	ROOM TEMP
No talking, time, or touching; fighting	Civil	Preoccupied	Proximity

WARM	HOT	HOTTER	BOILING
holding hands, hugs, talking	sharing fun, touching skin	Massages	Passionate kissing, expressing love

You want to let her know that you care about her, that you want her to feel good, that you are interested in her, and that you want to express your feelings sexually but you aren't simply interested in having sex for its own sake. You care about her and you're not using her just for sex.

You want to be intimate with her—emotionally intimate and then physically intimate. This means creating closeness and sharing and caring about her. When you create this intimate atmosphere, you're turning up the intimacy temperature and releasing her natural sexuality.

Begin by trying to imagine what it feels like to be a woman. Think about what it must be like to have a body with breasts and a vagina. Imagine what it might be like to be sexually aroused through being close and loved and to be aroused at a slower rate than a man. Think about her vulnerability and how often she's been told to be careful about having sex and how difficult it might be for her to let go completely. Close your eyes and picture your wife's body. Imagine her desire to be sensually touched before making love.

Now imagine what it would be like to be a woman and to be pushed to have sex before you are ready, to be felt or penetrated without being excited.

A woman may feel violated when her husband or boyfriend demands sex and does very little to make her feel loved or physically or emotionally receptive.

Of course, some women will go ahead and have sex even if they don't really want it, simply to keep the peace in the household, or because they're afraid of making him angry. A woman may be afraid her man will leave her. If she is financially dependent on him, she will suffer not only emotionally but financially as well. So she has sex, even if she doesn't feel loved, even if she isn't warmed up emotionally or physically, even if it hurts. Often she knows she must even pretend to like it, even pretend to be orgasmic. One study found that 59 percent of the women surveyed pretended orgasm at times. [10]

When women feel trapped into having sex they don't want, to one degree or another, they feel a sense of violation and all the anger and resentment that goes with it. This sense of violation and the resulting anger is what every man who wants to maintain a relationship with a woman must avoid. Instead she must want to have sex, and the single biggest key to making her feel like having sex, aside from letting her know you love her, is sensuality.

2. Take Action to Increase Sensuality

Touch your wife nonsexually at least once each day: hugs, kisses, holding hands, cuddling, arm around her shoulder, back massage, neck massage, foot massage.

Determine exactly what she likes and doesn't like and make it safe for her to tell you. Many women we interviewed said that their husbands, even after many years, didn't know what turned them on. "He thinks he knows, but he doesn't," said one woman, "and he doesn't because he's so sure he does that he's never really asked me. You see, *he* is the sexual 'expert,' not me. Never mind that it's my body."

Some women feel embarrassed to discuss this subject at all. Girls are sometimes taught not to touch their own genitals, and this often leaves them unsure of exactly what kind of touching does feel good. It is also difficult for some women to talk about their bodies or to ask to be touched in certain ways.

You can often solve this problem simply by touching her and asking her how it feels. If she is uncomfortable with this, you might make it easier by asking her to tell you how it feels on a scale of 1 to 10, with 10 being the best. Then try different variations until you find the 10s.

Other women can be more straightforward and will simply tell you what is most exciting and exactly how to do it. You can even make this into a game. There are sensual games on the market or you can create your own.

Smile at her when you're happy to see her. Say to her with your facial expression that you like her, care about her and want her to be happy and close to you.

Avoid the normal male tendencies to keep distance, talk little, and keep your feelings hidden. She wants intimacy, closeness, warmth, security, excitement, and sharing. So avoid behavior that turns the temperature down—being unemotional, aloof, cool, detached, or uncommunicative—and do the things that turn it up. That means adding words to your touches. The combination of her favorite massage and words of genuine appreciation and love are magical intoxicants for most women.

Relax and enjoy the experience of touching and being touched. Use sex as more than intercourse; use it as an opportunity to relax and be happy and enjoy yourself. Slow down. Stop the competitive drive to win. Use this chance to enjoy your life and the good things you have and can appreciate. Learn to breathe deeply and relax and enjoy yourself along the way. If you can calm your own breathing and slow down your pace, you're much more likely to find that she'll match your calmness and slowness and be more likely to open to you both emotionally and sexually.

Seduce her. Plan ahead and get her warmed up. Turn it into a fun day for both of you. She wants you to seduce her, but she wants you to do it in a way that works for both of you.

3. Use The Real Aphrodisiac

Allen said that he had never realized how infrequently he touched Carole aside from the times he wanted to have sex with her. Interestingly, he said he knew from working with his patients how much a hand on a shoulder or a hug could mean to another person, but he'd simply never thought about Carole's need to be touched nonsexually. Touching wasn't particularly hard for him; he said he liked to hold her hand and to hug her, but that he just was in the habit of keeping his hands to himself. His parents had never been physically affectionate, and he was simply continuing the family tradition.

Carole said that her family was very demonstrative and that her parents and her sisters were always touching each other's hands or arms or kissing each other on the cheek and that Allen's not touching her always made her feel that he didn't really like her: "My head said that was ridiculous and that I knew better, but my body felt lonely and pushed away."

Allen said he was surprised at the effect being touched had on Carole. She seemed warmer toward him once he started being more affectionate, and for the first time in their eight years of marriage "she went out and bought some lace panties and a see-through bra, did a striptease, and got us to go to bed together." She had never before initiated sex with Allen, who said, "In a sense it seems ridiculously simple, but I feel that I've discovered the real aphrodisiac—hugs and kisses."

Like Allen, any man can learn to help his woman release her natural sexuality if he follows the proper steps—up to and including doing it with love.

STEP 10: DOING IT WITH LOVE

The tenth male illusion about women is the notion that if she looks sexy, she must feel sexy.

What's the Problem?

This "erection projection" is another example of how men misunderstand female sexuality and, specifically, what are women's sexual signals and what are not.

If a man sees a woman who attracts him sexually, he is likely to think she is aware of being sexy and that she is feeling as sexy as she looks—and as sexy as she is making him feel. For example, if a woman has large breasts that excite him, he may assume (particularly if she is wearing something that makes them attractive or noticeable) that she is sexually available and excited, too. He essentially projects his excitement onto her and often assumes that she is experiencing the reaction she is creating in him.

Of course it is true that some women dress to attract men in order to have sex. This, however, is the exception rather than the rule. Women take great care with their clothes and makeup in order to be attractive. But sexy looks do not equate with sexy feelings. She may simply be dressing to feel attractive, to be stylish, to gain approval from other women, without even being aware that she looks sexy.

This reality is often difficult for men to accept. She is exciting him, and it is easy for him to simply project his excitement onto her. He may assume that she knows she looks sexy; he may even interpret any sign of interest in him—even a glance—as a sexual message saying that he might be able to move toward intercourse with her and that she knows she is exciting him. This causes tremendous misunderstanding between men and women, since a woman may feel surprised, even insulted, if a man approaches her sexually. The man, if he is rebuffed, often feels teased, betrayed, set up and led on. Unfortunately, too, he often will not recognize the source of his misunderstanding. He may assume that she is sexually excited and wants to have sex, but simply is turning him down personally.

Of course outside of the bar scene, in everyday situations, most men do not indulge in erection projection because of prior commitments to other relationships or work complications, but he still feels sexual desire for her and often will assume she is feeling as sexy as she looks. He will also use any excuse to assume she feels as much desire as he does. This, of course, is truly a setup for disappointment and difficulty.

What's the Truth?

If a man wants a woman to feel sexual, he should treat her in the ways we have discussed in the first nine steps of this program so that her natural sexual potential will be more readily available for release. Then, having prepared her emotionally, he should be careful to take her body into account. As Helen Singer Kaplan so clearly writes, "A penis does not make love to a vagina. Love requires two interacting people."[11]

What Can You Do?

1. Learn the Facts

1. The outer third of the vagina has nearly all the sense receptors needed to physically excite a woman. Penis size isn't the big issue to women that it is to so many men, since the place of greatest excitement for a woman does not lie deep within her vagina, but is rather at the entrance to her vagina, at the outer lips and the vaginal mouth.
2. Most women need more foreplay than men offer. Half the women in a *Cosmopolitan* magazine survey liked foreplay to last up to half an hour![12] Many women prefer the kissing and cuddling of foreplay and afterplay to intercourse.
3. Women take longer to become sexually aroused than men. The time varies from individual to individual, but generally women take considerably longer than men, so men need to learn sexual patience if they are to help women release their natural sexual potential.
4. Relaxation helps a woman become aroused, while tension may be a primary block to sexual arousal. A woman who feels pressured or upset is less likely to be excited than one who feels comfortable, relaxed, and loved.
5. Vaginal lubrication is one of the first signs of a woman's excitement, but it does not mean she is ready for intercourse. It means she is ready for further stimulation.
6. Lip and breast kisses are often very arousing to women.
7. The clitoris is a powerful center of sexual arousal that, in fact,

serves no other purpose. It is a firm spot covered by a hood of skin, and it is located where the intimate vaginal lips meet in the front. It is a highly sensitive organ with a tremendous number of nerve endings, making it highly sensitive to touch. The majority of women need clitoral or other nonvaginal stimulation to reach orgasm, and most women need continual stimulation to achieve orgasm. If stimulation ceases, the woman's progress toward climax ceases.

8. Orgasm is easiest for most woman to achieve through clitoral stimulation, though many women feel that the orgasm is preferable if they are penetrated at the same time. Most women climax through penetration and clitoral stimulation together, and few women achieve climax through penetration alone.

9. Unlike men who must wait a period of time before being able to have a second orgasm, many women are capable of having more than one orgasm in succession if they are stimulated after climaxing. Not all women want to have multiple orgasms or find it comfortable to do so. If she does want to climax more than one time, you can help her achieve additional orgasms through manual stimulation of the clitoris or its surrounding area. The clitoris itself may be highly sensitive and uncomfortable to direct touch after climaxing.

10. It is possible for a woman to have intercourse without having an orgasm and still feel satisfied. Obviously women differ, but if the sexual experience has been good, many women can feel relaxed and satisfied even if they have not climaxed.

11. Having a vagina and womb makes a woman feel extremely vulnerable. Imagine what it would be like to be penetrated the way she is by your penis. Be sensitive to her place of sexuality, sensuality, birth creation, and delivery.

12. Respect and appreciate that your woman has literally opened herself to you. After intercourse continue being intimate with her, helping her to feel filled with warmth and closeness and love.

2. Connect Sex with Love

Men are trained to be aggressive, to go for a home run. But when this goal-oriented, aggressive approach is used in sex, it can turn the woman totally off, reminding her of rape.

Try to slow down and *love her first*, then you can *make love to her second*. If you can be less goal-oriented in sex, you'll have a more aroused sexual partner and a better relationship.

Connect sex with love, so she will want to have intercourse for emotional as well as physical reasons.

How you approach sex mentally is as important as what you do physically. This is a time when you must convey to her your love for her. You must express the love you really do feel for her so she gets the message—use FemSpeak during sex. Share your heartfelt love with her, while taking her physical needs into account.

3. Learn to Handle Your Sexuality

You may want to have sex six times an hour, so how do you deal with the fact that she may never be sexual enough for you? Learn to handle your own sexuality so you can spend more time in sex and sensuality with her.

Learn to reduce your tension by breathing and relaxing and being more sensually focused, as opposed to genitally focused. This is a most important skill for men to learn. Slow down, enjoy the whole experience, concentrate on her whole body and yours in a sensual way. Learn to give and receive pleasure in nongenital ways. If you do this, she's going to find the whole experience more satisfying than ever before, and she'll be interested in having sex more often. This is going to be a change for you, too—maybe a very big one!

If you find the sexual tension is so powerful that you can't slow down, masturbate. Either enlist her help beforehand, or help yourself. Learn how your body works and take care of it so you function at peak performance, whatever that means for you and your body. If you can be loving and sensual with your woman if you have an orgasm an hour before lovemaking, then make sure this need is properly handled.

Bob said that he'd never realized what a powerful sex drive he had, but that it was simply the way he was and he couldn't remember a time that was much different. He said that it was torture to try to slow down and move at Julie's sexual speed. "She's going about twenty miles an hour," he said, "while I'm going about seventy-five—or at least I'd like to be going seventy-five."

Bob had never thought about "doing it ahead," but he liked the idea of coming twice while Julie was "only interested in doing it once." He liked the idea ten times better when Julie volunteered to help him out in advance of their lovemaking. They proceeded to experiment with different ways and with different amounts of advance time, so that he could "happily go twenty miles an hour right along with her."

4. The Warrior's Sexual Attitude

Let things warm up between you, keeping her differences in mind. It is likely that she will want more holding than you do prior to intercourse, so try to slow down. Breathe and relax and enjoy the closeness.

You might like diving into the sexual waters, but most likely your woman is more cautious. She probably wants to wade into the experience gradually. Focus on the here and now, using the sexual experience as a way of enjoying the moment, being together in closeness with the one you love and care about. Maybe you could massage her neck or back or hands, asking her where she'd like you to touch, how hard or easy, using this as an opportunity to slow and relax and enjoy a few moments, savoring the time together.

Try to be more whole-body oriented. Learn to touch the areas all over her body that excite her the most, not just her genitals. This gives you the aroused woman you desire while meeting her needs for closeness and touching and feeling loved for herself along the way, which naturally leads to intercourse.

Maybe you could think about a great vacation the two of you had together or that walk you took in the park, thinking about nice feelings between you as you let yourself feel closer to her. This is a time for more than intercourse; it is also a time to be happy in the midst of your life, to breathe and relax and be close. It's a time to slow down and smell the flowers, a time to be with her and enjoy your good feelings about her.

Let your sexual experience be wider than intercourse and wider than physical sensations, too.

Let it include your emotions and your thoughts.

Let yourself use this opportunity to feel the love you have for her, to focus on the nice things about her that you really think and feel. In this way sex includes a wider experience of happiness and goes beyond mere physical release.

A combat-ready soldier just wants to fuck; an intimate warrior wants to truly make love with his partner. He aims at being powerfully present, sensually alive, in touch, aware, able to experience intimacy as a route to further sexuality, savoring the lovemaking along the way.

5. Learn How to Make Love to a Woman

Remember that good lovemaking for a woman combines feeling, thinking, relating, and physical sex. Because her brain is her primary sex organ, she needs to be aroused in her mind and emotions before she has physical sex.

Try starting with sensuality. Maybe caressing her skin, giving her a massage, or holding her close will get her warmed up. The ultimate answer to her arousal lies within the woman herself. You can find out what she likes by asking her directly or by observing her bodily responses to your actions. And keep in mind that she is likely to vary in what she wants from one time to another.

Explore her body with your hands, stroking her in ways she enjoys. Let her know that she can trust you to help her to feel good and that you are responsive to her reactions or requests about what she likes and dislikes. The whole body can be a sexual instrument; it all depends on the individual's likes and dislikes.

Relax and enjoy being together. Breathe and let yourself slow down. This is one of the finite number of times in your life that you'll be together in a physically intimate way, so savor each moment and every touch.

Perhaps she wants to spend time kissing and being held; perhaps she is more eager this particular day.

Bring your strength and sensitivity to your lovemaking and create an atmosphere in which you both enjoy your time together. You can slow yourself down by masturbating beforehand or with her, if needed. Then she can move at the pace that is most exciting for her, leading her to be more interested in sex the next time. You can also pay attention to her cues and go with the flow.

Make her feel she can bring down whatever walls she has around her sexuality when she is with you; you love her, value her, and find her exciting sexually. You want her to open up fully to you and be close in an erotic way.

Practice this mind magic with her. Convey to her the picture of her as being a sexy and sexual person. Let her know how exciting you find her, how she gets you aroused when you see her beautiful face or smell her hair or think about her warmth. Let her know that she is a sexual person who can feel safe to open up with you, feel her own sexuality, be receptive to your body, safe in the knowledge that you have her best interests clearly in mind.

After being together for a while, touching and feeling close, you might move to her breasts if she enjoys this, touching or sucking or rubbing her in the ways she likes. You can feel her nipples become erect or stiffen in response to your touch when she enjoys what you're doing.

Maybe then you'll move to her genitals or touch her pubic hair. If she seems responsive you can enjoy touching her there, or if she seems tense and pulls back you may need to slow down.

Using KY jelly or some other lubricant you can gently move to the entrance of her vagina, touching the opening carefully. Her clitoris may be eager to be touched at this point, though most women find this a very sensitive area and prefer very gentle touching.

The highly sensitive clitoris may be most comfortably aroused by exerting a light pressure on the side of the clitoris through the vaginal lips.

Be careful not to become exclusively focused on her vagina and breasts, but continue to pay attention to the rest of her body as well, perhaps touching her or stroking her back and arms and face, whatever she likes.

Throughout the experience be sure to keep aware of her nonverbal cues as to what she does and does not like. She may like to talk and tell you what she enjoys, or she may be uncomfortable with words during sex and may prefer that you let her body language tell you what to do more or less of. If she's comfortable, you can ask her if you're going too fast or too slow, if your touch is too hard and rough or too soft or if she'd prefer that you touch her clitoris. You can no more read her mind than she can read yours.

You might tell her during the experience how you really feel about her, about how special she is to you, about how pretty her breasts are, about how she gets you excited, about how you think about her at work and wonder what she's doing. Keep her emotions aroused during lovemaking.

You might even recall a wonderful time you had together, like when you went to Hawaii and sat on the beach and felt you were in heaven. This brings good feelings into the experience and adds emotional closeness.

Once you have entered her sexually, realize that her clitoris is her key to orgasm. Simple penetration is usually insufficient for most women to be orgasmic, so clitoral stimulation is usually necessary. She may prefer touching her clitoris while you are inside her, or she may want you to touch her.

Breathe and relax. Allow yourself to be with her while you're in her. Let yourself be present, awake, fully alive.

IN CONCLUSION

This then has been the man's program, a step-by-step way to become a more exciting, romantic, and skilled lover—exactly the kind of man a woman wants to make love to. By doing these steps either alone or in conjunction with your partner doing Chapter 6—the woman's program —you have undoubtedly had a big impact on your relationship.

In Chapter 7 we'll look at exactly what you can do to help each other continue in this positive direction so that you can continue loving and making love more happily ever after.

NOTES, CHAPTER 5

1. *Los Angeles Times*, June 12, 1989.
2. Shere Hite, *Women and Love* (New York: St. Martin's Press, 1989), p. 27.
3. Michael Castleman, *Sexual Solutions* (New York: Simon & Schuster, 1989), p. 153.
4. Carol Tavris and Susan Sadd, *The Redbook Report on Female Sexuality*, 2nd ed. (New York: Dell, 1977).
5. Gilbert D. Nass and Mary Pat Fisher, *Sexuality Today:* (Boston: Jones and Bartlett, 1988), p. 193.
6. Helen S. Kaplan, *Disorders of Sexual Desire* (Washington, D.C.: American Psychiatric Press, 1985), pp. 68, 14.
7. Castleman, p. 171.
8. Nass and Fisher, p. 118.
9. Kaplan, p. 68.
10. Carol A. Darling and J. Kenneth Davidson, Sr. "Enhancing Relationships: Understanding the Feminine Mystique of Pretending Orgasm," *Journal of Sex and Marital Therapy* 12, no. 3 (1986): 182–96.
11. Kaplan, p. 60.
12. Nass and Fisher, p. 134.

6

The Woman's Program

Virtually every woman alive wants more love from her man, wants her life to be meaningful and fun, and wants to live in the security of knowing that the man she loves loves her in return.

What woman doesn't want to be flattered and drawn out by a man's interest, by his loving touches, by his exploration of who she is and what she wants?

What woman doesn't want to feel attractive, exciting, appreciated, admired?

Unfortunately, most men don't know how to make women feel this way. Many men know they love their women. Many men want to express this love. They just don't know how. And, as we've seen in previous chapters, they've been trained not to show the kind of tenderness that so many women recognize as an expression of love.

And of course by not knowing how to show women how they feel, not knowing the secrets of being seductive and exciting, they have been kept from getting the sex they want.

In Chapter 6 men were given step-by-step advice on how to remedy this situation by learning to be far more aware of their woman's emotional and sexual needs and how to become more and more the man of her dreams.

The problem is that it's far more difficult for a man to do this alone than it is if he has support and encouragement from you.

SECRETS TO MAKING THE
CHANGE HAPPEN

In this chapter we have provided a series of steps that parallel the man's program as well as a number of "secrets" to handling men. These are designed to help you understand more about your man, what his emotional and sexual needs are, and how to become the woman of *his* dreams—the woman to whom he wants to show all this loving attention.

These "secrets" are as follows:

1. *Forgive him.* One of the biggest problems men and women now face is that so many millions of women are at the end of their ropes with men, and men are confused about what women want from them. The whole problem is so complicated and poorly understood, that the root of the difficulty remains buried and both women and men are frustrated.

Many women have been trying for years to get their man to be closer to the man of their dreams, but for the most part, they feel their efforts have amounted to very little.

It's important to see three points: (1) change is possible; (2) it isn't his fault that he is the way he is; and (3) there is no better alternative. Let's look at these three points more closely.

Most people behave according to the conditioning they've received, but change, as we said, is possible. The truth is that men are not the way they are out of choice. If you are raised to be a certain way from infancy, the odds of your being otherwise are slim indeed. Men are trained to be emotionless, isolated, and alone; to maintain a strong facade and never to show self-doubt, fear, wounds, or sadness; to control anger and frustrated sexual desire beneath a calm exterior.

Many men feel set up. A man tries hard to be what he is expected to be, but then his woman blames him for being "just like a man." But this is who he is and how he thinks and feels. Don't blame him; help him change.

Most women are aware that there is no better alternative. Women are stuck with the responsibility for the relationship. Surveys show that both men and women agree on this point. So if women have no better choice, it's largely their problem since they're still responsible for the relationship. And since women are, at least at present, the ones who most overtly value closeness and love, then certainly the greater burden falls on women, like it or not.

2. *Give him a safety zone free of judgment and criticism.* Let bygones be bygones. You may have many resentments and points of anger that have built up over time. As much as possible release them and try to give him the opportunity to change in a safe atmosphere.

3. *Reinforce his efforts.* He won't do things exactly right the first time; neither will you. What he needs is encouragement, not an expectation that he must be perfect. Give him the message that you appreciate his effort and all you are asking is that he continue to put forth an effort.

Remember to praise what he does right and, as much as possible, ignore what he does wrong. Do this by saying encouraging and appreciative things when he does something you want him to do: "It's so wonderful of you to help me with this gardening project," or "I love it when you kiss me like that." If you are having trouble finding something to praise, give him a positive example of someone else's behavior: "Did you notice how Joe was holding Sally's hand after dinner? That is so nice and so romantic."

Also remember that when he does something you want, it's important to consider what he might like you to do as a reciprocal gesture. Always try to keep in mind that change will occur much more readily if he can see that it is making him happier, letting him feel more satisfied, or in some way making him feel better.

Be vividly aware of how things are when you are starting to work toward change. Any time you notice any improvement you should solidify it and encourage it by commenting on it or by rewarding it. Work to develop a new radar system designed to pick up progress in the desired direction. Notice any improvement *compared to the starting point.* This will encourage both of you to keep moving toward your goals: "Be careful, big guy, you're turning me on," or "If you keep that up you're going to have a tigress on your hands," or "I was thinking about how much better we're doing and I bought this" (hold up the very sexy lingerie you bought). Sit on his lap and whisper about the surprise you're going to give him later for making you feel good about yourself: "You make me so happy and proud of you when I see you really trying to make me feel loved. You really do love me, don't you?"

Men are often surprised to discover their woman doesn't feel loved and that it is actually so simple to make her happy. Your encouraging responses will help him keep working toward a better relationship with you and striving to shed the armor and anesthesia he's been living with all his life.

People need strong motivation to overcome a deeply ingrained pattern. Think about what he already likes and what he might like if he tried it, and try giving that to him as an incentive to keep working at something that's probably going to be hard for him.

4. *Keep in mind the differences in the male and female styles of loving.* Be aware of how he might feel, even though he isn't showing his feelings in exactly the ways you might like. He's going to be learning how to speak your language along the way, but keep him on track by encouraging him and recognizing his male style of loving as love.

5. *Keep in mind he is human, too.*

Remind yourself that there's a wounded orphan in him who's been this way for years, maybe decades. He may have been armored, separated from other people, and emotionally anesthetized for virtually his whole life, and he needs healing, teaching, and help. He needs forgiveness, too. So realize how hard all this may be for him, even though it may not seem so hard to you. Take a long-term view, and avoid impatience.

If a man expresses any emotion or shows any degree of closeness or equality that was not previously present, don't say to yourself that he should have been this way all along, or it's too little too late. You're both going to suffer for this attitude. Keep in mind how hard emotions and closeness are for most men.

Being armored and anesthetized pays off handsomely for men in the boardroom as well as on the playing field and the battlefield. Remember also that men who are successful are highly rewarded and perceived as more desirable by women, who commonly choose men at least in part because of their level of success. Men have been rewarded for being armored and anesthetized. Now they are being criticized for the same traits that helped make them seem so desirable in the first place.

No wonder the whole man-woman struggle is so tough to resolve. But now we know why. Now we can do something about it. Try to build on every change you notice. Patience and perseverance are the routes to success.

6. *Keep your own motivation in mind.* Is love important to you? Would you like him to be more like the man of your dreams? If so, it's up to you to do your part. Keep the program alive and running. Make it happen. Don't let it get derailed or simply forgotten in the midst of your busy daily life. This may be your greatest danger, and it will be lurking all along the way every day for the rest of your life.

Once you've established some new patterns, the momentum will tend to carry you along, but you still have to remember there is a normal gravitational pull that's always resisting the change you're trying to make. For most couples there will be setbacks, times when making these changes, and getting closer emotionally, will stir up feelings and difficulties that you will have to handle. Know this will occur and don't let it throw you off track or make you give up. If the problem is too severe, get professional help. The point is to keep going. You can't do it all, but you can do your own part and both of you will appreciate the changes that are happening even as you keep the program going.

A Man Needs Help to Find His Heart

Men are like the Tin Man in *The Wizard of Oz*, rusted in place, needing oil, feeling an emptiness within himself, trying to find his own heart, but needing help. Many women want to give up or turn the responsibility over to someone else, some wizard, perhaps. The problem is, however, that no one except their woman can help a man change.

Most men have no close friends. They discuss personal issues with no one except their wives and girlfriends. And most men are uncomfortable seeking or even admitting they need professional help.

So if they are going to change, it is up to their women to help it happen.

The Master of the Heart

You're the master of the heart as far as your man is concerned. You're the one who can help him enter the Inner World—and it won't be an easy job.

Change can't and doesn't occur overnight, but little by little, day by day, persistent effort will make a difference, and the more persistent your effort the more change you are likely to see in the long run.

7. *Appreciate his sacrifice, too.* Sure women have and do make many sacrifices, but don't forget his. A man's role is not an easy one. Women often don't realize that when a man makes a commitment, it isn't just to loving them, but to much, much, more.

Warren Farrell writes about a man who said to him, "Hilda and I are talking marriage. This weekend we went looking at homes in a nice Atlanta suburb. Hilda feels it would be a good place to bring up children. Well, she fell in love with a $165,000 house. But at 13.5 percent interest, that was over a half a million dollars. Then I read that kids cost $140,000 per, and I figured, two kids times $140,000 equals $280,000. After taxes! Shiiiit . . . Then I got to figuring utilities, cars, gas, insurance, clothes, and, oh yes, eating. That was enough to send the acid through my stomach. I got so preoccupied with how to do it, I couldn't get in touch with my feelings until tonight. Well, my feelings are that I'm scared. Real scared. Hilda says I'm afraid of commitment."[1]

Women may be juggling 101 responsibilities, but the name of the game for the men is intensity. They intensify their drive to succeed because they're doomed to a lower life-style, and thus lower self-image, if they don't succeed. A man also isn't supposed to complain or let on that he's having any doubts or fears along the way.

Be angry about it if you want, but recognize the bind a man is in. Or has been in. Each day he bears his burden without crying or showing his pain. Each day he feels he is making an important contribution. And each day he feels that what he does is, to some extent, taken for granted and undervalued by his woman.

Many women who have relied on their husband's income don't understand what it means to shoulder the primary financial burden. But it is a heavy responsibility, and to place on top of it the expectation that he develop personally as well can seem like a crushing weight for some men. Bear with him. Move forward in the direction of change, but take his reality into account as much as you can understand and live with it. At least value and appreciate his already being a good provider—or at least his efforts at being a good provider.

In her penetrating book *Intimate Strangers*, Lillian Rubin discusses her unexpected reaction to taking over the financial burden of her family so her husband could change careers, a responsibility she eagerly anticipated: "Suddenly I wasn't sure whether I wanted to work anymore; it no longer seemed like such fun. It's one thing to work because you want to, another because you have to . . . It was only when the burden of supporting the family was dropped onto my shoulders that I could comprehend how oppressive a responsibility that is. It was then that I said to my husband, 'I think you men are crazy to live your whole life this way. If I were a man, I wouldn't have waited for women to call for a liberation movement; I'd have led it.'"[2]

Men are expected to be good providers, with all that it entails. That is what they are supposed to do, what they've been taught to regard as a mark of manhood as natural as striving for sex and success. Can you blame them for wanting appreciation for the burden they're carrying, or for wanting understanding for the toll it takes on them as shown in health statistics?

8. *Be aware of his limitations.* Men are different from each other. There is no one way for a man to be, and even though we have talked as if there were a stereotyped male style, there is also a wide range of individual variation from one man to another. In terms of ability to enter the Inner World, men range from 1 to 100 in their interest in and aptitude for it. Some men may start at 1 and be able to get further than you'd predict. Others seem to start out further along and never make much progress. The only way to know is to work at it with your man, trying to accomplish as much as possible.

Millions of men deeply value home, family, caring and relationships. They want more but aren't sure what to do. Many simply don't understand what seems so evident to women. Many are rusted in place. Some are filled with hurt, anger, fear, and frustration and feel like volcanoes ready to explode (their self-control is one of their underappreciated gifts of love). Some men are depressed. Some are very lonely. Others are so preoccupied with the daily struggle to be successful and to be a good provider that this takes up all their energies and, in their minds, *is* their way of showing love. Remember, just because he's self-contained and controlled doesn't mean he isn't needy.

One of the things you need to consider is just exactly what your man is like and how this compares to what you'd like him to be. Women vary in what they want from a man, and you should know what you want before you begin. Do you really want a man, for example, to tell you all his feelings, or are you more comfortable with a man who is the strong, silent type? Some women complain that their man isn't strong enough, yet would never want to relinquish any of their own power in their relationship to a stronger man. Think about what you want in a man so you'll be better able to bring about the changes you value.

9. *See it all through the eyes of love.* The best way to go through the program that follows is to do it with heart. Every step in the program that follows can be done with love. If you do this, you will increase the chances of your success with your man, and you will also give yourself what you want in your life.

Now let's get started in the program.

STEP 1: GETTING STARTED: THE KNIGHT'S ARRIVAL

The first female illusion about men says that a man who loves a woman will want to help her at home.

What's the Problem?

Women want help. Women need help. Women deserve help. While frequently both men and women work outside the home, women find themselves working many more hours because of all their additional responsibilities at home. They feel that their burden is not only unfair but in many cases simply impossible.

This leads to women being not only exhausted but angry as well. They believe that if their man really loved them, they would be interested in sharing this burden more equitably. The problem is, men *don't* generally share this burden, and women, as a result, feel unloved and uncared for. When you add this to the exhaustion from being overwhelmed by jobs, you have a prescription for resentment and a step toward marital coma or divorce.

What's the Truth?

So why are men unwilling to help around the house? Is it true that they simply don't love their women? The truth is that men are slow to help for several reasons.

1. *They are unaware of their partner's need for help.* Women, having been raised to believe that women's work and men's work are not the same, don't feel it's appropriate to ask him to help them, and so they don't.

Another part of the reality is that men are used to hearing women complain about chores. Your man probably heard his mother complain and saw his father not take the complaints seriously. He's probably heard other women, including those he works with, complain. Complaining, alone, will not bring about a change in his behavior.

Even though she complains, the work still gets done, so why should he help? Why fix something that isn't really broken?

2. *Men aren't sure what to do or how to do it.* Without specific instructions as to exactly what to do, a man is often unsure how to help. If a woman says, "I'm exhausted. There is so much to do and I can't get it all done,"

that doesn't give a man much of a course of action to follow. This is especially true if, on those occasions when he did try to help, he was criticized for his less than perfect beginner's efforts.

3. *Men have been conditioned to avoid "women's work."* One of the facts of our society is that men are waited on by their mothers at home and raised to believe that, like their fathers, they will be waited on by their wives when they grow up. Even today, in elementary school, it is common for the boys to be sent out to the schoolyard to play while the girls stay inside to help the teacher clean up.

This message is also delivered in cartoons, books, and movies where mothers are shown waiting on their sons and women are shown waiting on men.

As with all of human nature, what is familiar is what feels "right" and comfortable. And this message is delivered over and over. Men, particularly "important" men whom boys want to emulate, are often seen being waited on and are rarely seen doing household chores competently. This means to them that if they are cared for and considered important, things will be done for them at home.

This also leads to the conclusion that any man who does do household chores is not important and is not cared for by others. If he were, he wouldn't have to do these chores himself. For many men this brings into question his masculinity, his sense of success, and his sense of self-worth.

4. *He doesn't know what good it will bring him to do things differently.* The final barrier for men is a very practical, very human problem: if a man helps a woman at home, he has to have a compelling reason to do so. Most people in most situations, before exerting themselves, and certainly before changing a comfortable pattern for a less comfortable one, will ask, "What's in it for me?"

All these barriers were illustrated very well by Ron, one of the men we interviewed. Ron is a computer salesman. His wife, Tasha, works as an executive assistant at a large corporate headquarters. They have two children eight and twelve years old.

"I never knew that Tasha wanted me to help her," Ron said, "until one day I came home and she just blew up, screaming about everything that needed to get done and how I wasn't helping. I do my share, don't I? I cut the lawn on Sunday when I'd much rather be doing something that's more fun; and whenever anything goes wrong I'm the one she expects to fix it. I had no idea she really expected me to run errands or shop or clean. It just never seemed like my responsibility. Sure, I've heard her complain, but I complain about things, too, and I don't expect her to do them. Anyway, as much as she complained, all the work still seemed to be getting done, so how tough could it really be? And if she needs help, why can't she get it from Sammi, our twelve-year-old girl? Maybe she's the one who should be helping her mother with the household chores. I don't need any more to do when I'm already tired from a long day or when I want to unwind over a weekend."

Now, many women readers will want to strangle this man, but look at it from his perspective. He isn't trying to slight Tasha, he just isn't aware that helping her is truly important to her or that he really can or should do anything about it. And if her getting more help is important, she shouldn't be looking to him, a *man*, but instead another female. This is something he's been trained from birth to believe.

Also, and perhaps most important, he doesn't see clearly what reward he would get for being more helpful.

As infuriating as this attitude might be, it is real, it is common, it is the reality confronting most women today. It might help your own mental health to release your anger about this issue, but doing so probably won't help your relationship. Complaining about the situation won't be nearly as effective as doing something about it.

Among the new generation, many men are still quietly functioning under the old rules: men do men's work; women do women's work. Men's work is making a living; women's work is taking care of the home and children. Even if the woman earns part of the living, she's still responsible for the home.

It will help to:

1. Let him know you need and want help.
2. Let him know specifically what to do, and if necessary show him how to do it.
3. Help him realize that just as women have taken on part of the traditionally male burden of making a living, it's become essential for men to take on part of what has traditionally been the female burden of running a household and caring for the children.
4. Convince him that this does not reflect negatively on his masculinity, especially with you.
5. Show him that it is worth his while to change, to work harder, and to risk feeling silly, because something good will happen as a result.

What Can You Do?

1. *Your first task is to get him involved in this program.* Before you talk to him, you'll want to read the man's program to make yourself familiar with what is being asked of him.

This may open the conversation regarding this whole area of juggling responsibility. Try not to make this discussion confrontational or allow it to turn into an argument. You are trying to make a positive contribution to your relationship.

Here is one way you could begin: "More than anything in the world, I want us to get along well. The reason we picked each other is because we love each other and we want to be happy together. I know you want more from me, just as I want more from you, and I really believe this program can help us. Even if it's hard, it's going to be worthwhile, and not just for me; it's going to pay off for you, too, and for us as a couple. Let's try it and see how it goes. Let's do it together, okay?"

2. *Once he agrees to try the program, let him know exactly what to do and how to do it.* For example, many couples decide that running errands will be the most useful way for him to help because he can do some errands on the way to or from work. Let's say you both decide that he can pick up and deliver the laundry to the cleaners. Give him very specific instructions on how to handle this so there won't be any misunderstandings, but avoid making him feel controlled or emasculated.

How do you handle this? Let's say that you've been taking the laundry to the cleaners whenever you have an opportunity. Chores are most likely to get done if they are put on a regular schedule, so pick a day and a time that will be convenient for him. Decide if the laundry will be bagged and by whom and where it will be, and then stick with this plan. You may or may not write out instructions to save him time and avoid problems.

Chores that require more precision may take him longer to master. As one woman said after she first asked her husband to help her with household chores, "I think of him as a new bride. I think of how little I knew about running a household when I first began doing it. That makes me much more patient."

Make sure you don't undermine his efforts by expecting perfection or by picking at errors or incompetencies. One woman used coupons when she shopped to save 15 percent on her grocery bill. She was furious when her husband did the shopping and bought not only more expensive brands than she did but also failed to use any of the coupons. Her reaction was so negative that her husband, who had done his absolute best to do the shopping well, refused to ever shop for her again.

This kind of experience helps no one, so control your expectations and your reactions. Perfectionism will get you nowhere; understanding will get you what you want. Praise him for what he's able to do, and teach what he doesn't yet know how to do.

As best you can, engineer success. Don't set up tasks that will cause him to feel discouraged or embarrassed. Give him chores that are simple and easy to do. Some men will never learn to change a diaper or wash a dish, but Harold can drive Janie to her dance lesson—and who knows? He may find it fun, especially if he's prepared properly ahead of time and rewarded afterward. The important thing is to start with something he can easily do.

3. *Be sensitive to the masculine ego.* When Bob first started helping Julie, he agreed to prepare dinner every Tuesday and Thursday night when she had classes. Bob later said, "I was actually having a good time. I'd done some cooking before Julie and I were married, and I knew a few things to do. I was making spaghetti and experimenting with some creative spicing when she came in from classes. Julie tasted it and laughed. 'That's good,' she said. 'You're going to make a great wife after all.' Now what kind of a crack do you think that was? I'm not anyone's wife. I help her out and she calls me a wimp."

Julie was surprised that Bob took offense. "It's just a joke," she insisted. She hadn't taken into account Bob's sensitivity about doing the cooking, which he saw as somehow taking away from his masculine identity. It is very common for men to be sensitive to feeling weak, dependent, stupid, and unmasculine. Do your best to avoid triggering his defenses.

Also avoid situations in which he ends up doing "women's work" in the presence of other men. The last thing he needs is to have his buddies put him down for doing something different. We're all sensitive to other people's opinions of us, so avoid this obstacle if possible.

4. *Remember to encourage him, so that he gets some kind of a reward for trying to change.* No doubt he already has a heavier burden and more chores than he wants. If he doesn't see how it's going to benefit him to take on more work, there's little chance he will do more, at least for very long. So remember to give him a kiss, a hug, words of praise, and anything else that you think would make him feel loved and appreciated.

Of course you may say, "Why should I thank him? He should have been doing this all along." That may be true, but look at it from his side: he is making an effort to do something you want and to be nice to you. The smart move is to reciprocate and do the same for him.

STEP 2: A MUTUAL ADMIRATION SOCIETY

The second female illusion about men says that real men are strong enough not to need their ego fed.

What's the Problem?

Men are supposed to be strong, competent, and independent, and to show that they possess these traits, they aren't supposed to need to be told they have them.

This view is apparent in old-fashioned movie heroes who, whenever they received a wound, however terrible, would scoff as the heroine examined it and say, "It's just a scratch, ma'am." When the Lone Ranger finally brought the bad guys to justice, he always left before any praise or thanks could be given so that those he had helped would be prompted to say, "Who was that masked man?" The Lone Ranger made it clear to his entire audience that he didn't need praise or thanks. He was a man, and a real man doesn't need his ego fed.

This same attitude can be seen in virtually all male hero models to the present. None of them seek praise or seem to particularly value it. They simply appear to know that they are good and are so completely self-confident that they don't need anyone to tell them so.

This is one of the dilemmas for both men and women. Once again men are caught in the squeeze between what they are supposed to be and what they really are.

This image presented by our heroes has put men in the position of having to live up to an ideal that women generally have accepted as appropriate male behavior. Women need to be told nice things about themselves, to be openly praised and admired. Women expect this, but they expect men not to need praise. They may interpret a man's need for praise as childish, weak, or hypocritical.

"My husband is really a little boy at heart," says a woman who is married to a successful computer engineer. "He acts so confident and so utterly self-assured all the time, as though he has nerves of steel and is ready for anything. But last weekend when some friends of his got together to play baseball, he was upset because I wasn't in the bleachers watching him hit home runs over the fence.

"He wants everyone to think he doesn't care what people think of him, but he does care, and he especially cares what I think. But he'd never say that. Instead, he got mad at me about something insignificant, but I knew it was really because I wasn't there admiring his skill and flattering him. It's really so childish, even hypocritical. If he was really that confident he wouldn't need me to tell him he was terrific, but it's all a show."

This is the bind men are in. Men, like women, want to be given positive messages about themselves. But, unlike women, men have been socialized to think they should not want these messages.

Remember that men are trained to remain distant from others and to receive less affection, less touching, less holding, less emotional nourishment than girls and women receive—and even most women feel emotionally undernourished!

A man may, therefore, try to get positive feedback and emotional nourishment in an indirect way while his woman reacts by quietly labeling him as childish. She feels he shouldn't need such ego building and ends up feeling annoyed at him for wanting the same kind of affection that she wants from him.

A woman, therefore, will often avoid giving her man praise and compliments because:

1. He acts so confident that she feels he doesn't or shouldn't need praise.
2. She may feel he is already too confident about himself and she doesn't want to give him a swelled head.
3. She thinks he doesn't deserve to be told nice things about himself because he isn't saying nice things about her.
4. She may be afraid that if she makes him feel too good about himself he will begin to think he's too good for her.
5. She may be stretched so thin emotionally that she has nothing extra to give him.

What's the Truth?

The truth is that men need praise and encouragement; they want to be told they are valuable, attractive, and important, at least as much as women do, even if they can't ask for it as directly. Everyone craves appreciation and recognition, and men need reassurance they are doing a great job, are good providers, and are competent in all the ways men are supposed to be.

They may actually need this loving reassurance even more than women do because women are allowed to seek praise more overtly and as a result are often given more positive feedback more directly. Women can also talk more honestly with more people than most men do.

Men can't be as direct as women. They are taught they shouldn't want or need ego food. Therefore they don't normally get it and are often embarrassed when they do.

Often, despite his great show of confidence, a man is covering up a lot of self-doubt. Even if he is very successful, he may have an insatiable ego, demanding ever more. For some men there is always a higher mountain to climb, and they die from exhaustion and defeat before reaching the highest summit—an impossible task for those who create ever higher summits. Pity these poor mountain climbers, forever struggling to prove their worth, never feeling at peace.

You may be angry that your man doesn't give you recognition, but if you play the game of "I'll start if you start," you're likely to end up with no one starting and nothing changing.

"Well, what if I do make him think he's the most wonderful man in the world? Won't he start to ask himself, 'If I'm so great, what am I doing with her?'" In our discussions of this subject, women voiced this concern again and again. The truth is, however, that a woman can build her partner's ego in a way that will reflect well on her.

"I'm just so exhausted," one woman said when discussing this subject. "I feel as if I have nothing to give to anyone at the end of the day."

"I don't even think good things about myself," said another woman. "How am I supposed to say good things about him?"

"I'm just so furious with him. It might be nice if I could think of something nice to tell him, but I can't think of anything."

Many women are too tired, too angry, or too emotionally bankrupt themselves to give any more emotional support to anyone else. But the only way to reverse this whole process is to break this cycle and turn things around so that everyone benefits.

What Can You Do?

A woman must accept that a man, in spite of the myths to the contrary, needs ego-building messages just as much if not more than a woman does and that this is a powerful tool to building a better relationship.

An essential factor in getting a man to love you is to make him feel better about himself.

Men typically report that while they may have dated many women, when they met that special one, they knew it by how they felt. This feeling is the magic for men who, in their own way, are often more romantic than women. They rely much more on this special feeling to tell them they are in love.

Making a man feel good when he is with you doesn't stop at courtship. The way to keep a man in love with you forever is to make him feel better when he is with you than when he is with anyone else.

Learn what to say, how to say it, and when.

1. Count the Ways

"All right," you might say, "I can see that it's important for a man to be told good things about himself, but what do I say? I've never really thought about it."

This situation is often the same for women as it is for men. You might want to say something nice, but what *can* you say? Just as we suggested in the man's program, you need to learn to "count the ways."

Begin by reading through the following traits, circling the ones you honestly feel your man possesses.

PHYSICAL traits that I especially like, love, value, or admire include his hair, face, eyes, eyebrows, eyelashes, cheeks, chin, forehead, ears, skin, teeth, nose, lips, mouth, smile, laugh, neck, back, shoulders, chest, arms, hands, stomach, waist, thighs, buttocks, legs, knees, height, weight, feet, penis, muscles, athletic skills, physical coordination, physical health, posture, clothes.

MENTAL traits that I especially like, love, value, or admire about him. He is: abstract, artistic, bright, creative, able to solve problems, alert, aware, astute, bold, original, clever, complex, curious, detail-oriented, honest, imaginative, improvising, ingenious, innovative, inventive, knowledgeable, musical, objective, observant, open-minded, perceptive, practical, precise, reasonable, reflective, sensible, thoughtful, understanding.

EMOTIONAL traits that I especially like, love, value, or admire in him. He is: accepting, agreeable, balanced, calm, carefree, caring, cheerful, controlled, cool, dreamy, easygoing, gentle, happy, hot, intense, intuitive, jovial, loving, patient, playful, powerful, relaxed, sensitive, shy, sincere, stable, strong, sweet, vulnerable, warm.

SOCIAL traits that I especially like, love, value, or admire in him. He is: candid, caring, committed, community-minded, considerate, cooperative, diplomatic, expressive, fair, friendly, generous, loyal, well-mannered, a good father, motivating, an organizer, respectful, sensitive to others, willing to share credit, sociable, supportive, tactful, a good teacher, well liked, a good husband.

BEHAVIORAL traits that I especially like, love, value, or admire about him. He is: adaptable, adventurous, ambitious, assertive, authoritative, capable, competent, cooperative, courageous, decisive, a good decorator, dependable, disciplined, dynamic, efficient, energetic, enthusiastic, expressive, able to follow through, free, giving, neat, independent, industrious, a leader, mechanical, orderly, organized, an outdoor person, good under pressure, persistent, playful, polite, good at solving problems, punctual, quick, quiet, reliable, responsible, resourceful, risk-taking, spontaneous, success-oriented, successful, talented in cooking, a gardener, a sport, zestful.

EGO traits I especially like, love, value, or admire in him. He is: authentic, balanced, confident, determined, dignified, extroverted, firm, flexible, generous, growing, healthy, honorable, idealistic, introverted, mature, modest, mystical, normal, optimistic, poised, principled, progressive, proud, realistic, resourceful, self-accepting, self-aware, self-reliant, sensible, serious, spiritual, spontaneous, stable, strong, tenacious, thorough, trustworthy, unassuming, versatile, wise, witty, youthful.

Read through the traits you circled, picking out those you consider the most important to you and the ones that are probably most important to him.

Look especially for those about which he has the most insecurity or self-doubts. This will help you care for him in a way that will build him up in the areas most in need of strengthening. For instance, if he doubts his strength, praise him when he's strong. If he absolutely is never going to be physically strong, then point out he is strong mentally and that is what is important to you.

Most men want to hear things about themselves that say they are masculine. Look for his best traits and tie them to his masculinity. For example, if he is very calm, say how wonderful it is to have his calm, manly strength around. If he is very energetic, say how wonderful it is to have all his male energy around.

He may be very good with his hands and feel confident in his skills in his workshop. He may also be successful in his work, but never feel that he has achieved what his father did. He may compare himself unfavorably with someone else, never feeling satisfied with any of his career accomplishments. He would certainly like to hear you say that you were awed by his skill with a band saw, but it wouldn't be nearly as valuable as your comments about how much he's done and how proud you are of his accomplishments. He may wave your comments away, but if you persevere, he might say, "Do you really mean it?" Then you know you've hit the bull's-eye—a sore spot in need of healing words.

Remember, how you make him feel will determine to a great extent how he feels about you. Make him feel wonderful when he is with you and he will love you forever. If you make him feel insecure about himself, don't be surprised if he is suddenly interested in another woman who *can* produce this magical feeling in him.

On the lines below, write down the traits that are the most important to you and those probably most important to him. Put one trait on each line.

_____

_____

_____

_____

_____

_____

_____

_____

_____

_____

_____

_____

_____

Now add specific details to each of these traits to make your positive feelings about him concrete and uniquely applicable to him. For example, if you listed "strong," you might add "never defeated by a project," "muscular," or "the man you'd most want to be with if you were lost in the woods."

When you're working on physical traits, think in terms of the five senses. For example, if you like his mustache, you could comment on its sexy tickle when you kiss him or its shiny red-brown color.

Here are a few top items from some sample lists.

Julie's list about Bob:
   great wavy hair
   sexy muscular legs
   clever at business
   organized
   spontaneous

Rita's list about George:
   healthy-looking
   calm in the rough times
   capable ally
   a great steady provider
   can fix anything

Carole's list about Allen:
   wonderful green eyes
   big muscular chest
   terrific horseman
   sensitive and ingenious
   my best friend

Give him one compliment a day. You now have fabulous emotional nourishment to feed him each day—and you'll come up with more as you go through life if you keep your radar attuned to positives about him. Keep this information about him handy. This is a source of tremendous power that can carry you forward through the rest of the steps. Refer to it over and over to refresh your memory about all the nice things that you can say to him. In so doing you will also feel more love for him.

The secret from here on is to *express* these traits to him, feeding him the nurturing you've just created. It does him little good if you do this exercise and fail to follow through in action, though thinking positive things about him is always valuable.

2. Tell Him How You Feel

Now that you know what you feel, you can begin to let him know. The following are some things to keep in mind:

DON'T tell him all these things at once and then not mention anything positive for weeks. A steady diet of small things is better than a cycle of feast and famine.

DON'T just tell him in words. Notes can be just as effective, and for the man who has difficulty accepting praise or feels shy or embarrassed when it is given, putting a note somewhere where he will find it when he is alone is one way of letting him accept praise in private until you get him ready to hear more in person.

DO be willing to break the cycle. If you haven't been saying things that are nice about each other and expressing feelings of love, then someone has to start. Having you express caring in this manner will open the way for him to do the same.

DO tell him at a time when he can really hear you, not when he's concentrating on something else.

DO repeat something nice over and over. You will probably change how you say it, but you can continue to make the same point over and over, particularly if it's something you know he wants to hear.

DO consider carefully which compliments he would most like to hear. These are usually the things he feels least confident about. For example, he might feel very competent as a businessman but not competent as a lover. He needs to feel better about himself as a lover, and this is where to put your emphasis. Decide which positive things are true about him as a lover and find opportunities to say them.

DO let him hear you praise him to other people. This has double power: he knows that you think it, and now that someone else is being told the same thing, he values you more because you are spreading around such nice comments about him.

DO tell him any time you hear someone else say something you think will make him feel better—unless, of course, it's another woman who's after your man.

DO find creative ways of helping him build himself up, such as helping him accomplish an important goal. For example, if there is a way that you can help him to be successful in his work, he will find it valuable and will value you as well. Julie was able to help Bob solve several personnel problems at work. Then she used her real-estate expertise to suggest moving a store to a different site that would have more potential. Soon he began consulting her on a regular basis, and he began to value her not only as a wife but as an ally.

DO keep in mind that being competent is central to a man's self-esteem. He's probably more sensitive to any sign of failure or error or inadequacy than you are. Therefore, being critical or pointing out when he is not competent cuts him more deeply than you may realize. For a woman, such criticism probably feels centered on just the situation of the moment. For a man it may feel as if his whole identity as a man is being challenged.

Women's sensitivity is often centered in her ability to be loved, her ability to mother, her attractiveness, as well as many other things, including her career. She has her ego eggs in more than one basket. If one basket is criticized (perhaps someone points out she has a blemish on her cheek), it may annoy her, but she probably has other areas of her life where she does feel good. A man's sensitivity is centered in his success and his competency. To challenge this is to challenge him as a man. He won't make himself feel better by saying, "Well, I'm still good-looking, I have lots of friends, and I can run a household like a top." His whole sense of himself is undermined because to be incompetent is to be less valuable as a man.

That's why he overreacts when you correct him about a detail in a story he's telling or his directions when he's driving. He's supposed to know what he's doing without error or dependency. Of course total competence is impossible to achieve, so overlook the things that can be overlooked and reinforce his expertise, his correct directions, his expert retelling of a story, and his success at work. He may act as if your praise doesn't affect him (remember the Lone Ranger), but it still counts with him. And when you criticize or correct him, make sure you use a sandwich of positives before and after to soften the blow to his ego.

For example, Rita said to George while driving to an office dinner party, "I'm always amazed at how you can find your way around so easily. I just wish you'd go slower around the curves so I wouldn't get nervous about these other unpredictable drivers. I'm looking forward to tonight and showing you off to my co-workers."

DO remember to build your own ego along the way, too. Make yourself feel good by finding the things you like about yourself. Notice your best traits and greatest accomplishments, the things that make you feel better about yourself. This is extremely important because if you don't have emotional wealth you can't distribute it to others—so take care of your own ego needs, too.

STEP 3: SHARED FUN

The third female illusion is the notion that a man wants to be with the woman he loves.

What's the Problem?

Women want to relate more closely and more emotionally than men do, and they more often want to spend time together in conversation or in other ways where the focus is more on the relationship and less on the activity.

Men, however, particularly after the courtship period, tend to want to be together, but not relating closely or as intimately, unless they are having sex. Men are inclined to focus on the activity rather than on the relationship.

This is frustrating and often hurtful to women, who interpret this avoidance of relating as a sign that their men don't want to be with them and therefore don't love them. As Rita put it, "Early in our marriage I went fishing with George, and he just sat there without saying a word. When I asked him if he wanted me with him, he said it was fine with him if I came along, but he hardly ever talked to me. I assumed he was just saying what he thought I wanted to hear. I always felt hurt, and after a while I stopped going."

What's the Truth?

In Chapter 2, we showed how boys are forced to sever their connection with their mothers and, in so doing, become in effect emotional orphans. This is part of the early male experience, which continues through life and which teaches boys to avoid close relationships and not to be like girls, who relate more closely and emotionally to each other.

The adult outcome of this is that men become intensely focused on women as the ones with whom they want to reunite and with whom they can heal their original and ongoing wound. At the same time, this early hurt, as well as adult male training, keeps men from wanting to unite too closely or be too vulnerable or seem too female.

A man, therefore, has the drive to merge and be healed, but this is counteracted by the drive to protect himself and to be independent and separate.

As a result, many men reach a compromise between these two needs, a strategy we call *proximity sharing*—they want to share the same space or activity with their partner, but they want to relate minimally.

This means, for example, that a man will want to watch TV or go to a movie or play golf or fish—activities where people can be together but where they usually don't talk to each other or relate very intimately. He will also avoid those activities where there is a need to relate closely or emotionally or to share many of his thoughts and feelings.

So we can see that a man's desire to be with his partner but to avoid emotional closeness does not result from a lack of love. It is a consequence of his desire to protect himself and to maintain his separateness and his maleness. However understandable this may be, it still leaves a woman feeling as if she's in an emotional desert where her man no longer loves her.

She may complain about this, feeling hurt, disappointed, and angry. Sooner or later this will translate into her protecting herself by pulling away from him emotionally, and then the sex-love erosion disease will take hold, moving the couple toward marital coma or divorce.

What Can You Do?

1. Find a Common Interest

An essential step toward solving this difficulty is to find activities you can enjoy together. That's not to say that couples should do everything together. But couples who fail to have shared activities are like two people trying to have a conversation without having anything to say to each other; their intentions may be good, but they don't have sufficient raw materials to work with.

Finding activities to share can revive the couple's interest in each other and in enjoying and sharing life. Activities provide a source of communication and intimacy, a basis for being together, for fun, for discussion, and for good memories. Having a good time together can create a bridge of shared positive feeling. Nurturing this bond between a couple also promotes warm, caring feelings for each other that will translate into a better relationship, more emotional satisfaction, and as a result, more love and better sex.

In Step 3 of the man's program, your partner is asked to identify activities you can share as a couple and which would be fun for both of you. Your part in this step is to help him accomplish this task.

Work with your man to identify activities you can both enjoy. Frequently it is difficult for couples to find activities they can share, and they resort to the easy solution of watching TV. Some television viewing is fine, but as a constant diet, it lacks nourishment.

Instead, perhaps you could take short walks together, listen to music, go to a museum, take up photography, go to classic car shows, or volunteer at a local hospital. Maybe you could take up tennis or swimming or golf; maybe you could play Scrabble or Monopoly or go dancing. Perhaps you could take a class in painting. Maybe you could take sailing lessons or go to the park or the zoo on a regular basis. Any activity you both enjoy can add new life and zest to your relationship and to you as individuals. Break out of your daily routine, especially the routines where you are together without interacting.

At first activities may be difficult to identify. Don't give up. Be creative. Try to think about each of your interests and find a common ground. What areas of interest do you have that overlap? Use these to turn them into a shared activity that enriches you as a couple.

Julie and Bob both like the water, so they started swimming together. While they swam at different speeds, it was still something they shared and enjoyed. They decided to build their next vacation around swimming and went scuba-diving in the Caribbean. Julie was also interested in photography, and together they took up underwater photography. After their Caribbean trip and their discovery of this common interest in photography, they started going to camera shows together, buying equipment for their hobby whenever they could afford it. They mounted their underwater photographs and entered them in contests. What started as a swim together developed into a fascinating, invigorating source of excitement for them as individuals and as a couple.

2. Schedule Activities Together

After you've identified one or more possible activities, make sure they happen. Schedule each activity on your calendar in the kitchen and decide together what you need to do to make it happen.

After each activity, plan what you'll do next time. Don't drop the ball after just one outing. If one event doesn't work out well, come up with another idea that might work out better. Don't give up. Persevere. Overcome the obstacles in your path. Eliminate the roadblocks.

After Rita and George failed at fishing together, they felt they had nothing in common. George didn't want to do anything at first. Rita kept bringing up different ideas, including dancing, but George turned these down, too. She began to despair, feeling that there was nothing they could share together, until she began to consider why he was turning down her ideas. He would say he didn't have time or they couldn't afford it, but she knew none of this was really true. She'd wanted most to go dancing, and in considering this again she realized that George didn't really know how to dance. He was embarrassed on the dance floor, especially if she tried to teach him in public. The answer came in a flash: Why not enroll in a ballroom-dancing class at the local adult school?

At first George balked, but he finally agreed. Rita couldn't believe it was so easy to overcome his hesitancy once she understood the reason. They started with a beginning class and kept at it. They began to take other classes at adult school and branch out into other areas, but they kept up with the dancing, attending a special ballroom dance session at a local club every Sunday night. They began to revive their relationship, sharing more and more together until they were never bored, because they now had seemingly endless subjects for discussion when they were alone. At first, Rita had to be the one who got them to the activities. She had to get the information and make the suggestion and generally make it happen. After the first few times, however, George started looking forward to the outings and began doing some of the legwork himself. Rita learned not to force an activity that wasn't going well. She recalled an archery class where things went badly for George in the first class and worse in the second. "If I had forced the issue, it might have turned him off to classes altogether. Instead, we enrolled in a painting class, and one night they had nude models. George is so prim and proper, but he actually surprised me by sitting in the front row and painting away. And talk about an enlivening experience! George took me home, and we made love like we hadn't in years. It was so wonderful. It was the turning point for us as far as really trying to work on our relationship."

Classes, such as the ones Rita and George became involved in, are only one possibility. Look in local papers for ideas. Ask friends and relatives for things that they've heard people do. Keep your eyes open for possibilities. Experiment. Try plays, movies, or different kinds of music. If you go to a concert and he hates it, that doesn't mean he wouldn't like jazz or pop rock instead. Keep trying different things until you come up with something you can do together. And let the search be fun. You *both* have to enjoy it or it's not the right activity for you as a couple.

Remember, there is a whole world of activities out there but someone must get the ball rolling. Most people find it too easy to slip into the habit of hanging around the house and watching television. They have to learn to be constantly on the lookout for things to do together.

The favorite shared activity of Dan and Melissa is horseback riding in the mountains, dressing up in cowboy duds and trotting through the hills. It's great exercise and, for them, nothing is quite so satisfying as a trip into nature. But they also have other activities. When they had another child recently and couldn't be away from home for so long, they began to find things closer at hand. Tending an extensive rose garden in their own backyard has become a shared activity. They also found an elegant resort near their home where they go to listen to the piano player, who willingly plays all their romantic favorites. It's become their own special romantic hideaway.

Another couple discovered a common interest in showing and breeding cats and dogs. A third couple started bicycling together. They found out about great trails over which they could ride their bikes. This gave them hours of exercise and fun and more hours of planning for their next bike trip and talking about the ones they had been on.

You and your partner might enjoy traveling together, spending time planning your next trip, and reading aloud to each other about places you plan to visit.

3. Make the Best of Silent Proximity

Proximity sharing is frustrating as a steady diet, but once you begin to do other things, you'll find that watching television together can be very satisfying sometimes.

Let him have the silent proximity he desires, but turn it to your own advantage. While you are with him, instead of feeling frustrated because he's not talking to you, let him have his separate space while you focus on your heartfelt love and caring. He can be quiet, but you can practice the heartwarming exercise described in Step 6. In this way you will both have some of what you both want.

STEP 4: WORDS OF LOVE

The fourth female illusion is that if a man loves a woman he'll take the time to understand what she's saying.

What's the Problem?

How many times have you said something to a man and been misunderstood? Perhaps he understood your words but didn't understand what you meant. Misunderstanding each other's meaning is a major source of difficulty between men and women. This often leads to more serious problems between a man and a woman, which might have been avoided.

How can you solve a highly charged communication problem when you don't even understand its source?

What's the Truth?

Most men and women don't disagree nearly as often as they think they do. Actually, much disagreement is a result of misunderstanding each other. They don't realize this because they both speak the same language. They therefore believe they understand each other and just don't like what they hear. The truth is they don't understand each other and would like what they heard much better if they did.

The barrier to understanding is that men and women often attach different meanings to certain words and phrases. These different meanings are based on their different styles, points of view, and conditioning. Sometimes it seems that men and women even speak different languages: MaleSpeak and FemSpeak.

For example, let's say you are a passenger in a car traveling on a freeway where you are more familiar with the area than the driver. As you are nearing your destination you may say, "You can take that exit. It will get us there faster." If the driver is another woman, she is likely to interpret these words as advice that is intended to help her, and she will probably take it. If the driver is a man, however, he may accuse you of backseat driving and remind you that he knows where he is going.

Instead of interpreting your words as helpful advice, he may assume that you think he is incompetent and that he needs you to keep him from making a mistake. In MaleSpeak, you have just called him stupid and incompetent, and since he is aware that a man gets respect and love through being competent, he thinks you're saying he is unworthy and unlovable. This leaves him even more isolated and separated than he already was.

This may sound hard to believe, but it is frequently true. It only seems strange because his interpretation of the woman's comment is so different from her intended meaning.

If he understood that she really meant to be helpful and was actually showing her love by trying to help, and if she understood that he felt attacked and criticized and unlovable as a result of the comment, the entire misunderstanding wouldn't have occurred at all.

Instead, every day millions of couples arrive at their destinations angry because of a lack of communication that isn't likely to be cleared up and will undoubtedly recur later, causing even greater miscommunication, hurt, and separation. It feeds the sex-love erosion disease.

Take another example: you run into an old friend one afternoon and spend a pleasant few hours catching up on old times and old friends. That night over dinner you happily relate to your partner all the events that have happened to your friend since you last saw her.

Another woman would probably be very interested, nod frequently, and ask questions about the story and about your old friend. But if your listener is a man he is likely to show little interest and even, after a time, become annoyed. "Why are you so interested in all this gossip?" he might ask.

You are hurt by his comment. You aren't gossiping, you're just trying to tell him about someone who is important to you and to have a pleasant conversation with him. Why does he have to be so rude? Why does he call you a gossip?

The truth is that, for men, the purpose of talking is much different than it is for women: men talk to convey information, not simply to relate. This causes men to make direct statements and get right to the point. And since a man's self-esteem is always shaky, he must find ways to express things that reflect positively on him, making him seem competent and successful. So in keeping with this male style, which includes intimacy avoidance, a man is inclined to use few words and to speak with the specific purpose of communicating something he considers worthwhile enough to put into words, something that often contains a hidden message about his competency.

By contrast, while a woman will also talk to convey information, she is also inclined to use conversation to express herself, her dreams, her hopes, her fears, and her problems.

As a result she will enjoy the verbal exchange itself. Brevity, or the simple conveying of information, may not be a goal at all.

FemSpeak, therefore, contains a flow of words that, like poetry, is designed to convey feelings, images, closeness, and sharing.

MaleSpeak, on the other hand, is briefer, more logical and intellectual, designed to convey information, solve problems, and get to the point. It is also useful in transmitting the man's self-reassurances that he is competent and successful.

Looking at male and female communication this way, it's easy to see why men and women so often have difficulty. If a woman doesn't convey any useful information, a man doesn't understand why she is talking and regards her conversation as meaningless gossip. He doesn't understand that for her the information was far less important than the chance to relate to him through talking.

When your man calls your conversation meaningless gossip and seems not to want to talk, you feel that he is rejecting not only your words but also your attempt to relate to him. He is therefore rejecting you as a person.

This difference in language makes communication often frustrating and infuriating for both sexes and causes endless and needless arguments.

Women find MaleSpeak very frustrating in its lack of sharing, intimacy, and feeling. It seems like a cold language, and women often hear it as a lack of caring and love. What's his problem? Why doesn't he ever want to really talk? they wonder. Doesn't he ever *feel* anything? Doesn't he really care? Women know that if they were to behave toward him the way he often does toward them, it would mean they didn't care. So they falsely assume it is the same for men. A woman, of course, may sense intuitively that he is somehow different, but since the difference is unclear, she remains puzzled and frustrated, continuing to believe the myth that men don't care and are unemotional.

From the man's point of view, FemSpeak goes on interminably in a droning, pointless flow of words that may irritate and frustrate him. He doesn't understand why a woman would take thirty minutes to express what could be conveyed in three minutes of carefully chosen words. He is likely to be annoyed that she is using so many words to get to the point when there is no real point, or when the point could have been stated in one or two sentences.

Then he gets angry and says something critical, which makes you furious. You feel that he is ridiculing you and that he doesn't understand you. Or he may tune you out and simply not listen to you, so you feel ignored and you end up complaining, "He just doesn't listen to me," all the time feeling that he also must not love you, since if you weren't listening to him that's exactly what it would mean.

In truth, since a man talks to convey information and the woman is not necessarily conveying any particular information, he feels justified in not listening at all. A woman, however, when she discovers this, feels unloved and rejected without realizing that he wasn't rejecting her; he was rejecting the seemingly superfluous words.

Another communication problem comes when a man tries to say he loves a woman but the woman doesn't get this message.

In Step 1 we discussed how having their laundry done and their meals prepared is a way that men see themselves as being cared for. Not surprisingly, then, men tend to express love in much the same way—by changing the oil in your car or by fixing the washer. The problem is that a woman doesn't interpret these actions as signs of love.

If a man says, "Your hair looks beautiful," a woman hears it as a sign of his love. But if he says, "Honey, I fixed the sink," she will not hear it as a sign of his love. A woman sees the action of fixing the sink as a chore that he is responsible for, just as she sees running the household as her responsibility. She doesn't see either one as an expression of love. She would prefer a hug, a kiss, an "I love you," or a compliment.

The truth is, however, that for him, fixing the sink *is* a sign of his feelings for her as well as a way of demonstrating his competence and therefore his lovability. That's why, after a man has spent the weekend mowing the lawn and doing chores, he may be furious when his wife says, "You never say you love me." He feels that she has overlooked everything he has done, that his efforts are unappreciated, and that his competency doesn't matter to her.

Women miss these expressions of love because they don't understand MaleSpeak and therefore don't hear the "I love you" that he has tucked in among the wrenches, the pipe dope, and the lawn mower.

He says, "What does she think I'm doing by going to work every day and bringing home my paycheck? What does she think that means?" He feels taken for granted, used.

This connects to yet another source of miscommunication between men and women—the whole issue of feelings. Often a woman will ask a man what he did today. Usually what he says is very informational and has little to do with feelings.

One woman related a conversation like this with her husband who was a personnel manager of a large firm. She asked him how his day went. "I fired a woman," he said. "She'd been late too many times, and the night manager wanted her out. Then I looked through some current applications and found some people to interview who seemed to have the right stuff. By five o'clock I'd found another woman without any day-care problems to take her place."

"Jim is just so cold about everything," his wife said. "I mean he hires and fires people like they're robots. He just has no feelings at all."

When Jim was interviewed and questioned more deeply, however, he expressed very deep feelings about letting employees go. He said, "I know it's a dirty rotten thing to fire someone, but it's the old saying, someone has to do it and the someone is me. I don't like it; in fact sometimes I hate it. That girl, for instance, couldn't help being late and I knew it, but it was my job to fire her and so I did. I've got a family to support and a man does what he has to do."

Jim was actually very upset about what he had to do, but he didn't discuss his feelings with his wife. He was doing something he didn't like because he wanted to keep supporting the family. On some level, then, he was sacrificing himself for her. Yet, far from seeing this, she saw him as uncaring and unemotional.

This problem is a typical result of male communication. Men will stick to the facts and will speak of solutions rather than problems. Men will think about a problem, and when they understand it as well as they're able, they may talk about the solution. Thus Jim didn't discuss his concern for the woman or how it had upset him to fire her, nor did he mention the efforts he had made to try to improve the situation. He simply told his wife the facts, the outcome, and she assumed that was all there was for him.

Men also tend to avoid discussing personal problems because they think it reveals a weakness. Consequently, when women want to talk FemSpeak to solve an issue, men want to use MaleSpeak to get to the point, not discuss the emotions, but focus on coming up with a rational solution. This male language also allows a man to maintain his armored distance and emotional anesthesia. The limited talking lets him avoid emotion while simply conveying information in a logical manner.

Since neither men nor women understand this difference in their use of language, problems arise that are never resolved because the misunderstanding is so deep and so confusing that they can't even begin to sort it out. It's frightening to think how many relationships have undoubtedly been derailed by misunderstandings of this sort. If they happen often enough, the partners may end up furious at each other without any hope of discovering the source of the difficulty and straightening things out.

If a man and woman are to have a good relationship that doesn't get bogged down in unnecessary and destructive misunderstanding, they must learn to talk to, and to understand, each other.

What Can You Do?

1. Learn MaleSpeak

Begin learning MaleSpeak by trying to communicate with your partner in his terms. Listen to how much he talks and how much is just relating and how much is conveying information. Then try to match him in about the same proportions. If your man speaks entirely in informational terms you will need to be more informational yourself. If he does some talking simply to relate, then you can do more of this. Generally try to use fewer, more carefully chosen words that convey information, logic, and action.

If he asks how your day went, give him a short and sweet answer that conveys information, that makes a point, and discuss what you're going to do. This will be less annoying to him and will make him start listening to you again.

Tell him what he does well that you appreciate (Step 2) and put into MaleSpeak your appreciation of his accomplishments, contributions, and caring: "Thanks, dear, for working so hard. You've certainly helped us to have a comfortable life when so many people have so much less than we do."

Remember his point of view and how he will interpret what you say in terms of his male values. Be very careful with criticism, particularly criticism that he might hear as saying that he is incompetent or unsuccessful as a man.

2. Teach Him FemSpeak

FemSpeak is a vehicle for conveying the Inner World, and with patience you can teach him to speak it.

He can start learning by reading Step 4 in the man's program, and you can help him by translating his "love actions" into words of love—FemSpeak. This is particularly effective with men who don't see their love actions as signs of love so much as they see them as part of their male duty. It's important to make him conscious of his love actions, however. If you let him know that you see what he does as a sign of love, he will eventually realize it is and, in time, come to see himself as a loving person. He will, in effect, learn to connect his caring and helping actions and thoughts with the emotions they actually represent. This will help him to learn to express his love more directly in words and in physical shows of affection.

Wait until he does something you know is meant as an expression of caring for you. Perhaps he stays late at the office hoping to get a promotion so you can buy a new car, or he fixes the sink on his day off. Now translate his actions into FemSpeak: "Thanks, honey, it means a lot to me when you work hard for us. I know it's your way of telling me you love me, and I really appreciate it."

When he gives you money or spends money on something that is at least in part for you, say something like, "Thanks for the money, honey. I know it's one way you tell me you care and love me." Combine this message with a kiss and a hug, and you'll make great progress toward getting him to connect his helping actions to his loving emotions.

Eventually you may even hear him speak FemSpeak. Bob finally spoke it to Julie: "Here's some money for you to buy a new dress for the party on Saturday night. You look so beautiful when you're dressed up, and I want you to have it so you feel good about yourself. I love you, you know."

Julie said that tears came to her eyes when he said this. She'd been wanting Bob to say things like that to her, but it wasn't until she realized he simply spoke a different language that she saw what the problem was. He had been saying he loved her, but he'd said it in a different language. He was saying "I love you" every time he worked late and every time he spent a weekend poring over the books and interviewing employees and doing all the other things that had made him successful. Using the technique of connecting his actions to his feelings of love, Julie taught him over several months how to speak her language.

Take the things he says in MaleSpeak and translate them into FemSpeak. For example, watch football with him and talk about the beauty of the wide receiver flying through the air to catch a pass, or comment on the thrill of watching a great basketball player leaping and sinking a basket that doesn't even seem possible to make. In this way you can share his interests and penetrate his male domain, infiltrating his world and building a bridge to the Inner World, the key to the loving relationship that you desire.

Try talking to your man in the dark. Some men feel more comfortable talking about personal and emotional things when they have the cover of darkness. (This might be compared to some women preferring to make love in the dark). Also, for some the end of the day when they are tired and more relaxed may be a good time to initiate nice, feeling discussions. You can get him in the habit of doing this if you keep your talks brief, pleasant, and positive. Let him get used to communicating more intimately in as safe an environment as you can create.

Remember that pushing too hard can backfire. Keep the long run in mind, and be aware that putting feelings into words can be painful for some men. Take his woundedness into account.

Ask him questions to draw him out: "How did your day go?" Then follow up with feeling questions about how the story or information he just told you affected him and made him feel (more about this in Step 6). "How are you getting along with your boss?" or "How are you handling all the stress at work? Can I give you a shoulder massage to help you unwind?"

Keep in mind that men and women are simply different; one is not better than the other. And there is obviously great value in maintaining the differences. What a loss if we all were the same! So just as women don't want to be forced to give up their Inner World emphasis, neither should men be forced to give up their Outer World focus. Women have modified their female style during the past thirty years, and now they want a modification of the male style.

Women need to appreciate that there is value in men being less emotional than women, in emphasizing strength and success, in expressing their warrior spirit. Men desire relationships, but they have other high priorities as well. These differences must be taken into account and allowed to exist. When women listen to MaleSpeak, they should appreciate that despite all the problems that these differences create, they also create excitement and electricity between men and women. Men want control and power, autonomy and independence, thinking and action and sexuality. That is not to say that men totally avoid feeling and relating and closeness. They simply emphasize different elements of life, and it is valuable that they do.

Avoid criticizing your man personally. Use informational language; speak in terms of the actions you dislike rather than what's wrong with him. For example, avoid saying, "You don't talk enough," or "You don't help enough with the kids." Instead, try to put things in terms of yourself and what's important to you: "It's really important to me that I hear what you think," or "It's really important to me that you help with the kids, especially at bedtime." This way, you are not putting him on the defensive, and thus you avoid an almost automatic conflict. Try saying, "I love it when you talk to me," or "I get interested in sex when you do the things that turn me on."

Put things in terms of yourself and what you want. Also let him know what he could be doing more of so that things would work out better. You can combine these statements with reminders about what he has done that worked well. This is helpful, valuable communication, as opposed to angry, inhibiting communication.

Instead of "You don't really love me," say, "I really like it when you give me a hug and a kiss when you come home after work."

Instead of "You never think of anyone but yourself," say, "I feel so much better when you call me if you're going to be late from work."

Instead of "You're self-centered," say, "I like it when you think about me and the kids."

Instead of "You only care about what you think," say, "I appreciate it when you take the time to listen to my opinion."

Learn to tell him what is most important to you. One of the problems that men and women have in communicating concerns the fact that one doesn't understand how important something is to the other. For example, men in therapy often say, "I just didn't know how *really* dissatisfied she was with the way we were getting along. Sure, we had fights, but I never expected her to leave me." Men are frequently shocked when their wives leave and they get divorced. They heard her say she was upset, but things always seemed to settle down and they assumed that meant things were okay. For him they were, but not for her.

This happens because in the male culture two men can have an argument, even a physical fight, and still remain best friends. On the sports field, for example, two men can curse at each other, call each other names, and five minutes later have a beer together. Men are used to keeping their relationships in spite of conflict.

This is one reason they are so surprised when a woman is ready to leave them over a fight. They don't realize that when two women have a fight, they may never speak to each other again.

This is why conveying how you really feel and what is important to you is so vital.

One way to handle his inability to grasp how important something is to you is to rate its value to you.

A man may be better able to get the message if you let him know the level of priority at which you're talking. You can also use this device to minimize conflict.

For example, you can say to him, "Please fix the sink. You said you would, and it's important to me, maybe a seven or eight on a scale of one to ten." Or you might say, "Listen, Bob, I want you to understand this. If we don't start to get along better, we're not going to make it together. This is a ten on a scale of one to ten. Please think about this, because the problem is not going away and we need to improve or we're going to fall apart."

Women and men often have disparaging thoughts and feelings about each other that are based on normal male-female misunderstandings. Do your best to eliminate this source of unnecessary conflict and create closeness to each other through understanding and words of love.

STEP 5: THE SIX WOMEN MEN WANT

The fifth female illusion about men is that men are impossible to please.

What's the Problem?

As we've seen, men and women are very different. These differences may, in some ways, be complementary, but they often lead to misunderstanding and interfere with the potential harmony.

From a woman's point of view, men seem to want their women to be everything. They want them not to talk, but to be interesting; to be feminine and sweet, but also to make it in the competitive male world; to care for the kids and the house, but also to be out earning a paycheck.

Women can and have made lists of inequities and incongruities, but the bottom line is that it feels impossible to be everything a man needs.

What's the Truth?

Just as women want men to fulfill four different roles—hero, friend, playmate, and lover—men want women to fulfill six different roles—lover, cheerleader, mom, best friend, animal tamer, and competent adult—although each man's desires will vary to some extent from other men's. Let's look closely at these six roles.

1. *Lover:* Men have a strong sexual drive. To meet their physical needs they want a willing and eager lover who will have sex only with them. Men may fantasize about having sex with different women, but most men are realistic enough to know the impracticality of this. They want their woman to be inventive and exciting enough to make up for this lack of variety.

2. *Cheerleader:* Men need someone to encourage them and keep them going in the midst of their personal battle for success and self-worth. Since men have difficulty forming close relationships, it's especially important for them to know someone is in their corner cheering them on in the face of all the obstacles they meet.

3. *Mom:* A man wants someone to look after him. He wants a nurturer who will make him feel cared about and who will pick up where his own mom left off when he was a boy (though now that he's a man, he shouldn't be made to feel like a boy). He wants a mom who will look after him when he's sick, help him find his keys, and (though it's never discussed) heal the woundedness his male training has inflicted.

4. *Best friend:* A man wants an ally with whom he can share the burdens of daily life. He wants a confidante and a good adviser who can help him handle problems, make decisions, and cope with daily existence. Also, he wants a best friend to have fun with doing things they both enjoy.

5. *Animal tamer:* Men depend on women to be the bridge from the raw animal inside them to the rest of humanity. Woman is the social glue, the bridge to other couples, the one who invites, entertains, and develops relationships with others. Some men also want someone to teach them social graces, help choose their clothes, decorate their home, and generally make their house a home. Men are often caught between wanting this closeness and fighting it. Men know they're supposed to remain untamed, and to be tamed seems, at least in part, to mean losing their combat-readiness.

   But deep down men know the necessity and value of harnessing their animal power and channeling it constructively, so men seek this out more powerfully than they resist it. This is one reason so many men are so eager to marry and to remarry after divorce or widowhood: they don't want to be alone in their cold caves.

6. *Competent adult:* Men also want a competent, capable, adult who is worthy of respect and who can be depended upon and admired. Whether she is a housewife or a career person, she is capable, competent, and effective. He wants to feel proud of who she is as a person. He may take pride in her crocheting and cooking, her child-rearing skills, her degrees, or her career accomplishments; this enhances his ego and makes him feel that he can take pride in her and rely on her. It is also a relief for him to know that she is dependable and capable, someone with whom he can share life's responsibilities.

What Can You Do?

1. Find Out What He Needs

A first step is to discover specifically what he wants you to be, what you are, and how you can come closer to being the woman of his dreams, just as he is busy trying to become the man of your dreams.

As every woman is different in terms of which of the four male roles she wants in her man, so are men different in their idea of what is most important to them in a woman. Your man, for example, may be beginning his career or be in a highly competitive one. He may want you most of all to be a cheerleader, helping him to achieve. He may be working so hard that his sexual interest is not particularly high and having an exciting lover is not so important.

For another man, of course, it might be just the opposite. Also, at different times of his life he may need or want different things. A younger man may be more interested in a lover and a cheerleader; a mature man may be more interested in a best friend and competent adult. To make this most helpful and specific to you, let's try to determine exactly what he wants and where you stand in relation to this. You can then make the changes he wants, just as he is making the changes you want.

SIX WOMEN ASSESSMENT

Rate yourself on where you are now and on where you would like to be. 1 = rarely or very little; 2 = sometimes or moderate; 3 = usually or very much

	Where I Am Now	Where I Want to Be
AS A LOVER		
I enjoy sex with my man	_____	_____
I like variety in lovemaking	_____	_____
My natural sexual potential is readily available	_____	_____
I look forward to our lovemaking	_____	_____
I try to satisfy him sexually	_____	_____
TOTALS AS A LOVER	_____	_____
AS A CHEERLEADER		
I help him feel good about himself	_____	_____
I encourage him to be successful	_____	_____
I'm in his corner cheering him on	_____	_____
He knows I see him positively	_____	_____
I like to build his esteem	_____	_____
TOTALS AS A CHEERLEADER	_____	_____
AS A MOM		
I take care of the boy in my man	_____	_____
I nurse him when he's sick	_____	_____
I help heal his wounds	_____	_____
He knows he can depend on me	_____	_____
I keep his best interests in mind	_____	_____
TOTALS AS A MOM	_____	_____
AS A BEST FRIEND		
We're good buddies and partners	_____	_____
I'm his confidante and adviser	_____	_____

	Where I Am Now	*Where I Want to Be*
We share responsibilities	_____	_____
We share good times	_____	_____
I help him handle problems	_____	_____
TOTALS AS A BEST FRIEND	_____	_____

AS AN ANIMAL TAMER

I create a bridge between him and other people	_____	_____
I help him be more socially adept	_____	_____
I make our house a home	_____	_____
I help him harness his power and channel it constructively	_____	_____
I help him control his temper	_____	_____
TOTALS AS AN ANIMAL TAMER	_____	_____

AS A COMPETENT ADULT

He feels proud of me as an adult	_____	_____
I contribute to the family's welfare	_____	_____
I'm dependable and capable	_____	_____
He knows he can rely on me	_____	_____
I have skills he values	_____	_____
TOTALS AS A COMPETENT ADULT	_____	_____

Now have him rate you so you can understand how well he thinks you fulfill the six roles for him. This is important in helping you decide what changes you could be making to help him feel more satisfied.

Rate your woman as you see her now and on where you would like her to be: 1 = rarely or very little; 2 = sometimes or moderate; 3 = usually or very much

	Where I See Her Now	Where I Would Like Her to Be

AS A LOVER

She enjoys sex with me   _____   _____

She likes variety in lovemaking   _____   _____

Her natural sexual potential is
readily available   _____   _____

She looks forward to our
lovemaking   _____   _____

She tries to satisfy me sexually   _____   _____

TOTALS AS A LOVER   _____   _____

AS A CHEERLEADER

She helps me feel good about
myself   _____   _____

She encourages me to be successful   _____   _____

She's in my corner cheering me on   _____   _____

I know she sees me positively   _____   _____

She likes to build my esteem   _____   _____

TOTALS AS A CHEERLEADER   _____   _____

AS A MOM

She takes care of the boy in me   _____   _____

She nurses me when I'm sick   _____   _____

She helps heal my wounds   _____   _____

I know I can depend on her   _____   _____

She keeps my best interests
in mind   _____   _____

TOTALS AS A MOM   _____   _____

	Where I Am Now	*Where I Want to Be*
AS A BEST FRIEND		
We're good buddies and partners	_____	_____
She's my confidante and adviser	_____	_____
We share responsibilities	_____	_____
We share good times	_____	_____
She helps me handle problems	_____	_____
TOTALS AS A BEST FRIEND	_____	_____
AS AN ANIMAL TAMER		
She creates a bridge between me and other people	_____	_____
She helps me be more socially adept	_____	_____
She makes our house a home	_____	_____
She helps me harness my power and channel it constructively	_____	_____
She helps me control my temper	_____	_____
TOTALS AS AN ANIMAL TAMER	_____	_____
AS A COMPETENT ADULT		
I feel proud of her as an adult	_____	_____
She contributes to the family's welfare	_____	_____
She's dependable and capable	_____	_____
I know I can rely on her	_____	_____
She has skills I value	_____	_____
TOTALS AS A COMPETENT ADULT	_____	_____

Now it's time to compare the four ratings and see how they match up; this will help you more clearly decide what you could be working on to change. Transfer the totals from the above charts to the lines below.

	Where I Am Now	Where He Sees Me Now	Where I Want to Be	Where He Wants Me to Be
LOVER				
CHEERLEADER				
MOM				
BEST FRIEND				
ANIMAL TAMER				
COMPETENT ADULT				

If couples are to get along well, they need to be well matched in these areas. In other words, if a woman rates high as a mom and her man wants her to rate high as a mom, then they are compatible in this area. If she rates low as a lover and he wants her to rate high, then there is an incompatibility that is likely to translate into frustration and conflict.

2. Start Working Toward Change

The aim of this step is to figure out what you can do to have a better, more compatible balance in your relationship so that your man is happier and more satisfied and so that the two of you get along better.

From the profile totals above, decide which roles you should be working on. Use the information below to steer yourself toward change.

If the steps recommended lie ahead in the program, work your way forward, keeping the needed changes in mind.

If you need to be more of a lover, start trying to bring out your natural sexual potential, overcome any sexual suppression that is interfering, and find the physical lover within you. At the same time initiate him into the world of intimacy and sensitivity by pointing out the deeper aspects of sexuality (see Chapter 8), enabling him to have a more sensual lovemaking experience.

If you need to be more of a cheerleader, keep reminding yourself to build him up. Find ways to help him feel good about himself. Let him know you're on his side by encouraging him to feel strong and successful. Talk about the things he does well, and encourage him to tell you about any successes he has. Help identify his good points, and try to find out what his inner sense of right says, as well as what his inner heart wants. Get him involved with kids or pets. These involvements, if he has responsibility for them at all, bring out the nurturer in him. This can be very hard and uncomfortable at first for a man with no experience, but it can also be a wonderful way to help a man grow and develop a healthy nurturing side of his own personality, bringing out the hero and the father in him.

If you need to be more of a mom, emphasize the caretaking aspects of your personality with him. Love the boy in your man without making him feel belittled or weak. Care for him when he needs help. Help him grow stronger and be happy with himself, and appreciate all he has accomplished so he doesn't think you take the good things in life for granted.

Be aware of how wounded he has been in growing up, and recognize the toll this has taken on him as a man; help heal this woundedness with sensitivity and care.

Realize that by cooking and cleaning for him, you may actually help to heal the wounded, lonely boy in him who still needs good mothering. Appreciate any progress he makes from where he began, and avoid being the one to wear the pants in the family. Help him feel replenished by looking after his best interests, especially when he isn't doing this for himself.

If you need to be more of a best friend, emphasize the partnership aspects of your relationship, making sure he knows you're in this life journey together. You are equal partners who value each other and feel safe with each other. Share responsibilities, problems, and successes. Encourage him to talk about his work if he wants to, and try to help solve problems, or at least be a good listener so he feels less alone in the world. Encourage him to increase his Outer World success, while also being his partner as he moves into the Inner World of feelings and sensitivity and close relationships.

If you need to be more of an animal tamer, emphasize the strong part of yourself so that you can serve as a bridge between him and the world, helping him control and channel his powerful energies into constructive outlets. Teach him social skills so he can be more successful in dealing with other people. At the same time, make sure his warrior spirit remains strong; help him to feel his power while keeping it under control. Use the magic of clear vision to help him see himself as strong, powerful, yet sensitive and in control. Help him be a warrior who has his Inner and Outer World power under his control. Help him overcome the combat-ready aspect of his male training and learn to channel his power into constructive, life-serving directions.

If you need to be more of a competent adult, develop your own skills and strengths. Let him know you can be depended upon to follow through, to shoulder adult responsibilities, and to be an individual in whom he can take pride.

Handle money effectively, keeping spending within your budget. Make good decisions that are well thought out. For example, if you're in charge of buying a new sofa, have some clear ideas about style, color, price and stores to shop in before discussing the final decision with him. Give him the feeling that you know what you're doing and he can rely on your good judgment.

STEP 6: HOW TO DEAL WITH A MAN'S FEELINGS

The sixth female illusion about men says that a man shares his inner feelings with the woman he loves, and he wants to know how she feels.

What's the Problem?

For a woman, sharing feelings is a part of any deep, intimate relationship. It shows caring, trust, and a desire to connect that women associate with love. Women don't expect their men to share their feelings with other people, but they do expect their men to share their innermost feelings with them and to want to hear and understand the woman's feelings.

During courtship, a man will often express his love, talk about his memories and experiences, let the woman see who he is in a deeper way, and listen to her talk about her feelings. Later, however, after the relationship is established, much of his willingness to express his feelings disappears. He begins to talk to her mainly about facts, revealing very little of what he feels, often discouraging her from expressing her own deep feelings.

This can be very painful for many women. She may have fallen in love with this man partly because he talked about his feelings with her and seemed to be interested in hers. So when he stops talking about his emotions and discourages her from expressing hers, she thinks he no longer trusts or cares about her and no longer loves her.

What's the Truth?

Because men have been conditioned to avoid feelings, both in themselves and others, they often give women the message not to be emotional. They seem to think that emotions are foolish and inappropriate. One result of this common male message is that many women, like most men, have been trained by either fathers or husbands not to express emotion. These women would benefit from doing this step in the man's program as well as the woman's.

Ask a man to tell you something about himself, and he will usually speak in terms of ideas and actions—what he thought and what he did—rather than in terms women value—what he felt and how his actions were affected by his relationships with other people. If you ask a man what he did today he will tell you the facts and focus on his actions or the actions of others, while staying away from his own and others' emotions and relationships: "I drove to work, the traffic was terrible. Someone should put a traffic light on Black Mountain Road. Then I got to the office. My secretary was sick so I took my own calls and got personnel to give me a fill-in by ten o'clock. The Randall account is looking good. I made an appointment with their buyer for next Tuesday. If I can sell them, I'll definitely be in line for a promotion."

By contrast, if you ask a woman the same question, she is likely to answer in terms of feelings. Actions are important to her, too, but she will discuss them in terms of relationships and emotions: "I drove to work and the traffic was terrible. People were furious and honking. I just turned up my radio and tried to ignore it. Then I got to the office. Madeline is sick. She just had a baby, a darling little boy. But poor Madeline is having some kind of complication. She won't be in until next week, so I brought Marcie in from next door. I've given her lots of rides home and she said she wouldn't mind taking both my calls and her boss's. I'm just thrilled about how the Randall account is going. I developed a relationship with one of the buyer's assistants. It turns out we both have daughters the same age. Anyway, she is setting up a meeting with the buyer because she really thinks our products are terrific. I know how impressed my boss is going to be if I can get this account, and I get a really strong feeling from him that he'll give me a promotion if I can make this happen."

This woman was aware of her emotional reactions as well as those of others and spoke not only about her actions but also about how her relationships affected those actions. The man in this case stayed away from his emotional reactions. He talked about taking action through channels rather than looking to his relationships to help him solve problems.

This is not to say that men have no emotional reactions. Men have as many emotions as women do. The difference is that men often simply don't acknowledge their emotions, even to themselves, and they are often uncomfortable when others do so.

That doesn't mean, however, that a man can succeed in actually getting rid of the emotions. What all of us have seen in men and women alike is that we may suppress an emotion, but it just comes out somewhere else, over a different subject or in a different form.

For example, a man may not get a promotion that he felt he deserved. He may feel sad, disappointed, and vulnerable. But he suppresses these threatening emotions and may not even be aware of them. What he does feel is a sense of discontentment and frustration that he may not be able to identify and which he may turn into a more familiar emotion, frequently anger, or into some activity, frequently work.

Later, when he gets home and finds the house in disarray and children's toys all over the floor, he explodes at his wife and kids, releasing all the suppressed emotion—now transformed into anger.

This is a common occurrence. By burying and denying the emotions, the man lost control of them. His warrior spirit was partially siphoned off in the way that a side channel takes away from the power of the main river. The original emotional energy is transformed into another, more familiar emotion, such as anger, and it comes out in a different way through an indirect outlet. Had the man directly dealt with the loss of the promotion, both emotionally and in terms of action, the anger that he expressed at the disarray probably would not have come out at all, or would have been expressed in a much milder form.

There are, of course, some feelings men are comfortable with and which they do express. Excitement and the thrill of victory, for example, are commonly accepted by men. They will also feel and express pride and satisfaction, particularly over an action taken. They can also feel anger, as we know, and aggression, both feelings men have been trained to be in touch with. Sometimes men will feel sadness and fear, but they try to keep it in check as much as they can and will rarely express these emotions unless they seem perfectly justified. Happiness, joy, contentment, satisfaction, and peace of mind are not on most men's lists of frequently felt emotions.

He has difficulty with the more personal, more intimate emotions, particularly those that reveal his vulnerability. Sadness, for example, is too vulnerable a feeling for the majority of men. If something makes a man sad he is likely to take action to avoid the sadness or turn the sadness into another emotion.

When Bob and Julie's dog died, Julie cried while Bob comforted her. He said it bothered him, but they'd get another dog. When a man loses a pet that he cares about, he often will not let himself feel sad. Instead he may turn this feeling to action, as in Bob's case, or into anger. The dog had been hit by a car after escaping from the fenced backyard. Bob was really angry. He said the driver, a teenager, had probably been going too fast and maybe he should sue the kid and his family.

The man may direct his feelings away from sadness and instead be angry at whatever or whoever was responsible for the dog getting out or whoever was driving the car that hit the dog. Bob focused all his feelings on angry action and on future good feelings with a new dog.

A man may also focus on other actions, which might include scolding or punishing whoever was responsible for the dog escaping. Bob went over to the teenager's home and ended up in a shouting match with the boy and his father. They ended up deciding that the boy would buy Bob and Julie any dog they wanted (they got Chanel, a large standard poodle). Another man might have taken action by patching the fence where the dog escaped. He could also get another pet. On the other hand, he might simply bury the sadness, try to remember all the trouble the animal caused, and vow never to have another. Anything and everything to avoid feeling the pain of sadness.

A woman, on the other hand, may take some or all of the same actions, but she will also let herself mourn for her pet, because women are far less likely to avoid or suppress sadness.

Another emotion men usually avoid or bury is fear. Everyone experiences fear, but men are supposed to be in control. They have a strong need to maintain control and avoid weakness and vulnerability.

This, of course, is to be expected. How could it be otherwise? Think about how different you might be if you knew you might someday have to go off to war, or if you were responsible every day and every night for your family's defense. You would harden yourself and be prepared to defend your own life and the lives of your family even if it meant wearing some armor.

Also, if anesthesia could keep you from panicking under violent attack and if it helped you do the many less than palatable tasks men are asked to do as well as help you be accepted by others, it would only make sense for you to become anesthetized.

Boys are raised with this mind-set. They're trained to keep control and to be strong, and virtually all men have some armor and anesthesia and, as a result, some combat-readiness.

Women, as we've seen, encouraged this attitude in men, because having a powerful, combat-ready protector helped guarantee their survival and their children's. Therefore, women can't blame men for being the way they are. Women needed combat-ready men, and society has forced men to be warriors. The truth is, however, that a woman also wants her man to be sensitive, and as we end the twentieth century and social roles and rules are shifting, this call for sensitive men grows ever louder.

The trouble is, few men know what being sensitive really means and just hearing that women want them to be more sensitive puts men in a bind. They are hearing she wants more sensitivity but they know that women don't want a man to be wimpy—something they certainly don't want to be, either. The trouble, then, is understanding how to be sensitive in ways acceptable to both sexes.

Women vary in exactly how sensitive they want a man to be. For example, some women wouldn't mind a man crying over a problem he had at work or refusing to kill a roach in the kitchen. Other women would be shocked to see a man cry over anything less than a major tragedy and would lose all respect for him if he couldn't kill a roach. Each woman has to determine exactly what she means by sensitive and when sensitive is too sensitive, and of course she also needs to know just how sensitive her man is capable of being and willing to be.

There is actually a balance between strength and sensitivity considered ideal by the majority of women and men alike. The problem is that this balance is usually found only in heroes because it is so difficult to achieve.

It is often said that a true hero is not a man who isn't afraid, but rather one who experiences the fear and is able to control it. An ideal man, then, is one who is sensitive to his own feelings, who knows what he is feeling, but who is able to handle his emotions and decide how and when to act upon them. Certainly the ideal man is not so sensitive that his emotions control him. He isn't weak, and he doesn't fall apart when he needs to be strong. This man's relationship to his emotions is ideal because it allows him to be effective and sensitive at once.

A woman doesn't want her man to be overly emotional. She doesn't want him to be weak, needy, overly sexual, or dangerously angry. If something threatens him, she does not want him to dissolve in tears or be overcome by rage. She does want a man she can count on to be strong, but who is aware of his emotions and who will talk about his feelings and not belittle or criticize hers. We saw in Step 2 how you can build his strength, but how do you build up his sensitivity?

What Can You Do?

Keep in mind that making any changes in a person's ability to identify and deal with his own emotions can be very difficult, and you may accomplish the most by moving slowly and carefully. It is also important to consider just how sensitive your man is, how sensitive you really want him to be, and how much he's actually willing or able to change.

Ask yourself these questions: Do I want him to feel emotions the same way I do? How would I feel if he cried over a problem? Do I really want him to reveal to me his deepest feelings of disappointment, fear, insecurity, and vulnerability, or do I prefer that he keep these emotions to himself? Do I really want him to be in touch with my emotions and react to them, or do I just want him not to be upset or annoyed when I have them? Women vary on this, but the majority do want men to be more in touch with their loving emotions and to express more of them; they want men to be enough in touch with their emotions so that the women can express some of their emotions without fear of being made to feel hysterical or stupid.

1. Put Out the Emotional Welcome Mat.

You can help your man get in touch with emotion by putting out an emotional welcome mat.

One way of doing this is to develop an extrasensitive antenna to identify the emotion he is expressing, then labeling it for him. Start with the emotion with which he seems most comfortable. For example, many men are at ease with irritation and anger. The next time you sense his anger say, "Boy, you sound really angry." You don't have to do more than that.

He in turn may say, "Yes, I am angry," or he may need to deny the emotion. "Of course I'm not angry; it's just that Megan needs to learn not to leave her bicycle in the driveway."

If he does deny it, you can approach it from a point of logic by saying, "If that happened to me, I would be really angry." In other words, you are saying that in this situation it is logical to be angry.

He may still say, "Well, I'm not angry."

That's all right. The point has been made. If you do this often enough, he'll begin to see that indeed he is having emotions and it's okay.

Now let the subject go and move on, and avoid doing this so often that it becomes annoying to him. He should never feel as if he's being hit over the head; it's his standard that counts in this regard, not yours.

Be sure you are willing to let him express emotions; women frequently are not. Rita and George had tremendous difficulty with this exercise. As soon as Rita began identifying George's emotions for him, she discovered he specialized in anger but wouldn't really admit he felt angry. It was only after considering it carefully and watching how they interacted together that Rita discovered she was so threatened by his anger that she kept unconsciously trying to keep him from being angry by saying things like, "Now, George, Marcia didn't mean to say that," or "Calm down, dear, you'll give yourself high blood pressure."

Of course, anger is probably not an emotion that you want him to have, but by getting him in touch with this emotion you will find it easier to get him in touch with others. Therefore, try to be open even to his "undesirable" emotions and begin to label them.

After you've gotten him to acknowledge the emotions that he is most comfortable with, you can begin to work on those he is less comfortable with by proceeding the same way. If you notice he is sad or happy or feeling love, start to occasionally label those feelings for him—but remember not to overdo it.

You can speak about these emotions in terms of those things men are most comfortable with: information, logic, and action.

Information: Tell him when he seems mad, sad, scared, happy, or loving. Identify the emotion for him, saying, "Oh it's nice to see you feeling so happy today, dear," or "You seem kind of down and sad today." Familiarize yourself with feeling words that convey mild, moderate, and strong forms of emotion (see Step 6 in Chapter 5). This gives him information that will help him identify his emotions. Even if you guess wrong about his mood or if he denies the feeling, mentioning it still serves a purpose; it brings emotions out into the open and makes them seem normal and acceptable. He may even begin to wonder to himself how he is feeling after a while.

Logic: Let him know it makes sense for him to have feelings. Tell him it's normal to feel disappointed and sad when he has a setback at work; that's how human beings react when they want something and don't get it.

Help him see that it's normal for a person to feel down when he doesn't get the promotion he was banking on. It's understandable that he wouldn't want to cry when the dog dies, given all the training men get to be strong and in control, even when they're sad.

Action: Talk about how feelings can be handled. You might say, "If I felt angry like that, I would probably have shouted at him, too," or "If I felt sad about a promotion not coming through, I would certainly have gone off by myself and felt miserable for a while." Identify actions that he took or those he might have wanted to take. "I know you're mad about that teenager running over our cat. I'm really upset, too, maybe you could go talk to him and his parents. But what can you do about the sadness? It's made me feel a lot better to cry and be done with some of the feeling. Maybe you don't want to cry, but you can at least feel sad about it."

By talking about feelings in terms of information, logic, and action, you can make them more acceptable to your man, and you can also show him how to deal with his feelings constructively and let them guide his actions on a conscious rather than an unconscious level.

But what about you? Are you really ready to hear about his misgivings, fears, failings, low self-confidence, or anger? Most men don't think so; therefore, they are faced with a terrible dilemma. What is he to do with these feelings when she wants him to open up? Is she prepared to hear about his lust? His self-doubts? His rage? His deep disappointments and pain and loneliness? These are difficult questions to answer and are important, because a woman cannot just wish he didn't have those feelings. She can't expect him to share only his loving and pleasant feelings with her. If he is to open up, she must be prepared for all of his feelings to come out, even the ones that are not pretty. Emotions are a complex and difficult subject between men and women.

2. Teach Him to Feel Love

Is it really possible to teach a man to love? we hear you wondering. Can he learn to express his love to me?

Yes. Men can learn about loving feelings because they already have them inside. Many men keep those emotions just under cover or express them in ways women don't recognize as love. He undoubtedly has loving feelings for you, or you wouldn't be in a relationship; men do, in fact, marry for love more often than women do. Research has shown that men fall in love more quickly than women do, and 80 percent say they would remarry their wives because they love them.

So—this is what you do.

Your first step is to find the things he sincerely cares about and teach him to recognize when he is feeling love by pointing it out to him. When you're both standing there looking at the kids asleep, say, "Don't you just love them?"

When he's happy about his work, say, "You really love your work when it's going great, don't you?"

Or "You love to watch the L.A. Dodgers play baseball, don't you? It's nice to see you having fun."

Another way to open your man up to his feelings is to touch his heart. Wait for the right moment to do this; choose a time when he is in a receptive mode. Then point out the beauty of the sky, the smell of a rose, the look on your child's face, the ladybug on a leaf, or the colors of the sunset.

But don't just stay with your world of beauty. Go into his world of work and sports and point out the sensitive things to be seen there—the lush green of the infield, the beautiful colors in his favorite tie, the birds whistling outside the window of his office.

Remember the world you have in common. You can refresh his memory about a wonderful moment you shared by reminding him of the day your child was born or the time the two of you stood by the ocean and watched a flock of geese fly through the air. The point is to find something that touches him. Find his soft spot. In these ways you can touch his heart and awaken his sensitivity, helping him take another step toward being a warrior of the Inner World.

Try whispering in his ear: "I love you. You're a really good man." Do that once or twice a week for life.

Try just sitting together practicing the heartwarming exercise later in this section. Just feel the closeness without imposing your emotions on him, without demanding anything back. Trust in the power of your feelings; over time he will start to change.

Point him toward the world of emotions at least once each day by saying, "How do you feel today?" or "Did anything happen today to make you happy?" or "Is something bothering you today? You seem upset." The questions are part of the emotional welcome mat and point him in the direction of intimacy.

Use your shared activities as a way to encourage love and closeness while you're having fun. In the midst of having a good time lean over and whisper that you love him and have a good time being with him. Make him feel good about himself and connect this with the feeling of love by saying something true and nice about him. This will help him get more and more comfortable with love and connect it with other things that are pleasant and comfortable and safe.

Keep in mind that many men suffer from love anxiety. Not that they don't want love, they do. It's just that they are uncomfortable with the closeness and the softness that comes with these feelings and which creates such a sense of vulnerability. He will want to protect himself from this feeling, since that is exactly what is expected of him as a man. So keep the long-term view in mind and help him get used to opening his heart little by little over time.

3. Make Allowances for the Male Style of Love

Keep in mind that, because of the male style, a man's love will manifest itself in certain ways that women don't readily recognize, but those manifestations of love are valid all the same.

In most societies, love is defined in female terms. In other words, love is what women say it is and must be expressed in female terms, the way women want it to be shown. We are trying to show men how they can express their love in ways that women recognize, but it is also important for you to receive the love messages he is already giving.

One way your man says he loves you is by providing for you, by doing odd jobs around the house and by putting his skills to work to better your life together. When he carries packages for you, changes the tire on your car, or confronts an intruder in your home, he is showing his love. Even his combat-readiness is a sign of love, a very important and significant sign of love. Isn't it a sign of love, for example, that the men of nearly every generation have had to spill their blood in wars in order to keep their women and children safe? Isn't the fact that we can assume we will be protected a sign of the love our men have for us?

Learn to recognize these actions as his way of showing love. Sure, you'd rather get a hug or a kiss or be taken to a lovely restaurant for a romantic dinner, but that doesn't lessen the fact that he is saying he loves you every time he fixes a faulty light switch, mows the lawn, or destroys a bug you couldn't bear to kill.

Meet him halfway by letting him know that you realize he is showing love and that he is sacrificing his time and energy to make your life better. If you do not appreciate his efforts, you are missing an opportunity to receive his love. Reinterpret his actions as loving feelings.

Also be careful not to impose your own standards totally on him. Try to assess how much anesthesia he wants to maintain. Remember this anesthesia is also, from his point of view, one of the ways he loves you. His anesthesia prepares him to do those things that you don't have the anesthesia to do, be it killing a roach in the kitchen or killing other men in a war. You wouldn't want him to demand that you be anesthetized, so don't demand that he be totally loving in your terms. Work on loosening him up and see what happens. He may surprise you and himself.

Remember that people change little by little, not all at once. Learning to show love in a different way is something he must learn day by day, and he'll need continual ego food to keep going. So remember Step 2 and be sure to keep feeding his ego. The better he feels about himself, the better he's going to feel about you and the more likely he is to have some healing take place and be better able to open up his heart.

Keep in mind that any emotion and any sensitivity will make for less armor and anesthesia, rendering him more vulnerable. This will happen only if he feels that the environment is psychologically safe for him. That's why we suggest creating an emotional safety zone. Don't expect him to be a female clone; for many men it is a big step just to become closer and more able to appreciate your emotions. If both of you want more from him, that's great, but keep your expectations realistic.

Love is a feeling of intimacy, a oneness, a bond, a blurring of boundaries, and it threatens his very maleness, his sense of independence and separation and individuality. Love is a craving he feels deep within his soul at the same time that he runs from its threat to his sense of self.

Remember that the more deeply wounded he is the harder it will be for him to open up. A number of Vietnam vets have told us they could never allow themselves to open up again after being through combat. That is not true of all veterans, but it may be true for your man, whether he's been in war combat or not. Many boys are filled so full of combat-readiness training that they are severely wounded and find it difficult, or even impossible, to open up.

So be realistic about what you can get. With some men the best you'll get is a good provider who is willing to spend time watching TV with you. If you're committed to the relationship, you must remember that part of loving him is accepting the signs of love he can give and learning to do the best you can with what you've got.

4. Do the Heartwarming Exercise

Practice love. The Dalai Lama, Mother Teresa, and all of the other great spiritual leaders teach us this central lesson of life. It helps if we practice.

You can use this heartwarming exercise to generate an atmosphere of positive feeling toward your partner and toward your other loved ones as well. People will sense something when they're with you if you're generating a force field of love. It's like being bathed in the glow of a sunset; it makes people feel welcomed, at peace, at home.

Here's how to do the exercise: breathe and relax; feel your heart opening and visualize your man. With each in-breath, breathe in love; with each out-breath, breathe your love out into the world. Feel the glow in your heart spreading through your chest as the fire within you grows brighter with each breath you take.

Try it right now. Feel the love fill your whole body and expand beyond yourself to fill the room, as if you're the sun and the light of love is shining forth from you. Picture your man and let the light of your love shine on him, on yourself, on everyone you truly love. Don't worry about whether or not the other person is responding; just concentrate on being filled with the feeling and radiating it outward. The sun is not concerned with who receives its rays; it simply sends out its power. Similarly, allow your heart to be filled with genuine caring and love, allow it to build and fill you up, and then project it outward onto those around you. If it is hard to find your way to these feelings at first, simply practice and it will come clear in time. Practice this one minute or more each day you walk the earth.

This simple heartwarming exercise can change your life. Filling your heart with love each and every day can transform your own life and the lives of those around you, filling your world with good feeling, emotional safety, and closeness.

Be a model of love. Feel it and express it in your daily life. If you want him to feel love, you must be loving yourself. Be the love leader, the love wizard. If you don't do this for him, who is going to teach him? No one, and he'll never learn. Fill your own heart with love. This is the best way to get the love you want. If you fill your own heart with love, then you already have what you are seeking from him. It's not the same, of course, but nonetheless your heart is still filled with love.

Find ways to give, express, and feel love for him. Again, be careful not to create a hothouse atmosphere that will suffocate him and make him want to escape. Keep the long run in mind. Little by little. Day after day.

Love fosters life; it nourishes your partner and gives you the satisfaction of seeing him satisfied. Love the one you're with. And love yourself.

5. Be a Master of Intimacy

You're the master of the Inner World; you lead the way. Stand up for what you want and help it happen. Of course, many women also have problems with their feelings. If you fear your own pain or anger or sadness, you must come to grips with yourself before you can expect anything different from your man.

If you have trouble getting in touch with your own feelings, if you are numb or unsure yourself, try doing this exercise: study your emotions, write about them, chart them, try to understand the things that make you feel mad, sad, scared, happy, and loving. Think about the feelings you frequently have and about the ones you seem to avoid. Start to tune in to the ones you avoid, looking for them in your daily life. Perhaps you feel apathetic, bored, dull, uninterested in learning new things, or empty inside; this is a sign that you may be avoiding primary feelings of your own.

Study yourself. Anger is frequently a problem for women. They may hide from it or bathe in it. Better to let it bubble up and let it go. If your anger contains a message about some aspect of your life in need of changing, then try to change it.

Julie worked hard at becoming aware of her anger at Bob, trying to keep it from coming out in a destructive way. She started small, becoming aware of minor irritations. She learned to let herself have angry thoughts and feelings, to learn the lesson in the anger, and to let it go. She found that she was angry at Bob for his bad temper, his jokes that seemed condescending, and his lateness. She realized that she had more than one feeling at the same time: she was hurt by these things, but she was also angry. Her anger scared her, but she was determined to find the power in her emotions, and so she let herself feel her anger. "I'm having a great time fantasizing being really mad at Bob," she said. "Sometimes I'll say something to him, but much of the time I'll just imagine dumping his Coke on his head or yelling a curse at him. Wow! What a charge. I usually laugh and feel strong. Then I really do find the parts of him I sincerely love."

Julie found a lesson hidden in her anger: his snide remarks about women bothered her more than she had realized. She had always tried to laugh them off, but she came to see that they made her mad and she started telling him so. Bob was responsive (not all men are) and could see that she needed him to show her more respect, especially after she discussed Step 2 with him again.

If you never get angry, start to look for minor irritations or annoyances and learn to move toward this powerful emotion. This is extremely important for many women. If you have a storehouse of repressed anger and resentment, you will have a very hard time practicing love.

In addition to feeling the emotion, letting it go, and changing your situation, you can try forgiving him. Think about his woundedness. Remember that, given their emphasis on success, many men are deeply wounded on an ongoing basis, simply by failing to be successful in their own eyes. The depth of the wound depends on the relationship between a man's expectations, his potential, his view of his success, and his actual success, although his view is more important than the actual accomplishments. The bottom line emotionally is that in spite of himself he needs love and you're the only one who can give it to him, since he won't let anyone else get as close to him as you are.

STEP 7: ROMANCE: THE HEART OF LOVE

The seventh female illusion about men is that a man wants to be romantic with the woman he loves.

What's the Problem?

For women, romance and love are intertwined; they are one, or at least women want them to be. Women we interviewed consistently said they wanted their men to be more romantic and saw the lack of romance in their relationships as directly related to how much their husband did or did not love them. As one woman put it, "If Jack really cared about me, he'd be more romantic. If only romance could last forever."

What's the Truth?

While men do enjoy the excitement, mystery, and heightened pleasure of romance, the majority of men, even those who deeply love their partners, are more attuned to having sex than to being romantic.

Many men, in fact, view romance as the interest they feel for a woman they want to have sex with. And since, particularly in relationships of long standing, sex usually becomes part of a routine that is sandwiched somewhere between work schedules, chores, and the children, it often occurs without a man being romantic at all.

Ultimately men are usually happier with this state of affairs than women are. They may miss the excitement, but if the sex itself is still good, they are usually satisfied.

Women, conversely, often have sex in order to give and receive love, and when sex seems unrelated to love and romance, they begin to feel unloved or even used. A woman may feel annoyed, hurt, frustrated, rejected, or furious. She may say, "All you think about is sex," or "All you want me for is sex." When her need for love and romance goes unmet, she becomes less and less interested in having sex, which makes her man feel confused, annoyed, hurt, frustrated, and rejected.

This may be only one of the couple's problems, but sexual problems have a way of making every other relationship difficulty much worse. As we said before, when the marriage goes on the rocks, the rocks are often in the mattress. Soon both partners are failing to get what they want; they blame each other, and the situation grows worse until ultimately everyone loses as the unhappy relationship deteriorates into marital coma and divorce.

The challenge, then, is to turn this situation around so that both partners get what they want.

What Can You Do?

Men know they want more sex, and we've suggested a number of ways they can be more romantic, exciting, and loving and, as a result, get more sex. But romance, as any woman knows, is not a one-way street. It won't work if just one partner tries to be more romantic.

Every woman who wants more romance in her life needs to understand what romance is and what she can do to bring more romance into her life, by being more romantic herself and also by encouraging her mate to be more romantic and exciting, more like the man of her dreams, the kind of man she wants to make love to.

If your man is reading this book, chances are he will have some great ideas about how to be more romantic. You, however, as the other half of the team, must receive his romantic gestures in a way that encourages him so that his attempts don't end in a discouraging fizzle.

Of course, the first problem that nearly every modern woman faces is finding the time to be romantic.

Many women have to juggle a career, children, a home, and a social life. Given their work load, it's almost laughable for someone to come along and add to the list, "Now you need to be romantic."

The truth is, however, that being romantic is central to enjoying life. Being romantic means not only loving but also appreciating beauty, discovering, being curious and open to new experience, being flexible enough to do the unexpected, and being open to change. It is an attitude that brings inspiration and it means savoring life.

However, it seems that people, particularly women, now more than ever, have gotten on an endless treadmill of tasks and more tasks, of going and doing—so fast, so furiously, and with such intensity—that they don't have time to enjoy the life they are working so hard to create or even to notice that they aren't enjoying life.

Stop right now, this moment, and consider how you are spending your time.

No one can tell you what your priorities should be. But if you find that you are on an endless treadmill of more work and more juggling, and you want to get off—if you want to find more love in your life, take more time for your relationship, and be a more romantic person—then we have some suggestions.

1. Prepare Your Life for Romance

Give yourself permission to be less than perfect. Many of us have an unrealistic view of what we can and should accomplish. Many of us are literally trying to be two people. We are trying to mother and keep house, as our own mothers did, and we fail to recognize that they had only the house and the children to take care of. At the same time many of us are also trying to be as successful as our fathers were, again not taking into account that our fathers had only their careers to worry about.

To make it worse, just turn on the TV and it seems that everyone out there in the world is perfect. Television is a major culprit in promoting this erroneous and unhealthy idea. Have you ever seen a messy house on "Family Ties" or "The Brady Bunch?" Have you ever seen the female stars looking haggard, losing their temper, or being anything less than efficient and organized? What about Mrs. Huxtable on the Bill Cosby show? Here she is, the brilliant lawyer, always looking beautiful, rarely rattled, forever knowing what to say, having a wonderful sense of humor, and raising five children in a perfect house with a man who loves her dearly and where they always have time to do cute little things together.

This is the kind of model that's being beamed into our homes.

The truth is, this just isn't realistic. You can't do it all and no one else can either.

What, then, are you going to do? How do you get off the treadmill? How do you stop when everything is set in motion, when everyone is depending on you to keep going?

Take another look at the situation. Many of us get so caught up in what other people expect and want that we never ask ourselves what we expect and want. Take a look at what you really must do. Make a list of "must do's," tasks that must be done or someone's life will be jeopardized. These are the real priorities. Then see how many of these things really don't have to be done, at least by you.

For example, the family must have meals. Fine. But you don't have to cook them all. If you have a husband, if you have older children, they can help and should. We have seen situations where a woman was literally at the exhaustion level while her teenage daughter's only assignment was to empty the trash. We recently saw a woman trying to load her kids and several bags of groceries into the car. She repeated several times, "Please help load the car," but the kids kept going in one side of the car and out the other and not helping at all. To the kids it was a game, but their frazzled mom was at the end of her rope. Finally she screamed, "I can't do this anymore; I can't live like this anymore." We felt like putting our arms around her and saying, "Yes, it's impossible sometimes, isn't it? Kids, car pools, work schedules! How can anyone do it all? We understand." Like millions of other women, she had pushed herself near the breaking point trying to do it all.

Perhaps you were never required to help your mother, or perhaps you would like your children to be unencumbered by household responsibilities. But is this realistic? Ask yourself what's more important, a teenager without any responsibilities or your not enjoying what could and should be some of your best years.

Reevaluate each of your chores and see who else might be able to help out. Then make a second list. These are the "want to" chores, things that you would like to see accomplished but that are actually optional: washing the car, cleaning the house, or weeding the garden. Look at it this way: no one will die from driving in a dirty car. Or, put another way, is it worth exhausting yourself to have a clean car or a clean house? Sure, people expect things of you, but you have to set limits. Very few people will say to you, "Hey, don't bother doing the laundry, you're exhausted." By and large people will let you do as much as you will do. You are the one who has to set limits.

Remember, you don't have to be perfect. A house that is messy is not a sin, neither is buying easily prepared food rather than slaving over complex meals. Lower your standards in areas that don't really matter and save your best efforts for the important aspects of life. No one can do everything wonderfully when there is so much to do. Change the quantity of what you do where you can, and lower the quality of what you must do when it doesn't really matter.

Guilt is an enormous problem for women. Instead of feeling guilty for what you're not doing, appreciate all you are doing. Self-appreciation is a powerful source of self-nourishment, and it counteracts guilt for being less than perfect.

Years ago, the man was responsible for bringing money into the household and the woman was responsible for everything else. Now women are also responsible for making a living, but they still think they're responsible for everything else. Remember, no one can do it all. It's time to delegate and to eliminate and learn to say no.

Get outside help. If you have eliminated, delegated, and lowered your standards and you are still overwhelmed with work, it's time to get outside help. This can mean hiring a housecleaner, hiring a baby-sitter, paying to have your car washed, or sending the laundry out.

Also, get outside help with emotional problems. If you find that you are overwhelmed and for some reason nothing seems to help, it's time to get professional help from a therapist or counselor. Don't wait for things to get worse. In most cases, the sooner you get outside help, the better chance you have of solving the problems before they get worse.

Learn to put aside those problems you can't solve. Problems vary from individual to individual. How we deal with these problems is key to surviving in this hectic world. Our suggestion is that you begin dividing your problems into two categories, those you can solve and those you can't.

The solvable problems are the only ones that merit an expenditure of your energy. Worrying about something you can't change is an unnecessary drain of your precious energy. When something happens that you can't change, let it go. Say to yourself, "There's nothing I can do about this, so I'm going to set it aside and focus on something I can affect."

When you have a problem, ask yourself if worrying about it will change anything. If not, try to put it out of your mind.

Try to put a cap on how much you strive and work. Don't get caught up in trying to have more and more things, endlessly. The Buddha taught that the root of human suffering was endless desiring. Unfortunately, it seems a universal and eternal fact that no matter how much people have, they want still more.

Before you take extra time away from your loved ones to earn more money, ask yourself what is really important, the money or the time together? Enjoying life means taking time out. Take it when you can. What good is life if you spend it harried and miserable? This isn't romantic, and if you never have a moment of peace or a moment to enjoy, you're not taking time for romance.

Dare to put your relationship first. It is often impossible not to put a child, particularly a baby, first. Babies are helpless and they must have their mothers. Often, however, because we love our children so much, it is easy to make a habit of putting them first even when it isn't absolutely necessary. The problem is a woman often makes her man feel that he is in second place in every way, thus risking the very relationship that she and her children need so much.

Look at it this way. Perhaps you do end up spending less time with your child in order to spend more time with your man, but if your lack of attention to him ends the relationship, then your child will be deprived of a father and you, as a single parent, will spend even less time with that child because of the other responsibilities you will have to undertake.

Remember to let your man know he's also primary to you.

Be true to who you are as a woman. Unfortunately, it seems that the women's liberation movement didn't free women to pursue the role of being more female or womanly. Instead, it freed women to fulfill the role traditionally taken by men. We think this is an important and necessary step in achieving the respect and equality women deserve, but in the midst of this it is easy to leave one's femininity behind.

The next revolution for women is going to involve a rebalancing that will create a better relation between strength and femininity. Part of this femininity is our need for love. Love is central to our Inner World. Every woman should guard and keep and fight for love in her relationship, just as we are suggesting you fight for time away from being all things to all people so that you can be yourself and be romantic.

The actress Jane Seymour writes about the importance of being romantic and strong:

It took me a long time to have the confidence to be my feminine self—to be both strong and feminine. To be each was easy; to combine them was the problem. It was only when I came to terms with who I really was that I found a happy, stable marriage. For me, as for so many, it was hard to combine the two meanings of the word "romantic"—the search for self and the sharing. It was only when I found myself that I could share.

There is a lesson here, I think, for all women who want to be strong and feminine. Learn from my mistakes. First of all, learn to be your own person. Learn to be alone sometimes. Build up your strong, romantic self. Then you will have the strength to cope with the demands of marriage and children as well as the demands of being a woman in the twentieth century; of being expected to have a career, or a job, or at least some impressive talents.[3]

When all else fails, laugh. Laugh at yourself, laugh at the problem. Developing a sense of humor about ourselves and our lives and problems is sometimes the only way to survive. This helps you to put your problems in proper perspective. When you have a problem, ask yourself what is the worst that can happen? For instance, "Is this fatal?"

Sometimes it's easy to get wound up in relatively trivial problems. Diane says that when she was sixteen years old and feeling, like many teenagers, that she had lots of horrible problems, her mother urged her to volunteer at a local hospital as a candystriper, something she did. She found that there is no better way of understanding the true extent of one's own problems than to look at other people's. Whenever Diane felt sorry for herself—about how skinny she was or some other typical teenage problem—she would go to the hospital and see what real problems were like.

2. Put Romance Back in Your Life

Remember when you first fell in love? Part of the wonder and magic of those times was that it was all new. You didn't know what to expect from your partner or how he might react. There were all kinds of things you didn't know about him and he didn't know about you. It was mysterious. You couldn't be sure what would happen next, and there was probably also some element of danger in the situation, perhaps because you wanted to be together but weren't sure if your dream would come true.

You can put romance back in your life by restoring these elements back to your life. Here's how.

Give him reinforcement for his efforts. In the man's program your partner is learning about the romantic things he might do with you. Don't pour water on any sparks he might try to light. Add to his efforts with some of your own.

Give yourself permission to have fun. Many people treat fun as something highly suspect. Many of the people we interviewed seemed to feel that having fun was for children. Some thought it was foolish and too immature and that others would not take them seriously if they were seen to have fun.

Nonsense! It is important to have a good time in life, and giving yourself permission is the first step. You deserve it. Of course, you don't have to cavort in public. If you feel shy or feel you have an image to keep, then cut loose only in private with your partner.

Think about what you consider fun. Make a list of fun activities. Some of us who have been busy working have almost forgotten what fun is. If that's your situation, look back to your childhood. What did you think was fun then? If you loved your bike, maybe you'd still enjoy bicycling. Look at other people. What are they doing that's fun? Look through college extension bulletins. Many of them have fun activities. Give yourself permission to have a good time.

Put more spontaneity in your life. One of the things that made courtship interesting was not being able to predict what the other person would do. This spontaneity in relationships tends to fade over time as you get to know your partner and can predict with great accuracy what he will do or say on any given occasion. We've interviewed people who not only could predict how the other would respond to any given question, but would even say the same thing at the same time.

Don't let this be true of you. Do something he absolutely doesn't expect. This can include anything from having your hair done differently to painting the living room a new color. Show up at his office with a picnic. Take a different side on a political issue. Buy tickets to an event neither of you ever attended before.

Do something unpredictable once a week or once a month. One of the best ways to keep a man on his toes is not by making him jealous; it's making sure that he can never accurately predict what you will do next. Don't expect everything to be a big hit, however. One client took this advice and brought home a Persian kitten and tucked it in bed with her husband, only to find he was allergic to cats.

If you have a failure or two, just try something else. The failures in times to come will be things to laugh at together. Boredom is a far greater enemy than failed attempts at making things interesting.

Make the most of whatever happens. Don't assume too soon that something is a failure. One woman surprised her husband by taking him driving in the mountains along an isolated dirt road. A storm broke, and the flash flooding trapped them for twenty-four hours. At first the adventure seemed like a failure. But then they realized they had enough clothes to keep them warm, the car to keep them dry, and a picnic meal that included a bottle of champagne. That kept them happy. They ended up having a wonderful time and a great adventure for their memory file together.

Do something different and make it special. This can be achieved simply by adding flair to your everyday life. We all tend to fall into routines, and we need to alter some of our patterns to awaken ourselves to the energy and life we contain.

Eat breakfast outside under a tree. Serve a meal of all his favorite foods even if they don't go together. For example, perhaps he likes lobster, bean dip, and strawberries. Why not serve them all at once? It's zany, but it's different and it will serve the purpose of jerking things out of the humdrum everyday routine. He may think you are crazy. But he won't be bored. He'll find you more interesting.

Suggest an outrageous outing. Better yet, just kidnap him and take him on an adventure where even you aren't sure where you're going. Go to the harbor and take the first excursion boat available. Or go to the bus or train station and do the same. You never know where you'll end up or what the adventure will be like.

Write down the names of restaurants you haven't tried, put them in a hat, have him draw one out, and go there. Don't have any particular expectations. Just go with the flow and have fun being together.

Don't be discouraged if your man doesn't join in the fun at first. One woman made a special meal and served it on the patio by candlelight. Her husband, a very serious man, was not impressed. He was used to his routine and was not accustomed to having it varied. At first all he did was complain about the bugs and not being able to see to cut his meat. She refused to let him discourage her. Instead, she kept the conversation very pleasant and began asking him about subjects she knew he liked to talk about. Soon enough he was happily talking and enjoying himself, and at the end of the meal he suggested they do it again. The next time she did something more off-beat and took him for a ferry ride. By then he was primed to have a good time.

When you're thinking up these outings, consider what your man might have enjoyed doing as a boy. Remember also what the two of you used to do together. How did you spend your first date? Returning there could bring back a whole mood.

Do something sexy and wicked. Why not do something that's a touch on the risqué side? What about meeting him somewhere with a coat on and only your skimpiest underwear underneath? One woman we know met her husband after work dressed exactly that way. She let him catch a peek just before they had to leave the car to catch a dinner reservation. All through dinner he was almost beside himself with excitement, but the fun part was that he couldn't do anything until they got home. She told us it was almost the same feeling as a date with someone you knew wanted you but couldn't touch you until later. It was very exciting. In the restaurant, she took off her shoe and ran her stocking toes up his leg, and he almost died. By the time they got home, he was so excited he made love to her with more passion than he'd shown since they first became lovers.

Another woman greeted her husband at the door on his birthday wearing nothing but a bright red ribbon around her waist. He said she was the best present he'd ever gotten.

Make love in unusual places or in unusual ways. Get a copy of a book showing any number of positions and pick one or have him pick one, or devise a way to pick it at random.

Do something to make your bedroom more conducive to lovemaking. Line one wall or the ceiling with mirrors. Get a bigger bed. Buy some satin sheets.

Dress up for him in something wild and give him something wild to put on for you. Play out your fantasies. One woman rented a Superman costume for her man and got him to wear it. At first he felt awkward, but when he saw her supercharged reaction to him, he rented it himself the very next week.

Dress up in something virginal and Victorian. Remember that a woman with some clothes on is far sexier than a woman who is naked. Some clothes lend an air of mystery. A naked woman has very little mystery and unless you have a perfect body, a few ribbons and other things will be more attractive. Decide what your man likes most. Some men like the naughty girl image of black and red or leather. Others prefer the sweet girl-next-door image. Decide what he will like best or vary your images. Remember not to be predictable. Do something he does not expect. Do something daring, even slightly dangerous or forbidden. He may not entirely approve, but it will probably excite him anyway. Besides, men don't leave women for being sexy, unpredictable, and slightly dangerous. They leave them for being boring.

Of course all this will be more difficult if you have children, but you still have the privacy of your bedroom. And be sure to get a lock.

Watch sexy movies together, or make your own.

Do something special and loving. Put a flower on his pillow or in a vase on his dresser. Put a little card in his lunch box or briefcase that says you love him. Buy him a special toy or other present he would like.

Play a role. Dress up in a special way. Be the heroine of a romantic book or movie. Stay in your home or go out on the town.

Pretend you've only just met and that you're on your first date.

Remember, being romantic is thinking romantically. Get into the moment together and make it special. Leave all the humdrum behind. Learn to go deeper into the experience you are having together. Focus more fully on it and let the rest of the world slip away.

Don't create a mood and then talk about the plumbing. Don't go to all this trouble to take a moment out of time and be romantic and then talk about mundane things that will ruin everything. Unfortunately, some couples are so used to doing this that they don't know what else to talk about. If that is the case, do something to change it. Go to a movie ahead of time and have that to discuss. Or, if you must, discuss politics. Try to keep things upbeat and create pleasant memories. Talk about what you feel grateful for, plans for the future, what you enjoy.

Remember the most loving times you have ever spent together. Recall your honeymoon, your best vacation together, the day you met, the first time you made love, or a quiet evening together when you were loving with each other. Recall the details of these experiences as much as you can. Dwell on these romantic and special moments. They are the gold in the relationship that needs to be extracted from the daily pick-and-shovel work. Take out these golden nuggets and inspect them carefully. Look at their color and shine and glow. Remind him of these moments when he seems to be in the right mood for a heart touch (see Step 6). Talk them over and bathe in the glow of the golden moments you've shared. Then try to create opportunities for more special moments.

Create a Book of Love for you to share. Make a photo album of pictures you both enjoy, showing you happy together. Add loving pictures of each other whenever you can.

Carole said that the Book of Love seemed to be a focal point for her and Allen. It actually became an ongoing hobby to find things they could put in their album. In addition to pictures and cards, they began to include other mementos of their life together: postcards from places they visited, feathers they found on their walks, and flowers they gave each other ended up being pressed in the pages of their book.

This eventually will become habit-forming. Once you discover how to put the romance back in your life, it will make such a difference that you may well become addicted to finding new things to do all the time. Love and forming a relationship should be a beginning, not an end. Find time to be romantic; keep your time doing the survival necessities to a minimum, and learn to enjoy life together. There is no greater gift the two of you can have together.

Remember, as Jane Seymour says:

Romance is vital. We must bring it back into this century of office blocks and Super Woman. Romance matters to every woman, to the young girl who is not married, to the hard-working woman with a career and no children, and to the woman who has a marriage, career, and children. Nowadays we all have to struggle continually. There is never any time. But all the juggling will be pointless, a parade of a useless skill, if while parading that skill we forget to live. The precious moments, the grace and style and delight and tenderness, are all there, waiting to be found. But if you take things too seriously you'll never find them, and you'll regret the flowers you didn't buy, the walks you didn't take, the picnics you didn't plan. [4]

And the love you didn't share.

Develop your individual self and get stronger so you can go after your most important goals in life. Develop your power by coming back again and again to what you know is important to you—love and closeness. When we look back on our lives, the things that ultimately matter most of all are the close relationships, the love that's been shared, the people and other living things we have nurtured and felt close to.

This life and love focus can provide a solid ground on which to stand.

If love is your ultimate bull's-eye, you just keep aiming there for life. Once you are deeply embedded in the pattern of loving, you can relax and enjoy the journey. At least you are doing your part and you are fulfilling your great potential. Live a life of love.

STEP 8: TENDER TOUCHES

The eighth female illusion about men is the belief that when a man loves a woman he knows what will excite and arouse her.

What's the Problem?

When a relationship begins, the partners often give much of their attention to sending signals of interest, then of affection and caring, and eventually of love.

These gestures, or cues, can be a touch, a look, or anything that gives the message that you are attractive, interesting, and exciting. They can also be sexual signals, those seductive siren calls that start your blood pumping, even before the first kiss.

Unfortunately, while these gestures are plentiful during the courtship and early phases of a relationship, they may later be replaced by a more casual and direct sexual approach.

As one woman told us, "The first year of our marriage he used to feed me dessert with his own fork. He used to leave love notes in my lingerie drawer and undress me garment by garment before we made love. Now when I come to bed he just looks up from his magazine and says, "Well, do you want to do it?"

This cooling off between partners is typical, but it is very painful to women to whom these sexual cues and gestures are nearly as important as making love itself, sometimes more so.

Doesn't he love me anymore? she asks, wishing she knew what had gone wrong and how to regenerate the excitement they once had. Often she concludes that if her man really loved her he would excite and arouse her the way he used to; since he doesn't, he must not love her anymore.

What's the Truth?

The truth is that these gestures aren't nearly as exciting or important to men as they are to women. Men, remember, feel good as a result of having sex. Women want to feel good *before* having sex.

This means that men are much more focused on having sex and not so focused on what happens beforehand. It also means that in the early stages of a relationship, where seduction is still important, he is more likely to be seductive. But later, when he has a relationship of long standing of which sex is a regular part, he no longer feels the need to turn her on; he just wants to get to the good part, the part that makes him feel best, the actual act of having sex.

A man like this may seem callous, but he really isn't. Usually he just doesn't realize that these seductive cues are so important to his woman. Often he doesn't even know what they are or exactly how to do them. More typical is the man who understands what works for him (having sex) and assumes it is the same for his woman. As one man said to us, "Why bother with fancy hors d'oeuvres when the main course is what you really want and it's sitting right in front of you?" Unfortunately for men (and women), the result is that neither of them gets fed.

What Can You Do?

In Step 8 of the man's program your partner is being told exactly what these subtle cues are, why they are important to women, and how to use them to be more exciting and seductive.

Even if he isn't reading this book or doing these steps, you can still make a difference by reading Step 8 in his program and also considering what love cues appeal to you.

There are two ways to handle this. One is to be direct: tell him the kinds of things he can do and then reward him for doing them by being more loving in return. Or you can tell him when other men do similar things or talk about what a friend's husband does and how wonderful he is and how it's improved their sex life and their relationship.

This will give him an idea of what to do without direct pressure to do a certain thing.

If he is willing to read Step 8 of the man's program, now is a chance for you to help it happen. Your task in this step then is to:

1. Encourage His Efforts

Be aware of his attempts and encourage him by responding in a positive manner. Even if what he does isn't exactly right, if it seems difficult or awkward, remember he is making an honest attempt to give you what you want. Never embarrass him. Find what is good in what he is doing and encourage him to do that while ignoring what isn't perfect.

This means you are going to release your natural sexuality. Allow yourself to be turned on by his efforts as well as by what he does. See his efforts as a sign of love. If you do not find that his actions are exciting, he may need more practice or some very gentle, sensitive guidance on what would be exciting for you. Let him know what you do like, rather than criticizing what he tries. Again you can look at other relationships and men and say, for example, "Nancy told me that her husband sent her a card at the office that said he loved her. Isn't that wonderful?" You don't have to say "And you should do that, too." The message will be clear.

When he does excite you, let him know his efforts are succeeding so he will continue doing what works for you.

If nothing works, there may be a problem either between the two of you—unresolved anger, perhaps, or a hurt that needs healing before closeness can occur—or you may need to look more carefully at your own willingness to take down your sexual walls and overcome the sexual suppression you have been taught.

2. Teach Him About Love and Sensitivity

Try using your own subtle cues to induce love and sensitivity in him, just as he is using subtle cues to induce sexual openness in you. You can point out the majesty of the sunset, the interesting formation of the clouds, the smell of a rose, the grace of a wide receiver, the interesting pattern of grass on the baseball diamond, the smell of his new car, the fine quality of the material in his suit, or the workmanship in his briefcase. Use his interests to sensitize him to the beauty of the world, thus merging his Outer World with intimacy.

Julie realized that Bob was very sensitive to color, detail, shape, and sound—but most of his sensitivity was focused on cars; of course, that was how he ended up owning an auto parts store. She had once complained to him about his preoccupation with cars, and he had come back at her with the fact that this was what paid for their house and a lot else. Julie admitted there was some truth in his comment and started to pay attention to what he loved. She started noticing the craftsmanship in auto upholstery, the range of colors made for cars, and the depth of shine on a newly polished car. She said it wasn't her first choice as a focus, but it was one way to be close to Bob, to let him know she could share his world with him, and to educate his sensitivities even further. One result was that he agreed to go to a rose show, one of her long-standing interests, and thoroughly enjoyed their colors, perfumes, and shapes.

3. Learn to Flirt Again

Flirting with him can show him that you find him attractive and can bring him close to you. Show your interest in him by listening attentively, caring, and letting him know you feel drawn to him. You can reward his efforts to offer subtle cues to you by offering your own right back. When you do, you'll be able to feel the temperature in the room rise a few degrees.

4. Find Your Natural Sexuality

Find the part of yourself that can be sexually aroused, and when your lover does things that excite you, cooperate with the urge.

Think about the times you have been excited and what led up to the excitement. This tells you something important about your sexual self; it shows you the door through which you can find the sexual lover your man is searching for.

Rita said the door to her natural sexuality "closed years ago," and she had no idea how to get it open again. She found this step a bit uncomfortable at first, so she spent some time alone sexually exploring herself. She looked through some of George's magazines, and much to her surprise she found some of the pictures and letters arousing. Rita said that spending the time with herself this way brought her back in touch with her sexual self, which had been lost for years.

The effect of all this effort is that you are becoming more open to your beloved and want him to be closer. As he tries to meet you halfway, you are doing the same. And as you learn to give each other tender touches, you will find your natural sexuality growing even stronger.

STEP 9: ASSERTIVE AFFECTION

The ninth female illusion about men says that if he really loved me he'd be more affectionate.

What's the Problem?

Women associate affection with love. Women are affectionate with children, friends, relatives, and pets.

Men associate affection much more directly with sex. They show less affection to everyone. When they do show affection to a woman it is often intended as a prelude to sex.

This is the basis for a major and nearly universal misunderstanding between men and women. Women often want to be affectionate in order to feel love and intimacy. Men see affection of any kind as a sexual invitation.

Many women find this bewildering. She may just want to rub his neck to make him feel better. She begins to massage and he immediately returns the touching in a directly sexual manner. If she rubs his neck, for example, he may reach around to run a hand up her leg. Hers is an affectionate gesture; his is a sexual gesture. She didn't have sex in mind, but he clearly does. She realizes this and pulls away. "What are you doing," he asks. "I thought you wanted to do something."

"I just wanted to rub your neck," she says.

At this point responses vary. Some men are annoyed that she isn't interested in having sex. Some feel confused and teased. Some are angry that after seeming to say yes, she now is saying no.

Her responses also vary. She may simply move away, realizing that to give him any more affection is tantamount to saying yes to sex. She may also be annoyed or disappointed that once again all roads lead to Rome with him and that it is impossible to give him affection without him interpreting it sexually. She may even be furious and feel that once again, instead of expressing love in return for her expression of love, he just wants to have sex.

Both partners fail to get what they want.

What's the Truth?

The truth is that affection is frequently not related to a man's love for his woman. Affection for many men is related to the emotions and to closeness, both of which may be quite uncomfortable for him. Plus, affection may be sexually arousing and, if he's already aroused, any more physical contact may prove too powerful, even uncomfortable for him.

For one thing, boys are not touched as much or given as much affection as little girls, either in infancy or in childhood. Young men are allowed to touch each other only with pats on the back, handshakes, or quick hugs and high fives during victory celebrations.

The only physical contact many men have is with women during sex, and they've become conditioned to any contact at all as sexual contact. All of this is added on to most men's powerful, biochemically based sex drive.

Affection for women involves feelings of love, closeness, and sexual stimulation that may not be followed by sex, but men are often very uncomfortable expressing or receiving affection.

Men do become more interested in affection and intimacy after age forty as their sex drive slows down. However, what woman wants to wait that long? And also, if a man avoids all affection before forty, how will he find out that he likes it after forty?

The answer is to help bring out his affectionate side in a way with which he can be comfortable, while you bring out your natural sexuality in a way with which you can be comfortable. It is asking an enormous amount for any man to overcome his anesthesia, his armor, and his natural sexuality in order to be affectionate, and it is asking a great deal for women to open up more fully to the sexuality they've been trained to treat with caution. But there is hope.

What Can You Do?

1. Play Hit and Run

The hit-and-run technique allows a woman to be affectionate with her man without creating too much anxiety or discomfort. It means that she becomes briefly affectionate with him and then pulls back before her lover is sexually aroused.

For example, she may touch his hand momentarily or put her hand on his shoulder for a second. Maybe she gives him a brief kiss on the cheek or holds his hand as they walk. The old philosophy of leaving him wanting more is perfect here. You want to pull away from physical contact before he gets sexually excited or uncomfortable with the emotional closeness.

At the same time, you can practice hit and run with your sexuality. When he touches your arm and conveys love to you as best he can, allow your natural sexual self to come into your bodily feelings more strongly. Then let the feeling go. This will allow you to gradually become more open to the sexuality your conditioning has warned you to be careful about. But now you're being provided with the right cues so you can aim your sexual feelings at your man, as he strives to aim his loving feelings at you.

2. Reinforce His Attempts at Affection

In his own Step 9 your partner is being shown how to overcome some of his own barriers and be more affectionate. Again he needs you to show him what you want and to reward him for his efforts.

Read his Step 9 yourself and consider what you could do to help him. Keep in mind that you are trying to meet each other halfway. He is trying to be more loving and you are aiming to be more sexual. In this way you will both gain more of what you want. So if he touches you in a loving way, try to find your natural sexual reaction to his loving touch and respond accordingly.

3. Try a Hug a Day

A hug a day keeps the divorce lawyer away. Your man can satisfy your craving for physical affection by giving you a meaningful hug each day. You may crave more than that at first. Perhaps you feel a deep deprivation. In time, however, one hug a day will add up to a great deal of affection.

4. Aim at Your Heart

Aim at your heart, at feeling the caring and affection, when you hug. Close your eyes, do your heartwarming exercise (see Step 6), and hug.

By combining several steps you can build the power and intensity of the program. Give him a hug each day while practicing the heartwarming exercise. Then tell him that you love him and why. When you do this, you are creating a wonderful, nurturing moment in the midst of your daily lives. If you do this once a day for life, you will someday look back over your life and say that you were always making the effort to be close and loving—and you will be happy with the effort and direction of your life. What more can you ask for than this sense of inner contentment and satisfaction?

To some extent he'll catch your glow; he can't help but be affected to some degree. How much any individual changes depends on a great many factors. All you can do is to put out your best effort and find a way to live with the results. We cannot control more than that.

5. Help Him Slow Down

A big problem for men with strong sex drives (most men) is that they are too easily excited to stand any affection or closeness without moving quickly toward intercourse and orgasm. Perhaps your highly sexed man could tolerate closeness if you helped or encouraged him to relieve himself. This might take off some of the pressure to have intercourse that he's feeling and enable him to slow down enough to be nonsexually affectionate with you. Try it.

Julie said that Bob made a valiant attempt to be nonsexually affectionate and that she was trying hard to find her natural sexual self, but that as soon as she seemed even slightly aroused, he turned from affection to sex. "He's like a dog in heat, I swear," she said one summer afternoon. "If we hug for more than fifteen seconds he's got an erection and his hand is inside the front of my panties. So I tried the masturbation idea even though it seemed perverted to me at first. I said to him that I just wanted us to hug and that if he needed help from me, I'd help him. He said he did, and I helped him reach an orgasm. The result really surprised me. He was so relieved he actually gave me the kind of hug I wanted. He just held me for a long time, and he even said it felt good to him. But I see now that his sex drive is so strong he couldn't have held me nonsexually without being relieved first."

As your partner is trying to find his loving self, you are aiming at your natural sexual self. Now we'll see how the two merge as you move into lovemaking.

STEP 10: LOVEMAKING: FINDING YOUR NATURAL SEXUAL POTENTIAL

The tenth female illusion about men is that a man shouldn't need to be told how to make love.

What's the Problem?

From an early age women are taught, subtly and not so subtly, to believe that men know more about sex than women do. In most cases, too, the men with whom a woman has sex are older and therefore are assumed to be more experienced. This means they should know what to do sexually to excite a woman. At least most women assume this is true.

Unfortunately, many women are disappointed.

Some begin relationships on a honeymoon high, their emotions so involved that nearly any sexual contact is stimulating and wonderful. But as the glow wears off, so does the great sex. This means that any sexual problems that were there in the beginning now become more visible.

At this stage the woman is often surprised to find that her man doesn't excite her as he once did and she's not sure what's wrong or what to do about it.

Many women assume that this state of affairs is their own fault. This comes from a certain predisposition among women to blame themselves for any problems in their relationships. She may also assume that he knows what should turn her on and if she isn't excited, it must be because of her shortcomings. Even if she suspects that he could be doing something better or different, she is often reluctant to discuss it. Many women are embarrassed to tell their man that he isn't doing what excites them sexually. Many fear he will get angry or that it will be too much of a blow to his ego and further wound him.

One woman told us, "Mike and I have been married now for seven years, and I haven't really enjoyed sex since the first months of the marriage. I'd had quite a bit of experience before Mike, and I'd had better lovers, but I was so in love with him that in the beginning anything he did turned me on and I didn't care if I didn't have an orgasm. But then things changed. Six months after we were married I wasn't as eager anymore. I was already pregnant by then and I blamed it on that. Then, after my first child I was always exhausted. That's when I started faking orgasms. You see, I was just so tired, but Mike was so horny. I decided just to do it and try to keep him happy. But that wasn't enough. If I didn't have an orgasm, he wanted to do it again until I did. I learned to fake really well.

"This has been going on for years. Our two kids are at school now and can be on their own a lot, and Mike and I are getting our privacy back. I'd really like to have good sex with him, but I'm just not turned on anymore. I feel that love should be the answer, and I do love him. What I want, I guess, is for him to make love to me so I enjoy it. But how am I going to explain that I want him to make love to me better when he thinks I've been enjoying it all along? How do I explain all those 'orgasms'? Anyway, I don't think a woman should have to tell a man how to make love to her.

He's supposed to know what he's doing. The problem is Mike doesn't turn me on. Maybe it just means I really don't love him."

This is a problem for many women. Many women aren't enjoying sex but don't know what to do to change the situation. Many women think there is something wrong with them. They think their partner doesn't love them or that they no longer love their partner. They may realize that he could be making love to them better, but resent that he doesn't know how, and they feel reluctant to discuss the subject.

"I feel so embarrassed to teach him," says one woman. "It seems like it takes away from his masculinity for me to be the one to do the teaching."

Says another woman, "'Where did you learn that?' That's what my husband would ask. He is going to wonder where I learned something he doesn't know. He's very jealous, and I know it would cause a fight, so I just avoid the whole subject. Anyway, I want him just to know. A woman shouldn't have to teach a man how to have sex."

Another problem for many women is that they often have much less interest in sex than their man and may have even gotten to the point that their natural sexuality has been turned off or turned down. Most women, especially very attractive ones who have men coming on to them frequently, have learned to say no. One result may be that they end up saying no to their natural sexuality. If so, they may have trouble finding their sexual self and their normal sexual reactions. We discussed in Chapter 3 all the reasons women have had to learn to control their sex drive and how this control may end up causing a woman to avoid any genuine involvement in lovemaking. In fact, some women will put all the blame on their man, saying that the reason they're not turned on is because he isn't providing the right conditions for arousal. No doubt this is often true, but it is also often true that many women have learned to turn off their natural sexuality and have lost touch with their sexual self.

What's the Truth?

The woman may not realize that there might not be anything wrong with her or her mate or their relationship. The problem could be that the man just doesn't know what pleases her, or she may have closed off her own sexuality and may need to get in touch with what gives her pleasure.

Of course, traditionally it is the man who teaches the woman about sex. But the truth is that the woman probably knows more about her own body than he does, and since a man isn't a mind reader, it becomes her responsibility to teach him what she wants and what makes her feel sexually satisfied.

Part of the truth lies, therefore, in the woman knowing her own body and being comfortable with her own sexuality so that she can tell her man what she does and does not find pleasurable and exciting.

If the man is going to learn to make love, as opposed to simply having sex, he will need his partner to give him the feedback and, if necessary, some instructions. At the same time, the woman must be comfortable with her own sexuality so she can give him this feedback and enjoy the results. In this way they can meet each other halfway; she gets more of the love she wants, while he gets more of the sex he wants.

What to Do?

1. Release Your Natural Sexuality

The single biggest turn-off for men is an unresponsive partner. Men want their woman to be excited and involved sexually, just as a woman wants a man to be genuinely caring and loving. If he feels she is uninterested, he will be turned off and resentful.

Imagine being a man. Imagine that you have a penis that gets erect easily with a sex drive behind it instead of a drive for closeness, and it's driven to penetrate and release the pressure. Imagine that your woman doesn't seem very interested in sex. She wants you to go slow and be sensitive, but your penis is hard and calls out for relief.

You lust after women walking down the street, at work, in ads on TV, in magazines, and at the office. You're not supposed to be that sexual, and yet you can't help yourself—or so it seems. You're not supposed to have affairs, only sex with your woman, but she seems uninterested much of the time. You're frustrated, but you can't reveal your frustration or your irritation or be angry or upset about it, because that would create another problem with her. You make some efforts to be the man of her dreams, but you feel uncomfortable and she still wants something more or something different. You want to scream, but if you do, she'll think you've lost your mind.

When your man makes the effort to find his love for you, it makes sense for you to find your sexuality for him.

Try to release your natural sexual potential with him, extending your boundaries, especially in relation to his efforts to be loving and closer to you. Be aware of his efforts and make your own efforts to reach out to him.

Recall times in your life when you've been in touch with your natural sexuality, perhaps when you and your man were first in love or when you were first married. Close your eyes and recall the physical sensations of being sexual.

Keep in good physical shape to be sexier. Regular moderate exercise enhances sexuality. People who go for walks, swim, or do other forms of physical exercise in moderation have better and more active sex lives than people who do no exercise or who constantly exercise vigorously.

Buy lingerie, magazines, romance novels, sexy perfume—anything that will get you in touch with your sexual self. Think about how well things are going with your man, about the good aspects of your relationship that make you feel loved and safe. Then permit yourself to release your natural sexuality.

Take time by yourself to give yourself pleasure. Relax and enjoy finding the ways you enjoy being touched; then you will be better able to release your sexuality with him. Give yourself a chance to feel pleasure in an unhurried way and find the door to your own sexuality.

Rita said that she was always about ten pounds overweight, and none of the diets ever worked for her in the long run. What would happen if she lost the ten pounds? she was asked. Rita said she'd feel better about herself, she'd fit into her clothes and be more comfortable, she'd be relieved, and she'd be sexier.

"What would happen if you were sexier?"

Rita answered, "Well, I guess it's what George would like, but I don't know about that."

"You don't know about being sexier with George? Would there be a problem?"

"I don't know," said Rita. "George doesn't ever make me think he really wants me, if you know what I mean. He doesn't make advances much anymore, and I don't really feel turned on by him because he doesn't make me feel desirable. And you know how guys are, always flirting with me as it is."

"So if you lost those last ten pounds you'd feel sexier, and you wouldn't feel like directing your sexuality at George because he's not making you feel turned on. Meanwhile, there are these men coming on to you. What would happen then?"

"Then I'd just have another problem," Rita said with a frown. "Then I'd be turned on with nowhere to go and have these guys coming on to me and be tempted. I wouldn't do anything, of course. At least I never have before, but things are going so much better with George that I don't want to foul up what's going so well."

Rita was confronted with a common problem. If she did get more in tune with her sexuality, perhaps by losing weight, or by learning about her own needs, she'd have to find an outlet for it. And if she wasn't aiming it at her husband, other men would become more of a temptation. What quickly became clear to Rita was that she needed to help George learn to make her feel desirable and sexy with him. She needed to go toward her natural sexuality, but aim it at her lover and communicate to him what she needed him to do so she could open herself up with him.

Men often do not know what you like and do not like unless you tell them, so be a good communicator (this is the most important form of oral sex). He can't read your mind even if he loves you dearly, and his body works differently than yours in some important ways, so he can't go by what he knows from his own sexuality. Initiate sex some of the time to let him know you're interested and so he doesn't always have to put his ego on the line.

2. Tell Him What You Want

The man's program includes some basic techniques to help him more fully satisfy you, but he still needs you to tell him what you do and don't like.

"But it feels so cold then to make love while telling him what to do every step of the way," some women say. "When I have to tell him, it takes the romance completely out of it."

True, it is more exciting for a woman simply to give herself up to a man's lovemaking and not have to guide him, but you won't have to teach him every time. You just have to show him often enough for him to learn to do what you like.

Remember, though, that by just teaching him sexual techniques that please you, you are limiting your entire love experience.

Rita had never told George that she needed him to make sexual advances so she felt desired by him. "He was really surprised. We never talked much about sex, and when we did it was usually an argument. I sometimes told him to back off, and he said he never thought he'd hear me say that I wanted him to come on sexually. George said that he stopped being assertive because I was always turning him down and he couldn't stand the rejection and the frustration. He said he was mad at me over it and figured it was best just to back off, shut up, and not expect much in the sex department."

George said he had no problem letting Rita know he desired her as long as he knew they weren't going to argue over it. He understood that there was a difference in their sex drives, but that if she didn't reject him the way she used to, he could easily make her feel desired.

Rita said she worried about being unable to satisfy him and was afraid he'd stop loving her. "George took me in his arms and told me he'd never stop loving me," she said. "I cried and cried and we made love that afternoon. It was just wonderful. The best we've had in years."

3. Make Lovemaking Exciting, Fun, and Pleasurable

Don't let yourself fall into the wife trap, where the dating game is ended, the wedding is past, and the relationship has grown dull. Let this be a new beginning for you. Be a mistress, flirt with him, keep him interested. Men become sexually bored more easily than women do, and they are not supposed to seek variety outside of the relationship, though many do, of course. The secret is to keep variety within the relationship.

Imagine you are having an affair with your man. Recall what it was like when you first met—sex several times a week, looking each other in the eye, feeling turned on by the love you share. Find the experience again and let yourself be swept away.

Be open to sex, enjoy it, relax, experiment; this will help to keep your lovemaking exciting. Women are sexually aroused through intimacy, men through novelty. So avoid boredom for his sake as well as your own.

Communicate about your lovemaking. For example, tell him, "I like you to bite my ears," or "I love it when you touch my nipples," or "You get me so hot when you rub my clitoris." Also, ask him to be specific about what he wants you to do to make him feel good. "Do you like it when I touch you here?" or "What do you like me to do most of all to make you feel good?" or "Do you want me to touch you faster?"

Perhaps you could suggest a bath or massage first, or even a massage during a bath. Put on some favorite music. Take your time and enjoy the experience. Be both a receiver and a giver of pleasure and love.

Express your love to your man during lovemaking. Let him know you find him special and exciting. Tell him about the things he does that turns you on. Practice your heartwarming exercise during lovemaking.

Everything gets stale if it's repeated the same way over and over.

Experiment. Try making love in different rooms, in different positions, with different music, with candles, with sexy videos or movies before-hand. Prepare for the encounter: go out to dinner, wear a very sexy outfit, and tease him during the evening by telling him what you're going to do to him later. Get yourself excited and get comfortable being sexual with your man. Shower or bathe together. Wear something sexy to bed. Turn down the lights. Use perfume or other sensual aromas that appeal to both of you.

If you want him to be excited, avoid your usual bedtime attire of old nightgown, curlers, and no makeup. Prepare for lovemaking whenever you can so that will be a turn-on for both of you.

You might try using sex toys for fun. Games, vibrators, massage oils, and other paraphernalia are available through stores and catalogs.

Use your imagination to enhance your sexuality. Tell him a story or a fantasy, or if this gets him too excited, think about fantasies that turn you on. Buy him something sexy to wear, like tiny bikini underpants, or a muscle shirt, if you find that exciting.

Vary your lovemaking. If you never use oral sex, try it. You might find a way to enjoy it more than you thought you would.

Release your natural sexual potential. Be sexy with him, turn him on, let yourself go, and let him know he's done it to you. Let him know that his efforts to be closer, more loving, and more open really do turn you on and warm you up.

Maybe he'll need to reach orgasm twice if he's really aroused. If this is too much for you, perhaps you can help him reach a climax once through masturbation and then again through intercourse.

This way you can deal with the sexual pressure that prevents him from being the slow, sensitive lover you'd like. This pressure may make it hard or impossible for him to be slow and calm and take things easy. Simply asking him to slow down may not work and may even make him angry. Help him handle it by relieving the pressure for him.

4. Merge Love with Sex

Learn to help him please you on a physical level and on an emotional level as well by unifying the act of having sex with the love you feel for each other. A way of doing this is to be clear about the connection between making love and being loving and to feel that connection while you are having sex.

To do this you must learn how to have romantic sex. In romantic sex you open your heart to your feelings of caring during lovemaking, and you teach your lover to do the same for you. At some point in your lovemaking let him know your feelings for him, why you care, how good it feels to hold him close, why you respect him, what it is about him that excites you and turns you on. Sex with genuine feelings of caring, affection, and love adds up to romantic sex.

This is also an opportunity to get him to slow down so that his sexual drive doesn't overpower him and push him toward intercourse and orgasm. Create a sensitive sexual experience, bringing sensuality to your intimate time together. In this way you can make that your lovemaking will truly be filled with pleasure and love.

NOTES, CHAPTER 6

1. Warren Farrell, *Why Men Are the Way They Are*, (New York: McGraw-Hill, 1986), p. 168.
2. Lillian Rubin, *Intimate Strangers: Men and Women Together*, (New York: Harper & Row, 1983), p. 24.
3. Jane Seymour, *Jane Seymour's Guide to Romantic Living*, (New York: Atheneum, 1987), pp. 68–70.
4. Seymour, p. 12.

PART THREE

MORE HAPPILY
EVER AFTER

7

A Daily Dose of Vitamin L

For many of you, doing the Great Love, Great Sex program has created profound changes in your awareness and your relationships.

For others the changes may have been less dramatic and the progress more of an uphill climb.

Regardless of how much you've changed and improved your relationship, however, the next step always entails trying to maintain the gains you've made and to keep the momentum growing.

Too often we strive to change, only to find that what was a brief shining moment of success has been lost to the persistent force of our old patterns which, like some irresistible siren, call us back to the dissatisfying situation we want so much to change.

In a way it's like stopping any bad habit. We may have had the habit for years until something motivates us to change.

Perhaps you have been motivated to do this program because you wanted to get more out of life and love. Perhaps you wanted to improve an already good relationship. Perhaps you were dissatisfied with your sex life, or perhaps you realized that your troubled relationship was heading for divorce. Perhaps your partner simply put this book under your nose and said, "Read!"

Whatever your motivation, once your relationship begins to improve it is often a wonderful, renewing experience. Suddenly you feel more hopeful about everything. You aren't stuck in the dissatisfactions of the past. There is a way out. You're feeling great about each other and more alive and turned on than you have been in years. Your partner is more loving, romantic, and exciting, and so are you.

But then, just when you think you've licked the problem, some force 't

pulls you back toward the old pattern. It could be a disagreement, outside stresses, children, the arrival of a holiday, or any one of a thousand other possibilities. Your progress stops, and before anyone realizes it, you are losing ground and wondering what to do now.

Dealing with this situation is what this part of the book is about. Part III is going to help you keep this program going for the rest of your life and show you a way of taking your relationship to the next step by learning to love on a deeper, more intimate and spiritual level.

Just as we have a physical need for protein, vitamins, and minerals, we also have a social and emotional need for love and lovemaking—vitamin L. We look to our partner to meet this need. How can we nurture and nourish each other on a daily basis?

Here we offer a series of suggestions as to how you can maintain this program and the changes you have made. This is an ongoing process that will lead to ever more fulfilling love and satisfaction.

1. Expect a Relapse and Deal with It

All of the couples we know who have made major changes in their relationships have, at some point, fallen back into their old patterns, at least for a time. Change is hard to achieve, but even harder to keep, particularly when the old undesirable pattern has been in existence for years.

Remember that this relapse is to be expected and shouldn't be grounds for guilt or despair. It's normal, and it *can* be dealt with.

These relapses are to be expected for three basic reasons.

First, we must remember that many of the destructive patterns come from the way we've been conditioned by our parents and through hundreds of generations. The sex-love erosion disease is not something that just some couples are subject to; it is part of our culture because of the traditional roles of men and women. These roles helped both sexes survive, but they also ensured that men and women would have problems staying in love. Therefore, when you and your partner begin changing, it's important for both of you to see that you're up against a pattern that has been deeply woven into human society and our collective consciousness; it isn't unique to you.

The second reason is that it is human nature to stay with what is familiar. The positive changes that you have made are fragile because of this human reality. You may go along very well for a while, but eventually the old familiar patterns will call you back. Often a relapse is caused by stress. Usually it is something that gets one or both of you suddenly preoccupied. It could be a serious illness in the family, a problem at work, financial troubles, or even planning for a holiday, something that preoccupies your attention for some period of time so that you have no time to give to the new pattern. You switch to automatic pilot and give your attention to the problems that are causing the stress.

Being on automatic pilot means that at least one of you will begin to slip back into the earlier way of behaving with each other. That old pattern can be done on automatic pilot because it doesn't require conscious awareness the way the new pattern probably still does. It is difficult to switch off the automatic pilot and return to rebuilding the new pattern again. It is often easier, if sadder, to continue in the old pattern and to say, "Well, it's just hopeless. We tried, but here we are again. I guess there's no way out."

Instead of letting this happen, you must do two things: (1) realize a relapse is coming when you are under stress; and (2) deal with it immediately and directly. Let's say, for example, that your mother becomes seriously ill and you need to care for her. Suddenly all romantic evenings are off. You are absorbed with reorganizing your schedule to deal with this new responsibility and are overwhelmed both by the task and by the emotional difficulties of seeing a parent dying. Before you know it your husband is back to sitting silently in front of TV or out playing cards with the boys, and you feel unloved once again.

Realize that this is a temporary situation and, while you have little time to work on your relationship for now, there are some measures you *can* take.

Discuss the situation with your partner. Say that this stress is likely to pull the two of you back into your old ways of operating, but that you don't want that to happen.

Discuss alternatives that would work better. See, for instance, how much of the emergency you can handle together. There is nothing like overcoming difficulties to bind people even more closely. Indeed, overcoming difficulties together is the stuff romance is made of. Most romantic stories deal with a couple who are drawn into a difficult situation which they conquer together and, after conquering it, live happily ever after. Now is the time for the two of you to pull together, not apart. See how much of this you can do together.

Even in the midst of this trouble, it may be possible to set an evening a week aside for the two of you, or perhaps a few hours on weekends. Plan for this time and keep it sacred.

At all times, try to keep the lines of communication open, letting your partner know that you care very much about him or her, that you must handle this difficulty, and that you want the two of you to help each other through it and not be divided by it.

The third reason that a relapse may occur is that the relationship may simply begin to deteriorate. The problem need not be precipitated by a specific stress. It may just happen little by little, the way your relationship began to erode in the first place. This erosion may begin with a slight that one person feels from the other and that starts a chain reaction going. For example, he is late from work, in a bad mood, or makes a cutting remark. She takes offense. He doesn't really love her. She is crushed and avoids having sex with him. He is annoyed and puzzled. He accuses her of being frigid. And so it goes on, dragging the couple down into the same old whirlpool, only faster this time, so they feel they've somehow failed and it's all hopeless.

The solution to this kind of erosion is, once again, to be aware it is coming and to look for it and not to let it ruin your efforts.

No matter which partner starts the chain reaction, it's up to both of you to try to stop it. Recognize it, discuss it, reaffirm your need and desire to continue moving forward instead of backward, and keep each other from becoming discouraged.

2. Master the Techniques You've Already Been Given

When the inevitable relapse comes, many people seek new answers and additional techniques instead of exploring more deeply the ones they already know. This is like planting a flower, digging it up before spring arrives, and allowing the weeds, which require so little effort, to grow instead. A good love relationship requires good gardeners with the patience to let their love develop. You can't make each other grow, but you can create a nurturing environment in which both of you can grow.

You already know what to do through the programs in Part II, so the answer is to use what you now know and master these techniques. No one says this is easy. In fact it's much easier to find another book to read, find a course to attend, or forget the whole thing. There's nothing wrong with reading and learning, but they can also serve to keep us from going more deeply into what we already know and understand.

What you want calls for depth. Only by deepening your understanding can you make true, lasting change come about—and change is what will bring you the physical and emotional love you are seeking.

For example, two months after Bob and Julie completed the program they were doing wonderfully. Then slowly things began to slip. Soon they had the same old fight over love and sex. "I was really disheartened," said Julie. "We had worked to get things better—and they were much better for a while—but then here we were back in the same old rut. What hope was there for us?"

Bob had been on a real high. He was surprised by the relapse, but having had a taste of a solution, he wanted to find the cure. Still, he felt the same discouragement.

"Maybe we should live apart," Julie suggested.

"But how will that help us get closer?" Bob asked.

Their immediate reaction was to look for a new answer, a different answer, rather than sticking with what had already worked. They began to look for different solutions, but the problems just became worse until Julie went to live with her sister. That's when Bob realized that what had worked before could work again, and now that he was more experienced he could implement many of the steps much better than he had the first time.

Instead of letting the relationship deteriorate further, Bob asked Julie out on a date. He told her how much he loved her and how much he knew she loved him. He assured her that they could and would work this out. They then read the steps again and both start implementing them.

Just as before, the suggestions worked—this time even better. Once again their relationship was closer than it had been in years and they vowed to stick with it and keep doing the steps they'd already been given instead of going off in a new direction.

It is essential to realize that basic changes are very hard to achieve and even harder to maintain. If they happen and are to last, they must be worked at on an ongoing basis. One must make the necessary effort.

3. Reward Each Other's Efforts

Don't be perfectionistic. Don't expect too much too quickly. A common reason why couples don't make their changes last is that they expect too much too soon. They are quick to find fault with each other, focusing on what is missing or wrong, rather than on the progress they've made or the effort that was put out. Yet if you are to deepen your mastery of the techniques and ideas you now know, you must encourage each other's efforts, however imperfect they may be.

Don't just count success, count effort. It is only through effort that we make progress, and if we fail to encourage attempts at change, then change will never take place.

Especially in areas where our partner is a beginner, it is vital to let him or her know that the effort made really counts: "Thanks for doing the shopping, honey. I really appreciate your handling that burden." This is much more likely to get your partner to continue working to bring about daily changes, to go shopping again, and to do a better job as he or she gets more practice, than "You forgot the soap, and this is the wrong type of cheese, and why didn't you use the coupons?"

Don't discourage your loved one; encourage your loved one.

A second part of this point is to measure yourself and your relationship from where you started instead of from where you want to be.

Too often people think about their ideal fantasy, about how things should be going, and when they compare this ideal to their own situation they feel critical and discouraged. Better to note where you began and then see yourself and your partner improving. This will encourage you along the way, and you will be much more likely to successfully continue working on yourselves and your relationship.

For example, if you began with a man who could hardly communicate any of his feelings and now he is able to tell you his emotional reaction to something, *this* is progress. You may want him to tell you he loves you every day and to express his tender emotions, but that is unrealistic to expect in the beginning, and if you use this as your measure, you will doom his efforts. Of course, it's valuable to keep an ideal in mind to be worked toward, but look at what he *has* done instead of what he *hasn't* yet done.

This is also true for you. Look at where you began and how you're improving. For example, Gayle, a young, very attractive model who, to avoid sleeping with the many men who approached her, had learned to say no to sex and turn herself off. Now as she did the program, she had great difficulty focusing on her sexuality and reconnecting her emotional love for her husband to her sexual feelings. She'd learned to say no and was now having a terrible time saying yes.

"At first I was doing really well," she told us. "I followed all the suggestions about reconnecting with my sexuality and I was amazed at how truly sexy I began to feel. I was always okay if Bill was just touching my arms or legs or even my thighs and bottom, but let him touch my breasts or vagina and I would just freeze up. It was like someone pushing an alarm button. But then I learned to get myself warmed up first, even before seeing Bill. I would set time aside, read a sexy romance, take a bath, really prepare my body, and even masturbate until I was already past my own inhibitions before I even got close to Bill. By the time he got to me I was ready for sex, and for the first time I had a really wonderful orgasm. This worked great, but then I got really busy. My schedule changed and I ended up working most Saturdays and Thursdays, the days both Bill and I used to have free. I didn't have the time to prepare, and the next thing I knew I was crawling into bed with him and I wasn't turned on at all. Of course, Bill was used to me being really hot and hadn't been paying as much attention to foreplay. He just went right for it. I was so disappointed that I wasn't excited and I ended up faking an orgasm just as I used to. Now I'm really discouraged about ever really being sexy."

The problem here is that Gayle is not looking at where she came from (being fearful and unresponsive to sex) and is comparing her reactions to her ideal. She stopped taking into account real life factors that interfered with her progress, and she needed to get back on track, since she was certainly still capable of being excited and orgasmic. Another problem was that she had learned to be excited, but now she needed to teach Bill to get her excited.

People often look at their difficulties rather than letting their progress encourage them to continue. They let what they haven't achieved stop them from putting in any more effort. This is a problem everyone has to avoid.

Keep your focus on what you've done instead of what you haven't yet done. If you constantly compare yourself and your relationship to an imaginary ideal and let yourself feel discouraged, you will constantly feel frustrated, angry, critical, resentful, bitter, defeated, and depressed. You may even seek outside relationships.

Focusing on imperfections is deadly and no doubt plays a role in early illness and death for many women and men. The surgeon general should print on every marriage license that "perfectionism is dangerous to your health."

Better to measure your progress from your starting point when you're beginning to seriously work on the relationship and keep yourself feeling optimistic and going forward. Reward each other's efforts and look for progress from where you began, you will both feel hopeful and encouraged.

4. Picture Your Goal

Keep in mind what you are trying to accomplish and go toward it. An obstacle that often blocks couples' progress is that they lose their sense of direction and, as a result, their motivation.

As clearly as you can, picture what your life can be like as you and your best beloved live out your programs, being more caring and loving with each other. This is your motivation to keep going forward and it is your bull's-eye to aim for.

See yourselves helping each other, building each other's good feelings, having fun together, being loving, and making love. In this way your vision of yourselves will pull you forward, give you clear direction, and provide a way to harness your efforts and energies. See yourselves as loving and lovemaking individuals and as a loving and lovemaking couple, and you will be more likely to make this a reality.

Allen and Carole said that they had a long history of arguing and debating with each other and that the main effect of this constant struggle was to make them feel alone in the world and rejected by each other. This, in turn, made them both resentful and angry. When they thought of themselves as a couple, their arguing stood out in their minds as a main element in their relationship.

"We're like two growling dogs," said Allen.

Carole laughed. "I've never heard you say that before, but it's true. We bark and snap at each other and I hate it. It makes me feel terrible because I want it to be so different."

When they looked into their relationship they both said that there were lots of things about it that were good, but snapping was one of the main ways they related to each other, and it had a powerful pull that drew them back to fighting over and over again. When they learned to see themselves as taking care of each other and made this a central focus in their vision of what they were as a couple, they found it much easier to let go of their fighting and to continue going after their goal of having a loving relationship in which they tried to meet each other's needs as much as they could.

Love and making love should be at the forefront of your relationship. Picture yourselves as a loving couple rather than focusing on fighting over bills and who was supposed to do the laundry. All couples have areas of sensitivity where they disagree or clash, but as you grow, you can learn to forgive, to talk over the problems in a constructive way, to let things go, and to come back over and over again to your caring and loving each other. Picture yourselves as a loving couple and you will be more likely to be a loving couple.

5. Aim at a Minimum

Another reason why couples fail to maintain positive change is that they aim too high and expect too much too soon.

Some of the results of this unrealistic overreaching are frustration, anger, stress, discouragement, and defeat. Any one of these can lead to a deepening of the sex-love erosion disease and cause a couple to sink into marital coma. Fortunately, there is an antidote.

This technique also works for dieting and exercising, as well as loving. When people set out to alter a normal pattern they typically say to themselves and their friends, "From now on I'm on a strict diet-exercise program. Each day I'm going to count calories, avoid ice cream, and run three miles." They do this for a week before collapsing back into their old pattern and feeling defeated because they couldn't accomplish their goals.

Dan and Melissa did the same thing years ago when they decided they needed to be in better physical shape by doing exercise after years of inactivity. They talked it over and decided to run two or three miles a day, which seemed easy enough because they'd both been fairly athletic before college. So out they went one fine spring morning, and after about two blocks, beet red, sweating, hearts pounding, they went home defeated.

When they talked over what happened they realized the only way to get going was to be realistic about their physical condition. Instead of aiming at two miles a day, they would walk a block or two and feel successful.

Instead of aiming for a maximum and failing, it is better to aim at a minimum and succeed. Once Dan and Melissa were able to walk two blocks, it became easy to go three and then four, until finally they could walk or run three, four, or more miles. The secret to success is to aim at a minimum that is realistically achievable, regardless of what your ideal fantasy tells you you should be doing.

The same is true for loving and making love. Aim at a realistic goal you can achieve on a regular daily and weekly basis. Of course, sometimes you'll do more, but it's the minimum that's more important in the long run, because that's how you keep yourself going. Repeatedly setting up goals that you fail to achieve is worse than doing nothing, because it leaves you with a greater and greater sense of failure and leads to discouragement; you want to arrange your goals so you feel encouragement.

In this way you can engineer success, not just in your relationship but in everything else in your life (and teach the same to your partner and children). Ask yourself what you can realistically accomplish on a regular basis from the man's or woman's program.

Can you do the count-the-ways exercise with your partner once a week? Once a day?

Can you do the heartwarming exercise once a day or once a week?

Can you do the heart-touching technique once a month?

What about shared activities? Can you find a fun activity to share once every week or two?

How about using subtle cues? Is that something you can do regularly? Weekly? Monthly? Not at all?

And assertive affection? Can you touch each other's hands or give each other a daily hug? A weekly hug?

Can you practice "letting it go" on a regular basis?

Can you communicate about feelings regularly?

What about the "I care enough to help" notion? Can you be of help to each other on a daily or weekly basis?

Find a time when it will be easy to carry out your goal. Could you hug in the morning or are you too busy? Do your schedules have you up and out at different times? Could you hug each other at bedtime, or tell each other ways you care during mealtimes?

Perhaps you could make a list of the activities you intend to do daily, weekly, or monthly and chart how you're doing until they become good habits you follow automatically.

Carole and Allen developed a pattern of telling each other during dinner each night if they missed each other during the day and whatever nice things they had thought about each other. Bob and Julie started to hold hands more often when they went out together on the weekend, and they started to set aside time just for themselves at least once each week.

Scheduling time together can be difficult, particularly for very busy couples. You may have to reorganize your priorities or look for opportunities to be together you hadn't thought of before. For example, some couples realized that they could get up early enough to take a walk together before going to work. This was good exercise and a time to be together. They discovered that early in the morning was a wonderful time to discuss things and to start the day off with a sense of closeness and loving. Another couple realized that there were times when she had a meeting and he was at home alone and vice versa. By simply reorganizing their schedule to have their meetings on the same night they managed to get an evening for themselves.

Another couple found that they were spending time on things that weren't as important to them as spending time together. A realization that they weren't living out what their real priorities were made them change how they were spending their time and led them to spend more together.

Rita and George got in the habit of giving each other long hugs in the morning and practicing the heartwarming exercise as a wonderful way to start their day. Gail and Michael leave notes of love and appreciation for each other around the house and on their computer. They are like little love bombs waiting to go off when they are unexpectedly discovered.

Aim at a minimum, aim at success, and you can truly keep your love alive and growing.

6. Take an Eagle's-Eye View

Have a long-range view. People get into relationships because they want them to last. No one gets involved and wants to break up or divorce. When people get married they vow to stay together. Yet they often act as if their relationship is the least important part of their lives.

If one of the partners is angry—let's say it's the woman—she may simply dump the anger on her best friend, often without regard for her commitment to be together with her partner, caring for each other on a daily basis. Many people even find another activity or another person to get involved with emotionally or sexually. We are often uncaring and unaware of the feelings of those closest to us.

Remember that you're not trying to run a sprint; you're in a marathon. You're trying to build a life together and what you do needs to fit what you want. If your goal were to be together for only a week or a month or a year, you could stay in an intense honeymoon atmosphere the whole time and then dissolve the relationship before any deeper intimacy and trust could grow. Many people spend years doing this and wonder why they can't stay in love. The problem is that partners who want to stay in a long, loving relationship need to develop a style of love and loving that will feed, nurture, and nourish each other for life.

This is not to say that you can never get angry at your partner and never have a disagreement. All relationships have difficulties. Everyone's life has ups and downs all along the way. The point is to put your relationship, complete with its difficulties and its joys, ahead of most other things instead of behind most things, as people so often do. Otherwise, over time, one or both of you will feel deprived, hurt, and angry, and your relationship will be doomed to break apart in divorce or lapse into a coma, to wither and die from sex-love erosion disease.

Of course, it is very easy to lose sight of where we are in the midst of our daily lives. We easily become wrapped up in paying bills, raising children, or getting ahead at work. Day by day we live our lives, too often with a rabbit's-eye view—our nose pressed up against the blade of grass in front of our face, concerned only with getting through the next few blades of grass. In the process we may lose what is most important in life.

Try to get an eagle's-eye view. Soaring far above the ground, an eagle can see what is and is not important. The eagle can see farther and with greater clarity than the rabbit down on the ground.

Strive to rise above the daily grind and protect and nurture what you value most highly. If you want more love and more lovemaking in your life, keep this focus in mind and don't get sidetracked by lower priorities.

7. Beware of the Hidden Dangers

When solving difficulties in a relationship, people often discover that small problems cover deeper, more serious ones.

This was exactly the experience of Audrey and her husband, Ted. For years Audrey had complained about Ted's anger, his silences, his lack of consideration, and the fact that he drank too much. When she brought Ted to therapy she recounted all the grief he was causing her and how, because of the continual aggravation in the relationship, she found herself often very unhappy, depressed, prone to eating binges, and therefore overweight.

"If only I wasn't so miserable in my relationship with Ted, everything would be so much better," she said. "But as it is I can hardly function."

Ted and Audrey stayed in therapy, began working on the Great Love,

Great Sex program together, and Ted immediately began to change. He had always wanted to make Audrey happy but hadn't had any idea how to do so. The program helped him realize what she really wanted him to do and exactly how to go about doing it. Slowly he began to reverse many of his old behaviors, and Audrey was thrilled. But then something else happened. Even though Ted began to change and to treat her much the way she'd always wanted to be treated, her eating and depression didn't stop. In fact they got worse. "Suddenly I realized that I wasn't as happy as I thought I should be and I was still angry, only now I wasn't sure what I was angry at. It was very confusing and painful."

Only after being in therapy did Audrey begin to understand that while the problems with Ted had certainly been real, she had falsely assumed that all the problems were because of Ted. Once Ted changed, it became clear that she had other problems. It was hard for her to receive love, and her self-esteem was low. She needed to work on these difficulties individually in order to be truly happy.

In another case Steve was tremendously frustrated in his sexual relationship with Trudy. She constantly teased him by dressing in sexy outfits and flirting with him and touching him all evening. Then later, when they were in bed, she didn't want to have sex. He said he was being driven crazy and they had to change something or he was going to have an affair.

They worked on their problem together, and Steve learned that Trudy was trying to be sexy in order to get him to say he loved her and to act as if he cared. From her point of view, he seemed to be interested only in sex instead of showing her the affection she wanted.

After both of them dealt with this problem, their relationship became better. But then something else happened. One day Trudy came to therapy and said she realized that Steve really wasn't the man for her. Her unwillingness to have sex wasn't just because he didn't show her any affection or love. Now that he was doing exactly that, she realized there were other problems that had been hidden below the ones she was aware of. Trudy felt they didn't have much in common except sex and that they weren't really communicating at all in any other way.

Again more work needed to be done to solve these additional difficulties.

The point here is that sometimes solving the initial problem and improving your relationship may open the way to discovering more difficulties. Unless they are also solved, the problem will continue. Some people, in fact, as much as they feel they want things to change, will sabotage their own efforts as well as their partner's, in order to keep things exactly the way they are, because even if there are problems, these people are benefiting from them in some way.

This is often unconscious, as it was with Sally and Mac. Mac came from a very troubled family with an alcoholic mother and father and a terrible childhood. As a result, Mac had trouble showing any tender emotion at all. He sometimes became violent and would lapse into terrible depressions.

Sally came from a devout Catholic background with a very nurturing and self-sacrificing mother and a father who was very similar to Mac. With great fortitude Sally put up with Mac's rages and lack of affection. She would frequently gather her children around her and explain that Daddy wasn't well but that he still loved them, telling herself the same thing in order to keep herself and the household running.

Sally was the constant focus of admiration and sympathy from her friends and family. People called her a saint and talked about how brave and compassionate she was and how impressed they were that she could maintain her family and her composure so well and even remain cheerful and seemingly happy while dealing with such a difficult husband. Sally would smile, say she trusted in God, and continue without complaint.

It was Mac who sought therapy after realizing that he was a terrible father and husband. He didn't want to continue the way he was and so was highly motivated to change quickly. Sally, however, suddenly stopped being the smiling and compliant woman she once was. Now instead of encouraging his efforts she seemed to go out of her way to aggravate him, remind him of how sick he was, and fight with him in a way she never had before.

Only after discussing it with her did it become clear to Mac that Sally had spent her whole life dealing with the same kind of man. Like her mother, she was used to being the saint who received praise and recognition for remaining healthy despite her relationship with a sick man. Now that he had stopped acting sick, she no longer received so much admiration. Instead, people began to say how fortunate she was that Mac had changed and how happy she must be now that he was behaving and not causing so many problems. Some even called her lucky.

The problem was that Sally had never lived this way. While Mac was difficult, she had always received a great deal of self-esteem from being the well one, the brave one, and the saint. Now that he was not such a problem, she was not so much of a saint. Unconsciously she had begun to sabotage his efforts, trying to get him to remain stuck so that she would continue to receive attention and admiration and remain in the familiar pattern which she'd learned to live with.

When dealing with old patterns, we need to change not only the patterns but also the part of ourselves that is invested in our staying the same. This can be very complicated, and professional therapy may be needed.

Another hidden danger for couples to guard against is the dragon of intimacy, which can sabotage and destroy a couple's progress. We know that men have been set up to avoid or even dread closeness. They may panic, but we don't usually think of women as fearing and being devoured by the dragon of intimacy. Yet it happens.

Women go through life striving to merge with others while also wanting to have a separate, individual identity. Women want intimacy, and they don't get enough of it from their men. But when a man truly does become capable of intimacy, strength, and closeness, the woman has to see how she reacts. She might be afraid that if she gets close to him, she will lose her individual self, or she will be hurt by him.

Sabotage in a relationship may be hard to detect. When a woman does something to undermine her partner's progress, she is unlikely to be caught, because her female friends will easily see it as the man's fault. This, by the way, is one of the sources of female bad advice that women frequently pass along to friends and relatives: the problem is with the man, and the woman is totally innocent. Sometimes some of the responsibility for a problem in intimacy belongs to the woman, but men are not adept enough in the Inner World skills to see through the subtle sabotage.

The sabotage can come in the form of perfectionism and fault-finding, impatience, provocation, pessimism, defeat, or lack of cooperation. If you are to avoid this dragon, you and your partner must be on the same side, encouraging each other to keep moving in the right direction, dealing with your fears and problems. If the problems persist regardless of your efforts, get professional help.

8. Heal and Forgive

Couples must confront another common obstacle before they can make changes in their life: they must learn to deal with past hurts or anger in a way that keeps it from damaging their relationship.

All of us get angry at times with our partner. Our expectations of each other are very high. We want our partner to meet our needs, cure our ills, heal our wounds, and fulfill many different roles for us, and we never get exactly what we'd like. Over and over again we must forgive our partner's failings and limitations, letting go of our small resentments and disappointments. If we fail to learn this lesson, we are nearly doomed to unhappiness in our relationship. As we learn this lesson, letting go of our anger, we clear the pathway of debris and allow ourselves to continue our forward movement toward what we want most of all.

Learn to let your anger go over and over again. If both partners continue to let go of the small grudges, rather than accumulating resentments, they may be able to approximate the love and lovemaking they desire and heal each other's wounds.

It is like meditating. In meditation you have a focus, such as your breathing. You realize that it is very hard to remain aware of your breathing and that your thoughts and feelings will constantly pull you away; the goal is to come back over and over again to your breath, learning to pay attention to the present in the present. Similarly with love. You will find many obstacles in your path to being a loving person, but that is normal. Simply come back to your loving and your forgiving over and over.

As you move forward through this program, you will find yourself feeling closer to your partner. You will suddenly be able to discuss disagreements and other problems, perhaps for the first time. Be careful this doesn't sidetrack you. Once you are closer and your relationship has more strength, it is easier to discuss old hurts and try and resolve them and get them out of the way. Do this as best you can. Once they are resolved there will be much less distrust and hurt to keep you apart. Simply try to forgive and go on, not letting things fester but bringing them up and forgiving them at the time they happen.

Simply forgive yourself and your loved one and come back to your heartfelt loving again. Keep aware of your human limitations and make your best effort. Over and over you will be pulled off target, and over and over you will simply get back on track. Over time, your love for your best friend will become more and more powerful, and when you both practice couple-love each day for life, you are bound to live more happily ever after. Along the way you will find that your old wounds from feeling unloved or not getting the respect you want start to heal. And you will feel healthier and stronger and your relationship will grow day by day.

9. Be on the Same Side

Try to be on the same team. A common obstacle couples face in trying to maintain the changes in their lives together is that they often revert to being individuals in a tug-of-war with each other, instead of working together toward the same goals.

Work at how you fit together and how you can care for each other, so that you are looking after each other's best interests. Keep your coupleness in mind, not just your individual needs. He should be asking himself how he can help give her daily doses of vitamin L so she will feel satisfied, loved, and happy. She should be asking herself how she can satisfy him and look after his needs, both emotionally and sexually. If they both do their part, they will create something larger than their individual selves searching for individual satisfaction.

10. Count Your Blessings

Don't take for granted or overlook all the good and pleasant things in your life together. Frequently, couples stop noticing the very assets that they first loved in each other. She no longer even notices his strong shoulders, which once excited her to passion; he no longer is aware of her preparing a special meal, a kindness that once seemed like the greatest gift he had received in years.

Bob said that he felt that Julie was like a hungry baby, always wanting more; Julie said Bob was like a demanding perfectionist, never satisfied, no matter what she tried to do for him. Their demands and needs were like a corrosive force that were causing their love and caring to rust away.

They came to learn that they needed to stop scanning their world for what was wrong or missing. Instead they needed to start appreciating what they were actually doing for each other and all that they had in their life together. Bob came to notice all the seemingly small chores Julie always did for him and began to thank her for the laundry, the shopping, the cooking, and cleaning up. He also stopped demanding that all of it be done perfectly and without error or oversight. He said he had to learn to accept less than the best and appreciate all that she did do. Bob said that when he did this, a surprising thing followed. He stopped being angry at her need for more love. He guessed that he started to feel that she was showing him love through all the things she was doing and that she "deserved more of a return on her investment" of time and energy and effort than his complaints that she hadn't done even more.

Julie said that when Bob stopped demanding that it all be done perfectly and started appreciating what she had been doing for him, that made her want to help him even more.

When asked to make a list of all the positives they had in their life together they both said they were amazed at how much they had been taking for granted. They had their health, a house, two cars, a good future, and they had found each other.

Look for what is going well and count your blessings. In this way you nourish each other with vitamin L and bring more love and lovemaking into your daily life.

JULIE AND BOB

"We're much closer now," Julie said. "Now we're good friends. Actually, it's more accurate to say that we're best friends again and we've learned to be real lovers so that I can feel how much I love him every day, even on our bad days."

"We're much happier now," Bob said. "I think for the first time I'm finally understanding women, especially Julie. I've even become the resident expert on women at work; the guys are always coming to me for advice on how to deal with their wives and girlfriends. I'm not nearly as frustrated as before. Sure, I could always go for more sex, but the sex we have is so much better than before that the dissatisfaction I used to feel just isn't there anymore."

Julie and Bob had traveled a long way from where they began toward greater love and sex; yet an even deeper dimension was possible in which they could achieve fusion.

8

Fusion: The Deeper Meaning of Sex and Love

A new person is emerging, a person who can successfully meet the challenges of the global society in the twenty-first century. And just as Eastern and Western cultures are merging, the new person of the future mirrors this blending together and seeks more wholeness and balance than individuals in the past.

In the past, men mastered the Outer World of work and action, while generally avoiding the Inner World of closeness, nurturing, feeling, and sensitivity. In the past, women did the opposite; they mastered the Inner World and had little experience with the Outer World. The new man and new woman master both the Outer World and the Inner World.

This new person is capable of living in a new type of relationship—an interdependent couple who can express themselves as individuals while also working to create a genuinely satisfying home life. They are both independent and yet are merged as one—merged in fusion.

For a man this means being an intimate warrior. For a woman this means being a liberated romantic.

INTIMATE WARRIOR

An intimate warrior is a man who is competent not only in the Outer World, but in the Inner World as well. He is strong, he is effective and successful, but he can now also be aware of and act upon his more tender emotions. In other words, he sends his male energy into the Outer World of work and action. He seeks to be powerful, effective, and successful in dealing with the Outer World, knowing what is important to him and going toward his goals. If he needs money to support his family, he strives to achieve career and financial success. If he is concerned about the quality of the environment, he takes action to stop its destruction and pollution. If he is concerned about the rights of children or animals or the elderly, he supports these causes. If he sees an opportunity to make his world a better place, he takes up the challenge. He is an adult who takes his adult responsibilities seriously; he is strong, competent, a formidable foe when he chooses to be, and worthy of respect as such.

At the same time, he is an intimate warrior sending his warrior spirit into the Inner World of love and sex, feeling, closeness, and sensitivity. He learns to open his heart to the love and pain and joy that lie within, coming to grips with the endlessly complex world of emotion as he strives toward ever greater awareness and experience of his feelings. Though he may not show all of his emotions, he is aware of them and free to show them if he chooses.

He opens his heart to those he loves, allowing himself to care deeply. He learns to handle the vulnerability of having feelings, and he also learns to be emotionally fed and renewed by them. He looks into the bright eyes of his children, holds his daughter's hand, hugs his son, and feels a glow of love in his heart. He brings his beloved woman close to his chest and allows himself to feel the important role she plays in his life. He is free to put his love for her into words and does so.

Like an artist, an intimate warrior is sensitive to the details of life. As the Buddhist master Chogyam Trungpa said, "A warrior is sensitive to every aspect of all phenomena—sight, smell, sound, and feelings. He appreciates everything in his world as an artist does. His experience is full and extremely vivid."[1]

The intimate warrior is aware of his world. He lets himself notice the pure white clouds floating slowly across the blue sky and the tiny wren chirping in the sage. He's aware of the smooth handling of his car on the road and how it makes him feel that he's flying. In this way, he removes his armor of distance from life, from others, feeling greater closeness and shedding the anesthesia that once deadened his feelings.

He knows that the Inner World has a power of its own and he seeks to use this power in the service of life, fostering the health and strength of that which he loves and values. He knows that the ability to be sensitive, to read other people and sense their inner state, is invaluable in being an effective human being, both in the workplace and at home. He knows that a deeper awareness, a quarterback's instinct, is a highly developed form of "woman's intuition" applied in the Outer World. He knows that when he gives up armor he gains in other skills.

As the intimate warrior grows in personal power and feels more at home in both worlds, he can open up to being a part of something larger than his individual self. We say he experiences *fusion*.

THE LIBERATED ROMANTIC

A liberated romantic uses her nurturing nature to bring herself the closeness and love she seeks. She seeks to master the Inner World of closeness, emotion, love, and sensitive living. At the same time she gains ever greater confidence in handling the Outer World of work and action, logic and information, money and success, as she strengthens and develops her individual self.

A liberated romantic has her priorities clear. She knows that love and closeness are important to her, and she uses her Outer World strength to help accomplish her Inner World goals. She can be assertively affectionate, teaching others to love and care and feel alive. She points out the dewdrops on the velvety red rose, the yellow gold sunrise, and the gray cottontail rabbit in the tall grass.

She does what she can to harness the powerful nurturer and lover within herself to bring this energy to her home and family and friends, as well as taking good care of herself. She tries to live her life in a positive, healthful way both for herself and for her loved ones.

She knows she can serve as a bridge for her man to the Inner World, and she can help him cross this bridge. She knows she contains a multitude of identities. She is a mother, wife, friend, teacher and student, coach and player, leader and follower.

A liberated romantic also welcomes her man as he becomes more and more an intimate warrior. She allows her natural sexuality to be brought forth by his strength and sensitivity and by his efforts to be an intimate warrior.

To be more of a liberated romantic or an intimate warrior means going toward fusion on many levels, especially in terms of love and sex.

LOVE AND SEX CREATE FUSION

Before we were born, we floated in a world of fusion, in a basic oneness. After we were born, we grew and developed, becoming more and more separate—divided within ourselves and separated from others and from the Outer World. In the adult world we continue to evolve and grow, but once again we seek oneness—we seek love.

Love and sex create union. Love creates an emotional bond between yourself and another. Sex is a physical joining with another. In both love and sex you transcend, at least momentarily, your boundaries and your separateness.

Love and sex create a larger oneness. Like two rivers merging to flow into a larger whole, love and sex penetrate and merge and affect each other. It is similar for a couple in a long-term relationship. Through love and sex they can form a greater whole than they form as individuals. It is often said that two heads are better than one, but it is also true that two hearts are better than one.

We can speak of an outer fusion in which two people are united through love and sex, and we can speak of an inner fusion in which both love and sex are united into one experience within an individual who is then capable of genuine loving sex.

But real life is filled with dangers, complications, and confusion. And many of us have been hurt, particularly where love is concerned; so being separated from others often seems safer. Genuine union with another is risky. It makes you feel vulnerable. So while you are drawn toward oneness and union, you also fear it and pull back toward separate individuality. You want both oneness and separation and are caught in a deep and subtle tug-of-war within. To resolve this inner dilemma and overcome the fear of oneness requires an inner fusion.

INTIMACY WITH AND LOVE FOR YOURSELF

Only after you are happy within yourself can you truly be close and happy with another.

This is because we tend to treat and think about others the same way we treat and think about ourselves. For example, those who have a perfectionistic and demanding attitude toward themselves tend to impose this attitude on their loved ones. If they think of themselves as stupid, lazy, or ugly, this creates an inner wound that affects others as well, particularly those at home.

If you have inner wounds that are affecting your happiness, you can change. To do so, you must first try to understand what about yourself makes you unhappy. Second, forgive yourself, and last, focus on ways to make yourself happier. Begin by seeing yourself as clearly and as honestly as possible.

Let's say you are frequently self-critical. Look at the reasons for this. Perhaps you expect a great deal of yourself, or perhaps you were raised to only notice your failings and errors. Perhaps your parents were self-critical. Try to understand and observe yourself. If you have difficulty doing this, perhaps you could talk it over with friends or seek professional help.

Then you must forgive yourself. Perhaps you can see how your parents' criticalness has been transferred to you. You can go about trying to change.

You can start to notice all the times you do things correctly, becoming aware of your strengths and your talents. If you think your problem has deep roots in your childhood, perhaps therapy would help. The important thing to do, however, is to forgive yourself. Everyone has imperfections. Accept the difficulty of living with dignity and wholeness. Then accept the fact that everyone has limitations and failings. Now you can be on your own side, and you can be closer to your loved ones.

ENJOY YOUR DAILY LIFE

Enjoy your daily life. A liberated romantic and an intimate warrior seek to live with dignity and respect, caring for themselves and each other, aiming at fusion within themselves and between themselves. The drama of life is played out not only on the Outer World stage but also deep within yourself and between yourself and others. One part of you may seek sexual satisfaction and release, but a deeper part of your nature strives to find the light of conscious union. You may focus your attention on another, but deep within, you are connected, and your partner is your mirror.

You can see that daily life contains a spiritual quality and ordinary events are also extraordinary happenings of cosmic significance. You awaken in the morning aware you are sharing the common human experience of returning from deep rest; you see your loved one and feel the special sense of having a partner with whom you share your life. You feel appreciation and respect for all you have.

You taste your coffee; rising from your chair you kiss your loved ones good-bye, wishing them a good day. You walk with the feel of their cheeks on your lips. Off into the world you go, aware and vulnerable, yet strong.

As you gain a more loving relationship with your self, you will find yourself closer to your real home within yourself, and you will feel more whole and complete.

Thus you find yourself free to open to the other as the other is less needed for your purposes and can be accepted without as much anger or hurt. It then becomes possible to love others for who they really are, rather than expecting them to give you inner happiness and blaming them because you are not happy.

THE GREATEST MAGICAL FORCE IN NATURE

When a couple has been able to experience some degree of fusion through love and nourishment, they may be able to move into a deeper level of sexuality. The Italian philosopher Julius Evola said, "Sex is the 'greatest magical force in nature'; an impulse acts in it which suggests the mystery of the One."[2]

In the sex act there is a penetration of the flesh, but it is also possible to have a penetration of the spirit, the emotions, and the mind. A merging of the two can happen, and as in prayer or meditation, a sense of boundary can dissolve. You gain a deeper physical sense that you are one with something or someone beyond your self.

In fact, men can use their hunger for sex in the service of their spiritual nature. Sexual union is a special opportunity, especially for men who are particularly focused on sex.

Women, too, can seek to release their natural sexuality by channeling it through their nurturing, loving spirit. They can seek loving sex. And they can communicate this sensitive sexuality to their man through each touch.

The natural magic in loving sex is like sunken treasure that is waiting to be discovered and brought to the surface, but few men or women know how to achieve true intimacy with another or how to create fusion. If you learn this, you achieve a new sexual and emotional relationship and learn to give the gift of love.

THE GIFT OF LOVE

Love is the most precious gift we can give one another, especially when it is expressed through physical, sexual intimacy.

Imagine yourself in bed with your loved one, who is smiling, relaxed, reaching toward you. You hold your lover closer. You want to feel a part of this person, to merge. But now there is not just the physical dimension; there is the spiritual-emotional-mental dimension as well. Touching has moved beyond simple physical touch. Now you are touching each other's heart and mind. This is love, the most precious gift we can give each other.

You are one as a man and a woman. You share a common ground. You share the electric current of caring and love. You share daily life. You share problems and successes, failures and accomplishments, transitions from one stage of life to another. You are a team.

In a sense it is artificial to say sex and love should be merged. In reality they should be accepted for what they are—variations on the theme of oneness. The electricity of life. We ordinarily separate elements of life into categories, as if real life were actually divided and chopped into pieces. The reality is that one thing flows into another; love flows into sex and two can be a larger one.

Our life with our loved one is a long journey. Like any road it changes as we travel. It has ups and downs, hard parts and easy parts, sometimes beautiful and sometimes unattractive, at times boring and at times exciting. Through it all we treat our best beloved with love and respect, over and over letting things go, and in so doing we gain dignity for ourselves.

There is no distance between the two of you for a moment, and the energy of your love for each other carries you outward, making all life seem touched with magic.

"I love you," you say. It is a simple statement and the two of you kiss. You see each other, accepting, respecting, honoring. You feel as if you belong and feel the very essence of what it means to be alive. You merge sexually. Now a heart-to-heart connection exists. Emotionally and bodily you are one in joy and wonder.

You can relax and savor the nourishment inherent in the intimacy. You need not race or rush, but rather feel at home in your lover's embrace. You can be filled up where once you felt empty. You can be healed where once you were wounded. You can feel connected where once you felt lonely.

It is like a dance between equal partners. Both lead and neither leads. You feel your way toward mutual satisfaction, knowing that one's satisfaction is the other's satisfaction.

Instead of racing to orgasm, you savor the moment. You slow down. You open to your senses. You allow the warmth in your hearts to glow more brightly. You breathe and relax. You allow yourselves to have a moment of peace in the midst of your lives. You find it is easier than it seemed. You breathe again and relax even more deeply. You feel as if your chest has opened and you can breathe through your heart. And as you go through your heart you also go beyond it, to fusion.

If you can carry this beyond the sexual experience, you can see how your combined lives lead to a greater good and serve a higher purpose. You can live your daily life as an expression of a larger, deeper self, as the life force flowing through you.

NOTES, CHAPTER 8

1. Chogyam Trungpa, *Shambhala: The Sacred Path of the Warrior* (Boulder, CO: Shambhala Publications, 1984), pp. 65–66.

2. John Welwood, ed., *Challenge of the Heart* (Boulder: Shambhala Publications, 1985), p. 216.

3. Quoted in T. P. Malone and P. T. Malone, *The Art of Intimacy* (Englewood Cliffs, NJ: Prentice-Hall, 1987), p. 195.

9

The Twenty-first-Century Couple

Early civilization caused over three hundred generations of men and women to live in a state of contained domestic warfare. But, as Bob Dylan sang, "The times they are a-changin'." A new century and a new millennium is coming and with it a new era in which men and women will never again live together in the old way.

One thing seems clear: the changes already forged in society have challenged the traditional relationships between men and women by opening up new opportunities for them to leave the confines of their traditional roles and become more whole, more balanced human beings living in healthier and more satisfying relationships.

What we have offered here is a new perspective on the past problems between men and women and an invitation to create new roles and new traditions in a more loving, more balanced, and more satisfying way. In essence, we are trying to create a new relationship in which couples can escape from the battle of the sexes and give more love and lovemaking to each other.

Now is a time of choice. The future is in the making. Our lives and actions mold and model the future for us, our partners, and our children, and we predict that in the new society of the twenty-first century, love and relationships will become ever more important and precious.

Indeed, in spite of our other varied endeavors, our relationships are still and will continue to be the one area of our lives able to produce the most universal ingredient for human happiness, the essence of life—love.

THE HEART OF LIFE

Sit back for a moment and consider your own life and remember when you have been happiest. You may have had recent happy times or they may have been long ago. Perhaps a happy time for you surrounded an important event as a child, one that made you proud or satisfied, or perhaps it was a shared experience with someone special. Perhaps it was falling in love, the birth of a child, or a reunion of old friends. If it was a career success, no doubt it was most valuable when shared with another who truly mattered.

Close your eyes for a moment and try to recall the happiness you experienced then, the buoyancy, the sense of all being good with the world, the sense of intense aliveness. And probably entwined in that special moment is the feeling of love.

Breathe and relax and allow yourself to float in this feeling right now. Let it fill you.

Now imagine it is the last day of your life. You are dying, but you are not in pain. You are calm, lying in bed, aware that the end has come. You are facing the closing of your life with acceptance. It doesn't matter whether you are lying on silk sheets or a dirt floor; neither condition can go with you. All the wealth or all the poverty in the world has become meaningless. All material possessions, all titles, all degrees, all earthly powers shrink into insignificance.

Lying here, facing eternity, you consider your life and feel acutely how you have lived. What stands out as the most important to you now? Is it how well you succeeded at work? How prestigious your last automobile or address? The net value of your financial assets? The number of "toys" or shoes you've acquired?

When looking deep into one's own soul we believe the triviality of these material pursuits becomes evident. What does stand out instead are those times when you were happy, those times you mattered to someone, those times you have loved and been loved in return.

Certainly our lifetime accomplishments can make us feel proud, giving us the satisfaction of knowing that we have lived out our abilities and talents as best we could. But in our hearts we know that some essential part of our basic human nature depends on our relationships with others.

Love is the life food, the sustenance, of our human connections. Love is our emotion of transcendence and the greatest gift we can give another and ourself. To merge with another person in utter honesty and communion is one of the most profound states a human being can experience. Yet how many of us lead harried, preoccupied lives, filled with activity that has little real meaning?

For millions of people love is a side dish when it could be the main course. We busy ourselves with our daily grind, with our careers, with fashions and fads, hurrying to work, hurrying to consume, and hurrying to have fun. These are the things that take our time and energy while our relationships to our loved ones often go untended or, worse, suffer the damage and corrosion that results from our daily preoccupations and the bumps and bruises along the way.

It is unfortunately true, as Ella Wheeler Wilcox, an American poet, once wrote, that:

We flatter those we scarcely know,
and please the fleeting guest,
and deal full many a thoughtless blow,
to those who love us best. [1]

Everyone needs love, and never more than now when our humanity is increasingly challenged, when families are spread across continents and extended families give way to single parents and childless couples. More and more people are alone where their ancestors were intricately intertwined in a close social network. Our circle of loved ones has diminished so that our best beloved partner, our husband or wife, our friend, is no longer simply one of many we might love, but increasingly the only one with whom we can share this most precious emotion.

We see that we must overcome the damage men and women inevitably do to each other. We must heal each other by creating a loving environment with emotional and physical intimacy.

Men and women *can* achieve what they both want most of all—a relationship filled with understanding and mutual caring and respect; a relationship where a balance of roles has been achieved and both people can give and receive love and lovemaking in satisfying measure.

The implications are profound. If we alter our own lives, we alter the world. Every person and every couple are like drops of water in the ocean of human life. As we live our own lives, we automatically affect the world. Indeed, we are the world. It is only through a transformation of the man-woman relationship that we can evolve to a higher level as a society and move toward our new world in harmony and peace.

The only way to retain our humanity and combat our isolation is to reach for that which makes us human—our ability to love.

Now is the right time. In truth there is no time but now. Doesn't it make sense, then, for each of us to rethink exactly how we are leading our lives and where we are putting our energies? Are we giving time to our loved ones, or are we devoting it to the passing parade? Are we pouring our heart into those we love, or spilling our life into ephemeral actions, giving our energies away to fleeting "guests"?

This is our hope: that we have offered all readers a way to refocus and give their relationships and their desire to love, to be loved, and to make love the attention it deserves.

We hope the warfare that fills so many couples' lives can be transformed into loving kindness and that all of us can live out our dreams, live more happily ever after, and make love, not war.

NOTES, CHAPTER 9

1. Hazel Felleman, ed., *Best Loved Poems of the American People* (New York: Doubleday, 1936), pg. 645.

Also available from Virgin

HOW TO MAKE LOVE TO THE SAME PERSON FOR THE REST OF YOUR LIFE
(and Still Love It)

by Dagmar O'Connor

'How can I possibly make love to the same person for the rest of my life?'

Sex therapist Dagmar O'Connor's witty and practical guide shows how a committed and monogamous relationship is not the life sentence many fear, but can lead instead to ultimate joy and ultimate sex. With her help, you can identify and overcome the common pitfalls, including:

- how to deal with the boredom backlash of 'I'm in the mood for sex – so why aren't you?'
- how to bridge the gap between family life and sex life
- how to free yourself for sex by booking time for it
- how to take the monotony out of monogamy by cancelling 'performance' sex
- how to let your bodies as well as your minds 'make friends'

Completely updated for the post-AIDS sexual revolution of the 1990s, *How to Make Love to the Same Person for the Rest of Your Life* shows how a loving and fulfilled sexual relationship with your long-term partner is a reality within everyone's reach.

ISBN 0 86369 663 5

FEMALE
SEXUAL AWARENESS

by Barry and Emily McCarthy

'You are a sexual woman from the day you are born to the day you die.'

Female Sexual Awareness is for the woman who recognises her sexuality as an integral part of her character, and who knows that it can, and should, enhance every part of her life. Barry and Emily McCarthy, authors of the best-selling *Sexual Awareness*, frankly yet sensitively confront the special challenges facing women in the 1990s. Topics include:

- intimacy and commitment
- pleasuring
- foreplay, intercourse and afterplay
- sexual fantasies
- sex and the single parent
- sex in later life
- women and AIDS

The ultimate guide to this most important part of our life, *Female Sexual Awareness* is a book about women – for women, for men and for couples.

ISBN 0 352 32594 1